C000256182

Faith and Uncertainty

Faith and Uncertainty

JOHN HABGOOD

DARTON·LONGMAN+TODD

First published in 1997 by
Darton, Longman and Todd Ltd
1 Spencer Court
140–142 Wandsworth High Street
London SW18 4JJ

ISBN 0–232–52227–8

A catalogue record for this book is available from the British Library.

The Scripture quotations used are, unless otherwise indicated, from the
Authorized Version.

Phototypeset by Intype London Ltd
Printed and bound in Great Britain by
Redwood Books, Trowbridge, Wiltshire

Contents

IV EDUCATION

V MORALITY

VI ENVOI

Acknowledgements

I am grateful to the following for permission to reprint some of the papers in this collection.

For 'Learning to like each other', from *Explorations in Science and Theology* pp. 89–95, to The Royal Society for the Encouragement of Arts, Manufactures and Commerce; for 'The sacramentality of the natural world', from *The Sense of the Sacramental* pp. 19–30, to SPCK; for 'Is there reliable knowledge about God?', from *Humanity, Environment and God* pp. 214–25, to Glasgow University and Blackwell; for 'The Church in society', from *Living Evangelism* pp. 43–56, to Affirming Catholicism; for 'The family and the new social order', from *The Christian Family – a Concept in Crisis* pp. 1–13, and for the Foreword to *Veritatis Splendor – A Response* pp. vii–xii, to the Canterbury Press; for 'The case for a national RE syllabus' to Culham College Institute.

I would also like to thank those who stimulated me to reflect on the variety of themes explored in this book, and especially Dr Idreos and the principal of Manchester College, Oxford for the invitation which produced 'A vote of thanks to Darwin' and 'Evolution and ethics'. Finally I want to express my gratitude to Raymond Barker, my lay assistant when I was Archbishop of York, whose criticism of many of my drafts, and wise advice, were invaluable.

Introduction

> Doubts are the messengers of the Living One to the honest. They are the first knock at our door of things that are not yet, but have to be, understood . . . Doubt must precede every deeper assurance; for uncertainties are what we first see when we look into a region hitherto unknown, unexplored, unannexed.
> (George MacDonald)

To entitle a book *Faith and Uncertainty* may seem to be asking for trouble. There are those who love to scoff at what one author has called 'the Church hesitant'. To couple faith with uncertainty may seem typical of a religion too weak-kneed to stand up for what it professes. I can already hear the tut-tuts of those who pride themselves on the robustness of their faith. Surely, they say, a faith worth having must inspire absolute conviction. There is no future in building a house on a wobbly rock, nor in following guides who have themselves lost their way. What is the point of a Church without a clear focus of authority, able and willing to distinguish truth from falsehood? Faith is a response to what God has authoritatively revealed, and the only uncertainty is whether our response to it is adequate. As a final flourish, out comes the familiar quotation, 'If the trumpet give an uncertain sound, who shall prepare himself to the battle?' It is a text commonly regarded as the knock-down answer to woolly liberalism, in serene disregard of the fact that it was originally used by St Paul as an argument for speaking rationally rather than in tongues.

Such sentiments are the stock-in-trade of popular commentators and letter-writers, many of whom are genuinely shocked by what they perceive as faithlessness. Others, while not being believers themselves, want a firm standard against which to measure their own unbelief. Fundamentalists are easier targets for ridicule than those whose faith

1

defies simple description. A faith which holds hands with uncertainty has to be denigrated, not for what is believed, but for what is apparently not believed. The usual accusation is that it has succumbed to the latest intellectual fashions. Dean Inge's famous remark, that a Church wedded to the spirit of the age becomes a widow in the next, makes regular appearances in anti-Christian and anti-liberal polemic.

There are yet others for whom faith and uncertainty are looked upon, not as curious bedfellows, but as identical twins. As they see it, faith *is* uncertainty. It is a speculative and ultimately futile attempt to discover meaning and reassurance where none are to be found. In sharp contrast to the progress of objective, scientifically-based knowledge, faith is dismissed as no more than the expression of personal hopes, a way of comforting ourselves in the dark, a reliance on what is unproven and unprovable. The only certainties in this world are to be had through the public process of gathering evidence and submitting it to rigorous testing.

I have briefly described these stereotypes because they are typical of many immediate reactions when matters of faith are raised. Examples of them constantly appear in newspapers, particularly in the letter columns; and in 24 years as a bishop I must have received sackfuls of such comment in personal letters, the most virulent of which, sad to say, were usually written by those who called themselves firmly believing Christians.

George MacDonald, the nineteenth-century Scottish author who inspired both J. R. R. Tolkein and C. S. Lewis, offers a wiser way of understanding faith. The passage quoted above occurs in one of his *Unspoken Sermons* (1891), a magnificent exposition of the book of Job. Of all the books in the Bible, Job takes us closest, I believe, to the religious issues which are uppermost in our own day. Old certainties about God's moral governance of the world can seem hard to sustain. Why do the innocent suffer and the wicked flourish? How is it possible to believe in the face of the appalling carnage of the twentieth century? Why does God seem so distant? And even if God were clearly present, on what basis could human beings make their case against him? Doesn't the very idea of God as an omnipotent authority, dictating what we must be, devalue and crush the dignity and worth of free, responsible human beings? Job has to discover, in ways which are not fully resolved in the book – and which could not be resolved before the death and resurrection of Christ – that there is an experience of God which can change his whole perspective. It is through being exposed to the true awesomeness of God that he comes to see himself as he truly is. And in the light of that new vision, his objections fall away.

But to reach that point, as George MacDonald rightly saw, Job has to step out into uncertainty. The faith his friends were urging on him was intellectually coherent and traditionally sound. But as a piece of intellectual baggage, it could not be taken on board and remain unchanged in the light of what he was experiencing. In George MacDonald's analogy, faith is more like a territory in which we live, whose contours and frontiers are uncertain, and which invites constant exploration. It is a progressive discovery of who we are, and what we must be and do, if we are to respond to the reality of the God in whom we live and move and have our being. And such exploration and discovery are only possible because this same God is the one who empowers us to undertake them.

In explaining the title and purpose of this book, I have run ahead of myself and assumed a definition of faith which needs to be spelt out more fully. Meanwhile I must defend the statement that Job's predicament, his obsession with God and yet the apparent absence of God, is one which resonates especially in our own times.

One of the major transitions in Western culture over the last 200 or so years has involved the loss of an awareness of God's reality which was previously almost universal, and which had seemed incontestable. Intense disputes about the nature and purposes of God, and the kind of reality claimed for him, did not detract from the conviction that there was a reality to argue about. The reason is not hard to discern. Quite apart from there being no alternative account of how the world and human beings came into existence, there was also simply no alternative way of underpinning the sense that life was meaningful, and that there was a moral order somehow written into the nature of things. God, however he was understood, was the ultimate source and guarantor of all that gave enduring shape to human life, including the gift of reason itself. To lose what had formed the linchpin of human self-understanding would be to spin down into chaos and nothingness, and there were few who were willing to go all the way down this dangerous path, despite some notable expressions of religious scepticism.

The modern world, by contrast, has a superabundance of alternatives on offer. Whether any of them are capable of substituting for the original is open to doubt. I doubt it myself. But what is not in doubt is that large numbers of people, not least many of those who shape public opinion, now feel free to find meaning for their lives, and to assert moral claims, without rooting these in any transcendent reality. Indeed, as I have already indicated, for some of them traditional ideas of God seem positively malign, in appearing to subject adult freedom and responsibility to an external power which effectively robs human life of its dignity. To Christians such a claim may seem perverse, and to miss the whole point of what is meant by dependence on God's grace. Nevertheless it is important to reckon with it, because those who hold the view that human freedom and dignity must be defended against God are tapping deep reservoirs of human feeling, definitively explored in the book of Job.

Among other alternatives, Romanticism and its modern offshoots continue to inspire those who look for meaning and direction in their lives through the mysteries and beauties of the natural world, or in the products of human creativeness. In their vulgarised forms these range from the assertion, as expressed by a mother who had artificially conceived octuplets, that 'It's only natural', to modern forms of pantheism, and even a small revival of paganism. In the aesthetic and intellectual world of the most avant-garde, there are paradoxical attempts to rediscover a sense of human dignity based on an unblinking acceptance of ultimate meaninglessness. There is no God, and Samuel Beckett is his prophet. The permutations are endless.

And there are, of course, other faiths. The consciousness that Christianity is not the only religion in the world need not threaten the incontestable role of God as the guarantor of meaning and morality. In fact, it may positively reinforce it by reminding us that religion is a universal phenomenon. But it also poses familiar questions about why religious truth, if there is such a thing, should take such a diversity of forms, some of them incompatible. The same problem arises in an even more acute form with the various fundamentalisms. The more loudly each trumpets that it, and it alone, possesses the whole truth, the more obvious it becomes that none can be exclusively true. Certainty of the kind proclaimed by some religious believers may be impressive in terms of the commitment it elicits, but seems absurd to those who are aware of how many other supposed certainties are on offer. Job was bewildered because the heavens seemed empty and, until the final disclosure of God, he received no answer. His twentieth-century counterparts are bewildered because there are too many answers, and they assume that these must therefore all be illusory.

If this is a fair, albeit grossly over-simplified, sketch of the climate of thought and feeling in Western society within which today's Christians have to make their mark, then perhaps a certain exploratory spirit and tentativeness of approach may have a good deal to commend it.

The late Bishop John Tinsley was fond of quoting Emily Dickinson's poem:

> Tell the truth but tell it slant,
> Success in Circuit lies.

In a culture in which there is no longer any single publicly accessible language for conveying religious ideas, and no publicly agreed basis from which to start, a kind of obliqueness may be the only way of making a point without falling foul of all the old stereotypes, stale images and popular misapprehensions. Truth must be felt, must resonate in our experience of life, as well as be reasoned about. It must be discerned within the context of things which matter to us here and now. In the world that is opening up, in which the accessibility of information and of different ideas and views is expanding explosively, the very multiplicity of opinions must put a question-mark against all exclusive claims and over-confident assertions. Thus people can hardly avoid becoming aware of the uncertainties which confront all claims to knowledge.

Nor is this just the case with religious truth. Science may have become the paradigm of reliable knowledge, but its reliability depends on its detachment from the very things which most concern us as human beings. The task of scientists who try to advise governments on the safety of foodstuffs, for instance, is fraught with perplexities, precisely because of the human interest involved. What are they supposed to do when faced with results which cannot be fully substantiated, which are going to have to run the gauntlet of intense public discussion against a background of insistent demands for certainty, and when they are conscious of the enormous human, political and financial consequences of their utterances? The lust for certainty is as strong in secular public sentiment as it is in religion, and it requires both courage and faith to resist it.

To take uncertainty seriously as one of the conditions of modern life is not the same as being wedded to the spirit of the age. Every age poses its own questions and sets limits on the kind of answers which can be heard. But religious faith has its own milieu in which it can nourish itself and learn how to straddle the different realities within which it has to manifest itself. To be tentative in theology and open to different kinds of experience need not entail being weak in commitment, half-hearted in worship, and morally gutless. The New Testament injunction is to be 'in the world but not of the world' – a difficult but not impossible balance.

One way of expressing how this works in practice is in terms of George MacDonald's analogy of a territory waiting to be explored. To be a Christian believer is to see oneself as part of a tradition of thinking and acting and belonging which, over millennia extending back to the dawn of recorded history, has provided great civilisations and countless people with access to sources of transcendent meaning. At any given time the tradition is likely to contain those who are conscious of living in secure territory at the centre, while others push out the boundaries – sometimes profitably, sometimes disastrously. In periods of general uncertainty there is greater consciousness of the boundaries, sometimes enhancing the sense of identity, sometimes threatening it. And there is a constant temptation to be self-enclosed, as if there were no world outside.

This is all very vague and general. Most Christians would, I am sure, feel able to assert something much sharper and more personal. Having faith means knowing God through Jesus Christ within the company of fellow-believers. But the advantage of a generalised description is that it brings out the kind of activity faith is, before we get caught up in the particular claims which give it substance.

The believer is part of a tradition which includes a way of life, a vocabulary and symbolism, certain practices (such as private prayer and public worship), certain attitudes to other people, and some vision of ultimate good which gives meaning to this whole range of activities and points to their goal. Different believers may inhabit such a tradition in different ways and with different emphases, and may justify their allegiance to it with different arguments. A tradition envisaged as a space in which these things happen allows much freedom of movement. But across all the differences the tradition of faith is recognisable to those who belong. And when all the historical, philosophical, theological and moral arguments have been exhausted, its ultimate vindication for most believers is that it does indeed give meaning to their lives.

To do this, however, the tradition of faith has to engage with the realities being experienced in the world as it is. If it fails to do so, it increasingly becomes a form of words and actions divorced from most of the life of the believer. In a pluralistic age, overwhelmed with novelty, diversity, sharp contentions about morality, and constant pressures for decision-making, the temptations to isolate faith from this confusing world are very strong. If this is to be avoided, the need to live and grapple with uncertainty, to find ways of being faithful without presuming to have all the answers, must be high on the agenda. The various essays, lectures and sermons which make up this book represent some of my attempts in the last few years to meet this demand.

An archbishop has many opportunities to address mixed audiences – of Christian believers, unbelievers, and those at the fringes of faith – on a wide variety of topics. I have consistently tried to make what I say accessible to those who do not start from Christian assumptions. This is why I seldom quote the Bible in such circumstances. Those in the know can, I hope, see the biblical basis of my theology, but outside the context of sermons there is nothing, in my view, more off-putting to those one is trying to reach than the idea that arguments can be clinched by quoting biblical texts. Let me stress again that this is not because the Bible is irrelevant. On the contrary, it is at the centre of the tradition in which all Christians live. Used as a set of texts for proving arguments about contemporary problems, however, it can give the quite misleading impression that there is some quick way of short-circuiting the struggle to bring faith to bear on them. Christians are not in the privileged position of being able to look up the answer in the back of the book.

As I see it, the route from biblical insight to contemporary application always runs through theology. When, for instance, the psalmist says, 'It was you who fashioned my inward parts; you knitted me together in my mother's womb' (Ps. 139:12), we are not being given a lesson in embryology with direct relevance to controversies about abortion or *in vitro* fertilisation. The theme of the psalm is the omniscience of God from whom it is impossible to hide, and who knows us through and through. What it means to be known by God may indeed inform our thinking on medical dilemmas, as well as on related issues about human identity. But it does so not just because a particular text happens to strike a chord, but because God's knowledge of us is an enduring theme in biblical and subsequent Christian tradition, defining what we are. The need to stand back, to see the large theological picture, to hold to the central truths without being distracted by contentious details, is to my mind the best means of picking one's way through our present intellectual and moral labyrinth – and I hope this will be apparent in what follows.

The contents of the book are divided into six main sections corresponding to major topics which have occupied me for most of my ministry.

1 Faith and science

Building bridges between scientific and religious ways of thinking has been a lifelong concern, ever since an early enthusiasm for science led me to a phase of adolescent unbelief. I now believe it is possible to have enthusiasm for both, and that is the theme of the first chapter in this section. 'Learning to like each other' was a lecture sponsored by the Templeton Foundation in 1993 and takes a historical look at the way in which science and faith have been intertwined. The two chapters on evolution which follow were the 1994 Idreos Lectures on Science and Religion, delivered to large mixed audiences in Manchester College, Oxford. Given that there are many Christians who still believe that Darwinian evolution is incompatible with their faith, and given also some strong scientific voices (not least in Oxford) proclaiming the same message of incompatibility from the opposite point of view, my aim was to show that even in Darwin's own time Christians could and did learn some valuable lessons from him.

Chapter 4, delivered as part of a lecture-series on sacramentality at Durham University in 1993, explores a different area of common concern between science and faith – the care of the environment. My 1994 Christmas sermon preached in York Minster (Chapter 5) also uses the theme of sacramentality as a way of discerning divine meaning even in the midst of apparent evolutionary chaos. Chapter 6, 'Life on Mars?', was written in 1996 for the *Church of England News-*

paper, and seeks to apply the same kind of incarnational theology within a wider cosmic frame.

The section ends with a lecture prepared for the centenary series of Gifford Lectures in 1988. As befits a Gifford Lecture, it is at a slightly higher academic level than the rest of the book, but is included as an example of a somewhat more rigorous attempt to justify belief. By linking belief to practice and to the need for dialogue, it also serves to introduce the next section on how people can live and work together, despite a diversity of beliefs.

2 The common good

Central to everything in this section is the question which haunts Western culture. How can we enjoy the advantages of a social order based on scientific and technological expertise, individual enterprise, personal choice, and democratic and bureaucratic control, without undermining the moral foundations needed to make such a social order work?

Chapter 8, originally a lecture given in 1994 to a mixed audience of British and Japanese industrialists in the Industry Churches Forum, was an attempt to open up this question by comparing the two cultures. Chapter 9, an address in 1995 to the Affirming Catholicism conference, looked at some of the effects of moral erosion, and the kind of response Christians might make to it. Chapter 10, an address on the family, which formed part of a series in the University of Leeds also in 1995, considered the mutual interaction between personal formation, family patterns and wider social assumptions.

'Religion and democracy' (1993), which is Chapter 11, was a Christian contribution to a multi-faith conference on democracy, and focused on the relation between freedom and order. Chapter 12, 'Paradoxes of freeedom' (1996), looks in more depth at the concept of freedom and some of its theological implications. Chapters 13 and 14 were sermons (both preached in May 1994), the first in King's College, Cambridge, and the second in Manchester Cathedral; both consider ways in which faith can influence secular societies by keeping open a door to the transcendent. Chapter 15, a lecture given in 1995 to an audience of politicians and theologians in Leuven, Belgium, attempts to use Christian experience of working for unity to throw light on the vexed question of European union. The audience evidently regarded my thesis as typically British.

3 The media

The Gerald Priestland Memorial Lecture (1995), which is Chapter 16, took up the same basic theme as the previous section, but in the context of the media. In a world where communication is universal and knowledge is growing faster than it can be assimilated, and where so much is in danger of being trivialised, how can one retain a sense of the moral and spiritual realities on which our culture depends?

Chapter 17, 'Preachers from outer space', is a light-hearted acknowledgement of the pressures on the media themselves. Chapter 18, which concludes this section, was a sermon preached before the Royal Family at Sandringham during Epiphany 1995 and, like the Christmas sermon before it (Chapter 5), draws heavily on a fascinating article by Angela Tilby in *Theology* (September 1994) in which she compared radio and television to Apollo and Dionysus.

4 Education

Chapters 19 and 20 were two addresses on education, both given to specialist audiences with the aim of stimulating thought, first on continuing adult education, and secondly on the need for national standards in religious education. 'Maps and dreams' (January 1995), which is Chapter 19, points out the importance of spiritual aspiration in motivating learning. My defence of religious education (Chapter 20) stressed its intrinsic educational value, and hence its proper place alongside other subjects in the National Curriculum. If our society is to rediscover its moral basis, educationalists cannot use pluralism as an excuse to contract out of their responsibility for laying some moral and spiritual foundations.

5 Morality

But how are such foundations to be laid without relapsing into an authoritarianism which could undermine the real gains in freedom and responsibility referred to in Section 2 of this book? An open society creates insecurities which make the voice of authority sound more attractive.

The first two essays in this section (Chapters 21 and 22) are critiques of two recent papal encyclicals which in my view go too far in seeking to re-establish moral absolutism. They are friendly critiques, because I believe that the pope is tapping into real and deeply felt public concern. But he does not, I believe, engage sufficiently with the kind of world I have been describing. Chapter 21, '*Veritatis Splendor*: a response' (1994), is the preface to a book of critical essays, mostly by Durham theologians, and Chapter 22, '*Evangelium Vitae*' (1995), was written for *The Independent*. The remaining chapters in this section, on particular moral issues, were first published as articles in *The Evening Standard*, the *York Diocesan Newspaper*, *The Independent*, *Parliamentary Review*, and a specialist medical publication.

This section also includes three sermons: Chapter 25, 'A nasty murder', the Mulligan sermon to lawyers at Grays Inn (1993); Chapter 28, 'Loving God', to members of the General Synod (1994), and Chapter 29, 'Innocence', my 1993 Christmas sermon in York Minster, following the murder of little James Bulger (1993).

6 Envoi

The book ends with my last sermon to the Diocese and Province of York. It sets out briefly some of the things which have held me to the task in nearly 50 years of exploring boundaries.

I

FAITH AND SCIENCE

1

Learning to like each other

All my life I have had a love affair with science. I see it as one of the greatest of human activities, demanding enormous resources of skill, intelligence, imagination and dedication. I enjoy the company of scientists, and admire them for their achievements. I was fortunate enough to work in the physiological laboratory in Cambridge during one of its golden periods: there was a strong awareness of fundamental problems being tackled and solved by researchers who were at the top of their profession. As a young researcher I sat at their feet and drank it all in, and have been grateful ever since. So I have no difficulty in liking science and scientists. Whether they like me, and what I now try to do, is another question.

Yet despite this starry-eyed beginning, the first serious piece of theology I published was entitled 'The uneasy truce between science and theology'. It appeared just over 30 years ago in a book called *Soundings: Essays concerning Christian Understanding*, edited by Alec Vidler. It was a composite effort by a group of Cambridge theologians, and grew out of a shared sense that something was wrong – that many Christians, theologians among them, were unduly complacent about the intellectual foundations of their faith, and that what was then called 'biblical theology' was inadequate to the task of meeting the real challenges to faith. *Soundings* was in fact the first shot in a campaign of theological reassessment which took its place as part of the process of radical rethinking which marked the 1960s. Our efforts were quickly superseded by John Robinson's *Honest to God*, which identified many of the same issues, but in a much more urgent and popular style.

The interconnectedness of science and religion

My contribution, as its title suggests, put a question-mark against some of the over-simple demarcations between science and theology. 'Science is concerned with empirical truth, theology with symbolic truth. Science deals with the objective world, theology with the existential world. Science tells us about efficient causes, theology about final causes.' These are the sort of terms in which writers then were trying to specify two independent realms of study which could exist side by side without conflict or interference. Still today one hears the formula that science deals with the hows, and theology with the whys of life. But how and why are actually, in most spheres of life, interconnected. *How* a TV set works may not be of immediate interest to most viewers, but the reason *why* some programmes assume the shape they do may to a considerable extent depend, at least indirectly, on the limitations and possibilities of the technology.

I went on to argue that an attempt to separate science and theology into two autonomous spheres was not only unreal but positively harmful. There are, of course, profound differences between them, both in subject-matter and in method. But theologians cannot afford to underestimate the psychological impact science has had through the grandeur and intellectual coherence of the scientific account of the universe and its workings. Scientists in turn cannot safely ignore fundamental questions about the nature of truth, nor the different kinds of explanation appropriate, say, in physics, biology, psychology, sociology and history, nor those insights into the nature of human existence which are part of the currency of theology. In fact there are continuities as well as discontinuities between science and theology, and that is why their practitioners need to listen to each other.

All this was 30 years ago, but I recall it to make the point that in learning to like one another we do not have to start from a position of alienation. As I hope to show later, there is and always has been, a relationship and overlap between science and theology. Sometimes this has involved unlawful trespassing – some of the great conflicts of the past can be seen now to have resulted from over-confident claims on both sides. Both are now humbler, more aware of the limitations of knowledge and of the way it is conditioned by its human instruments. I have always been attracted by the thought of knowledge as a kind of spectrum or hierarchy. At one end of the scale there is precise scientific knowledge of those features of experience which can be treated as objects existing independently of us; much of this can be expressed in mathematical terms. At the other end of the scale there is the knowledge we have of other persons by our involvement with them – the kind of knowledge we can only have when we stop treating them as objects; much of this is beyond verbal expression or definition. At one end of the scale we have extreme articulateness; at the other end, extreme inarticulateness. And in between there are kinds of knowledge which pull in both directions: in biology, say, there is on the one hand the attempt to reduce biological processes to highly complex interactions which are, at least in principle, capable of being analysed mathematically; on the other hand there is the knowledge of living creatures which depends on empathy with them, and which owes much to our own experience of being alive. The knowledge which depends on mathematical analysis or mechanical analogies, and the knowledge of the naturalist, can fruitfully relate to one another because in the end they are knowledge about the same objects – but the one cannot be reduced to the other. Both are needed. And I would want to argue that, in just the same way, the whole spectrum of knowledge is needed, from the knowledge of God to the knowledge of the atom – and that we impoverish ourselves if we limit the possibilities.

Complementarity and the spectrum of knowledge

The idea of a spectrum of knowledge fits well with current tendencies to favour holistic thinking. Scientists have been blamed for fragmenting knowledge, for concentrating on parts and ignoring the whole, for relying on crudely reductionist explanations of a kind described to me when I was a student by my physiology supervisor. 'Some scientists', he said, 'think of a gramophone record as a series of bumps in a groove. They have no interest in actually playing it.' Ecology has vividly exposed the dangers in all that. Part of its psychological impact has been to highlight the interconnectedness of phenomena which can only be understood with any degree of completeness as parts of a total system. Furthermore, since ecology has obvious practical implications for the way human beings need to live if we are not to destroy our environment, it has become one of those subjects in which science, ethics, human values, and political pro-

17

grammes are clearly seen as insufficient if pursued in isolation from one another.

But it is not just environmental issues which have emphasised the continuity between different ends of the spectrum. John Brooke's excellent historical study, *Science and Religion*, has shown in fascinating detail how science and religion are both hard to differentiate and define with any precision, and how they have been, and still are, in continuous interaction, sometimes fruitfully and sometimes unfruitfully.[1]

He cites Niels Bohr's concept of complementarity as a good example of the complexities of this interaction. The idea that there could be complementary ways of describing quantum phenomena was a key feature of the so-called Copenhagen interpretation of quantum theory. It held together two kinds of explanation of sub-atomic events, as waves or as particles, and asserted that there was no way of reducing the one to the other. The mathematical formalism is flexible. Equations for particles can be rewritten as equations for waves. Complementarity at this level simply implies the possibility of transformation from one mathematical form to another. The notion begins to bite, though, when one asks what 'really happens' in an atomic event, and the answer has to be that this depends on the way one observes it. All this nowadays is a twentieth-century commonplace, but there are three lessons to be drawn from it in relation to what I have called the spectrum of knowledge. The first is that in this description of quantum theory, the two ends of the spectrum meet – the abstract, impersonal mathematical end and the participatory end at which the observer's actions are determinative of what happens. Heisenberg, one of Bohr's colleagues, put it like this: 'Quantum theory reminds us of the old wisdom that when searching for harmony in life one must never forget that in the drama of existence we are ourselves both players and spectators'.[2]

The second lesson drawn out by John Brooke is that the notion of complementarity did not arise purely and simply out of quantum theory. Bohr justified its use on other grounds. His father was a physiologist, and he was well aware of the different and complementary frameworks of explanation needed in the description of living organisms. He was also interested in psychology, particularly the stream-of-consciousness psychology then popular. To explore a stream of consciousness is to disturb and change it, just as the investigation of

18

a quantum phenomenon determines the form of the phenomenon, and sets limits on what can be known about it. Bohr may even have been influenced by his fellow-Dane and theologian, Kierkegaard, with his emphasis on the incompatibility of different interpretations of life and the necessity of choice. It is also striking that quantum physics, with its seemingly nonsensical and contradictory descriptions of the ultimate nature of things, should have been developed during the inter-war years in Europe, in a social atmosphere dominated by nihilism, irrationalism and the break-up of established orders. Thomas Mann explored this theme in his novel *Doctor Faustus*, where he depicted a rather cynical group of scientists no longer concerned with truth but with what he called 'the creative fiction', and ultimately with power.[3]

Complementarity, therefore, has a somewhat murky history which extends beyond the purely scientific issues that provided the context for Bohr's use of it. This is no doubt one reason why some scientists, Einstein among them, always disliked it. It introduces a cloudiness into scientific explanation, as does Heisenberg's uncertainty principle, at the very point at which one might have expected the sharpest degree of precision. Einstein sympathised with Rutherford's claim: 'It should be possible to explain the laws of physics to a barmaid'. Alas, it is not. The belief that everything should be simple is just as socially conditioned as the belief that it is irreducibly complex. If the concept of complementarity is to be successfully challenged – and there are those who are highly critical of it – it can only happen if and when a more comprehensive explanation of the apparent dichotomy has become available.

The third lesson to be drawn from the story of complementarity concerns the use made of it by theologians. The idea of alternative, apparently incompatible, explanations of the same phenomenon, both of which are true, has proved irresistible. The contrasting descriptions of science and theology with which I began (and many others like them), have frequently appealed to quantum theory as a kind of justification that the holding together of apparent opposites is rationally and (even better) scientifically respectable. Other theologians have gone further, and have used it to undergird the paradoxes of the incarnation. Here is a physicist and lay theologian, Russell Stannard: 'Just as scientists have had to come to terms with complementary behavioural descriptions of the fundamental physical entities, so we, too, have to content ourselves with complementary descriptions of God and of Jesus'.[4]

There is a need for caution. If the attractiveness of complementarity as an intellectual device for holding on to the ambivalences of quantum theory stems in part from the fact that it has resonances in other fields of knowledge, then it ought not to be surprising when other fields of knowledge find it a useful concept. What has been read into it can be read out of it; but the fact that quantum physicists may find it useful too is not to be used as an argument that physics somehow justifies the forms of complementarity observable elsewhere. There is a risk of circularity. The late Donald MacKay, a careful writer on science and theology, made much use of the notion of complementary descriptions; but he rooted it in his own speciality, which was the study of brain-function in the light of information theory. The claim that there are different and complementary levels of understanding in the analysis of mind and brain need owe nothing to quantum physics. Descriptions of brain activities and mental processes are complementary, and cannot be reduced to one or the other, because there are necessarily two complementary ways of observing what is going on.

Darwinism and Christianity

I have dwelt on this concept because it illustrates rather nicely the degree to which, even in our fragmented culture, exchanges take place along the spectrum of knowledge. It also illustrates some of the pitfalls. I turn now to another familiar story, spurred on by Desmond and Moore's recent huge biography of Darwin.[5]

This gives an enthralling account of the social, political and ecclesiastical jungle which provided much of the background to Darwin's work. Yet for years it inhibited him from expressing his true mind, because he was afraid of the way in which his ideas might be misused. He dreaded the moral sustenance which he believed his theory might be claimed to offer to those who were preaching social revolution. He was conscious that allies like Huxley were in part fighting a different battle – the battle to liberate science from ecclesiastical domination, to professionalise it, and to give it status in the universities. He knew that the stability of Victorian society, already threatened by social unrest, could be put at risk by a levelling theory; a theory which not only levelled classes – though not in those days, races: Darwin never forgot his encounter with the miserable Fuegians – but threatened the dignity of human life itself. His science was certainly not socially and ethically neutral; nor had his ideas been conceived in a vacuum. The class struggles, the population explosion, the rise of a new breed of individualistic entrepreneur, Malthusian economics, the growth of poverty and crime – all these were raw material close at hand for a theory of natural selection. They set the scene. But the development of his thought entailed a constant struggle to insulate his scientific studies from this wider context by piling up more and more evidence of a strictly biological kind. It was vast, mind-boggling, detailed work which filled the 17 years between the first sketch of the theory of natural selection and the publication of *The Origin of Species*. In a sense it was the deliberate detachment of his science from the context in which it had begun – a detachment which, as he had foreseen, was immediately abandoned by evolutionary propagandists as soon as the book was published.

The message went out loud and clear that Darwinism and Christianity were incompatible – and there are those who still believe this, on both sides. Richard Dawkins, for example, is contemptuously dismissive of all religion on the supposed ground that evolutionary theory is in principle capable of explaining everything, because it demonstrates how complexity can be generated from simple beginnings.[6] At the other extreme there is an astonishing proportion of Christians, especially in North America, who use every anomaly and unresolved problem as evidence to prove Darwin wrong.

Fortunately there has remained a large middle ground. Christianity has had to adapt. It is no longer possible to think of creation in purely Panglossian terms, or to be complacent about the wise designs of providence. It no longer makes sense to regard the world as static, fixed according to a predetermined pattern by a distant and uninvolved deity. Interestingly, Darwinism brought the concepts of event and narrative to the centre of the scientific stage – concepts which are only now beginning to percolate into the exact sciences through chaos and complexity theories, and which ought to be congenial to a theology in which event and narrative are the key elements. Furthermore, seeing the world as involved in a process of becoming, has in a curious way brought God closer. One Victorian poet described earth as 'the star of suffering'.[7] In fact, as time went on, it came to be seen that Darwinism might actually help in providing some rationale for the pain and suffering and waste, now acknowledged as an inevitable part of a free-running creative process which is not simply preordained from above.

There have been other advantages too. Darwinism liberated theologians from increasingly absurd theories about God as a kind of craftsman-creator, enmeshed in the construction of all the minute variations in animal species which natural historians were then discovering. Furthermore, evolutionary ideas as applied to religion itself began to make sense of the false starts, the barbarities, and the outmoded ideas which had survived as embarrassing appendices, even in such a highly developed faith as Victorian Christianity.

Nor was evolutionary theory without some direct underpinning from theology. Darwin's nightmare had always been the problem of rationality. If the human mind is simply the product of an evolutionary process, what guarantee could there be that its so-called rational conclusions – say on the subject of evolution itself – could actually be trusted? It is a question which has surfaced again in our own day in the writings of Alasdair McIntyre. He has pointed out that rationality is not a concept with a single, clear meaning, but that there have been different, culturally conditioned traditions of rational thinking – not all of which agree on the same standards and methods. There is a further logical point. A system which seeks to explain everything always relies on some hidden assumptions which are not provable within the system itself. Darwinism, it is now seen, carried over into itself some assumptions about the order and rationality of the world which were a legacy from previous beliefs, even while it seemed to undermine those beliefs. The same was true in the moral sphere. What Darwin claimed about the evolution of morality, and the extreme and revolutionary form given to these claims by some of his followers, were belied by his own continuing adherence to liberal values, and by the liberalism of a society which had allowed him to look into the abyss of moral relativity to which evolution seemed to lead.

There is an important paradox here. The search for knowledge at the impersonal, precise, scientific end of the spectrum excludes all questions of meaning and value – as far as possible. It cannot, as we have seen, exclude all prior assumptions, because all science is practised in a social context which sets the standards of what counts as a rational explanation. But there is also a further sense in which science cannot keep questions of meaning and value at bay once it is allowed to escape from the laboratory. Darwin working on his barnacles and pigeons in Downe House could concentrate exclusively and disinterestedly on their minute variations from one another, and try to make sense of these. But the sense he made of them spilled over uncontrollably into a view of the world with profound personal and social implications, in which questions of meaning and value were inescapable. Different groups with different agendas seized on the theory in different ways. Its acceptability, even to Darwin himself, depended in part on the meaning he could give it in terms of his own life and family, and his biography traces the long, slow process by which the work finally became an end in itself.

Society and scientific meaning

The importance of finding an acceptable meaning for the world as disclosed by science is no less pressing in our own day, often for severely practical reasons. The conventional image of science as beneficent and disinterested exploration has changed radically, even within my own lifetime. The pursuit of power rather than the pursuit of knowledge is, however unfairly, now widely seen as the scientists' primary aim. And much of the power sought is perceived as threatening. The negative feelings aroused in many people's minds by biotechnology are a case in point. Claims made about its immense potential benefits tend to be treated with suspicion, except when they give promise of some miracle cure. The focus of popular feeling is usually on the perceived or imagined dangers. The perceived dangers in, say, the uncontrolled release of genetically engineered organisms should rightly make us cautious, and raise important questions about the international control of science. The largely imagined dangers of human genetic manipulation belong at present mostly to the realm of science fiction, but may in the long run demonstrate the need for much deeper thinking about the nature of human personality, and whether that which lies at the core of our being as persons should remain inviolable. The need to bring theological and ethical insights to bear on such issues, as well as scientific ones, is already apparent – and my hope is that this will grow into a fruitful field for interdisciplinary discussion.

Biotechnology is one example of a scientific subject in which different ends of the spectrum of knowledge are forced to interact and, one hopes, learn to like each other. Environmental issues provide many more such examples. Many environmental fears have a strong anti-science component. In general, the enormous range of new choices made available by science-based technology can bemuse or alarm as well as excite, can destroy established patterns of life as well as increase the possibilities of creative living. The meaning of science in our society is therefore increasingly seen as ambivalent: eating from the tree of knowledge has led to all that we now know as civilisation, and destroyed Eden. The ambivalence goes back to the Bible itself, but I believe that we in our generation are being forced to become more sharply conscious of it. I recall vividly a turning-point in my own awareness some 25 years ago, when I had been speaking to a highly intelligent sixth form on science and religion. Instead of there being the usual questions at the end on how any scientifically educated person could take religion seriously, I was surprised to find myself defending scientific rationality and integrity against an onslaught of teenage scepticism. It was not religion which was problematic for them, but science.

What science means to a society is also of vital practical significance to science itself for a very basic reason: society has to pay for it. This is an uncomfortable truth which nowadays has an ever greater bearing on the kind of research which is actually done, and the conditions under which it is performed. The best scientists have always believed passionately in the right to free, untrammelled research − but the reality is that most scientific research is now done under commercial contract, and is under strong pressure to produce results. There has always been a competitive element in science. The race to be first only shows that scientists are human. But when the future of jobs and institutions hangs on the result of the race, the scales become rather heavily weighted against scientific disinterestedness. The scandalous controversy between French and American scientists about the original discovery of HIV is an example of what can go wrong. The growing tendency to patent scientific knowledge is another cause for alarm. The patenting of strings of information about the human genome has been causing enormous concern to those who saw the project to map the whole human genetic structure as the medical equivalent of going to the moon, not as an attempt to corner a market in medical treatment.

There is an idealism at stake here which is not confined to traditional, high-minded science. I believe that both science and theology can usefully identify a common enemy. It comes in many guises, of which commercialism is today one of the most obvious. In saying this I have no wish to denigrate commerce as such: it is precisely because it is so important as a foundational ingredient of civilised life that its influence can become so pervasive. But this begins to be malign in science, and in many other spheres of life, when it distorts concern for the truth, and when it forecloses some avenues of research as commercially unpropitious. Christian writers frequently condemn commercialism in ways which may seem naïve, unfair and unrealistic. But I believe that what underlies these condemnations is this same concern for integrity, a sense that the reality of things is not discerned by putting a price on them. Some years ago I was a contributor to a report called *The Value of Useless Research*[8] in which I tried to make the point that the instincts which drive people to worship – from a non-believer's perspective, one of the most useless of human activities – are not unlike the instincts which lead scientists into the kind of adventures whose end cannot even be guessed. It seems to me that there are common interests here against an enemy which would only allow the asking of the immediately profitable question.

Another guise in which the enemy appears can perhaps be labelled indifferentism. I have in mind the cluster of attitudes and assumptions associated with the post-modernist movement. The great intellectual achievements of the post-Enlightenment period – the quest for objectivity, the reliance on reason, the belief that we live in an ordered and intelligible world – are derided and dismissed. Instead we are faced with fragmentation and discontinuity, with personal preference and unpredictability, with concentration on the ephemeral, the here-and-now, with what has been described as a 'laid-back pluralism'. Here is a quotation from *The Times Literary Supplement* (in 1987), which gives the flavour of it. The writer refers to 'the heterogeneous range of lifestyles and language games which has renounced the nostalgic urge to totalize and legitimate itself'; and he goes on: 'Science and philosophy must jettison their grandiose metaphysical claims and view· themselves more modestly as just another set of narratives'.[9] Science, in other words, tells its story which may be no more or no less true than any other story. It makes no difference, because the notion of objective truth has dropped out altogether. Feyerabend, the most extreme of all modern philosophers of science, made the same point:

> The sciences are after all our own creation, including all the severe standards they seem to impose on us. It is good to be constantly reminded of this fact and that science as we know it today is not inescapable and that we may construct a world in which it plays no role whatever . . . What better reminder is there than the realization that the choice between theories which are sufficiently general to provide us with a comprehensive world view and which are empirically disconnected may become a matter of taste? that the choice of our basic cosmology may become a matter of taste?[10]

Statements like these at the upper end of philosophical abstraction may not seem to matter much in the ordinary business of life. But they are in fact reflected in much everyday experience. Television – with its rapid succession of ephemeral images, with its supposed lack of commitment to any particular point of view, with its growing opportunities for choice – brings some of the assumptions of indifferentism into everybody's living-room. As with commercialism I am not denying the importance of the freedom and openness, the release from imposed cultural norms, which such indifference to a unitary understanding of the world can bring. It is a great thing to be able to think one's own thoughts and dream one's own dreams and create one's own life. Indifferentism becomes an enemy, though, if it undermines the belief that, beyond all this creating and choosing, there are truths which can actually be sought. They may – they almost certainly will – elude ultimate description. But they surely must remain as a goal outside ourselves.

I fear for science if scientists ever lose this vision. Science is a great intellectual adventure, but it is *not* a game which can be played simply according to self-chosen rules. Theology, too, is an attempt to discern and articulate transcendent truth, or it is nothing. To believe in the doctrine of creation is to take one's place alongside those who, in pre-scientific days, dared to trust in the orderliness and meaningfulness of a world in which much seemed chaotic and threatening, and who realised their dependence on a power outside themselves. Their story is the story of the vindication of those beliefs in the events through which they lived. And what we now, through our scientific eyes, perceive in terms of orderliness and meaningfulness, though it has had to be hammered out through centuries of huge intellectual effort, rests in part on this same experience of commitment and trust. Scientists and theologians have a common interest in maintaining it. And that is not a bad basis for liking each other.

My final point can be made more briefly because it is already well accepted. We have a common enemy in the huge sufferings of a world which seems to have outgrown its capacity to live at peace with itself. And we have a common interest in harnessing all our resources – scientific, technological, political, ethical and spiritual – to bear effectively on the problems of peace and justice. I have a little practical experience of this, in trying to mobilise religious and scientific bodies to work together in different parts of the world to tackle local issues – such as deforestation in Central America. It has been both revealing and heartening to see how the combination of technical expertise, religious commitment and community involvement can produce startling results in terms of changed public attitudes.

The moral is simple. Liking one another has to go beyond generalities. When it turns into a trust of each other's basic integrity, and a willingness to work together, things begin to happen.

In the two chapters which follow I look first in more detail at some of the implications of the Darwinian revolution, and then at a few of the ways in which a specifically Christian approach may help to shape more respectful attitudes towards the natural world.

2

A vote of thanks to Darwin

I was recently given a leather-bound presentation copy of the Bampton Lectures preached before the University of Oxford in 1884. The title is *The Relations between Religion and Science*, and the author was the then Bishop of Exeter, later to become Archbishop of Canterbury, Frederick Temple. My copy is signed by his son, William Temple, later himself to become Archbishop of York and then Canterbury.

William, who was more influential in shaping the twentieth-century Church of England than any other figure, confessed that his ignorance of science was so profound as to be distinguished. In many ways it might have been better if he had known more. Over the last 100 years science and theology have drifted apart. William Temple had the public stature and the intellect to have engaged in real dialogue, but even he could not have reversed the process whereby specialisms have become more narrow and isolated, and effective communication has become more difficult. This is not the whole story, as we shall see later. But in his father's day, things were different.

The acceptance of Darwinism

Frederick Temple had begun his career as a mathematician. In 1860, while headmaster of Rugby School, he had written an essay which had given him an undeserved reputation as a dangerous liberal. The years from 1860 to 1884 were a time of intense scientific and theological debate about Darwinism. But when in 1884 Temple delivered his lectures, which started from the assumption that evolution was proven beyond doubt, scarcely anybody thought it odd. At his translation to Canterbury in 1896, a solitary clergyman called Brownjohns protested on the grounds that Temple was a believer in evolution. Not all church leaders would have shared Temple's belief at that stage, but as a focus of major controversy, the issue was dead.

What then happened between 1860 and 1884 to bring about this change of atmosphere? In particular, what was it in Darwinism which proved positively attractive to some theologians, so that they received it, not as a new and unpalatable truth which had somehow to be assimilated, but as a solution of some of their own problems? I shall use Frederick Temple as my guide. But I must make it clear that I am not a historian, and that my primary interest in this little bit of history is in what it can tell us about adopting a positive attitude towards Darwin in our own day.

This unfortunately is a lesson which needs to be learnt afresh, because a curious thing has happened in the late twentieth century. Considerable numbers of Christians, particularly conservative evangelicals, are firmly committed to the view that evolutionary theory is false, or at best dubious. There are serious theologians, not necessarily fundamentalists, who are unwilling to accept its full implications. Conversely, among some evolutionary scientists there is an anti-religious aggressiveness which harks back to the nineteenth century. They deploy a dazzling battery of new insights and techniques with which to twist the tails of theologians. We might be back to the days of T. H. Huxley who wrote in 1860: 'Extinguished theologians lie about the cradle of every science as the strangled snakes beside that of Hercules'.[1]

Part of the struggle that took place between 1860 and 1884 was not about evolutionary theory at all, but about the respective roles of scientists and theologians – their place in the universities, the gradual professionalisation of both roles, and the overriding need for science to free itself from the limits set on it by claims to revealed truth. One of the wisest and gentlest theologians of his day, F. J. A. Hort, centred in his 1871 Hulsean lectures on the claim that Christ is himself the touchstone of truth – a belief from which he did not waver. Nevertheless he accepted that truth might have to enlarge its borders and diversify its understanding:

The pursuit of truth begins in a sense of freedom . . . If we accept the command to 'prove all things', and 'hold fast that which is good', we must be prepared for the possibility of having to cast aside at last, after the most patient and watchful trial, this or that which we have been accustomed to receive as true. How far the loss, if it comes, will be other than a semblance of loss, or how far it will be outweighed by unlooked-for gains, we may not know.[2]

It was a brave and far-sighted thing to say in 1871, though it has to be admitted that it was not published until after his death.

I referred in the last chapter to Desmond and Moore's account of the social, political and moral struggles which provided part of the context for Darwin's work. Huxley in particular is shown as seething with anti-clericalism. He spoke about 'a new Reformation', a revolt against ecclesiastical privilege: 'If I have a wish to live for 30 years, it is that I may see the foot of Science on the necks of her enemies'.[3] Social revolutionaries of other kinds saw in the new thinking an opportunity to overthrow the old order and to ridicule inherited power: if all descended from apes, then earls and dustmen shared the same pedigree. Darwin himself feared greatly the social and moral consequences of his work – which is one reason, say Desmond and Moore, why he hesitated so long, and accumulated such meticulously detailed evidence, before publishing it.

All this and much more was part of the background to the intellectual issues which had to be faced. And remember that the theologians of the day were not only having to come to terms with Darwinism but also, much nearer the bone, with the results of historical criticism and the new ways of reading the Bible which this necessitated. In fact, the two types of criticism, evolutionary and historical, were to interact in rather constructive ways. But to see how this happened we must go back to Frederick Temple's Bampton Lectures.

Darwinism and theology

In the first instance, Temple was grateful to Darwin for rescuing the theology of creation from what had become a scenario of increasing complexity and absurdity. When the world was small, individual experience limited, the known number of plants and animals not enormous, and historical time supposedly restricted to a few thousand years, it was not impossible to believe that each had been created separately, 'after its kind', as Genesis says. But when all those assumptions were blown apart – when the sheer size, age, diversity and fecundity of the natural world were revealed by explorers and scientists

– the multiplication of creative acts, which the creation of separate species seemed to presuppose, began to look like continual divine interference, not to say niggling. Such interference had already been rejected in physics and chemistry. Indeed Darwin had used a quotation from a clergyman scientist, William Whewell, on the title page of *The Origin of Species*: 'But with regard to the material world, we can at least go as far as this – we can perceive that events are brought about not by insulated interpositions of Divine power, exerted in each particular case, but by the establishment of general laws'.

Frederick Temple made the same point: 'The doctrine of Evolution restores to the science of Nature the unity which we should expect in the creation of God'.[4] That insight led him on to expound on the theme of the Genesis creation story as being the orderliness of creation, rather than the details of how it happened. All are related as part of a comprehensible process. And in our twentieth-century reading of Genesis we can see how this awareness of order, this sense of the controlling hand of God, was a key element in the story of creation. It had been vital to people whose lives were precarious, who (like the Israelites) were living in exile, who were deeply conscious of the forces of chaos threatening to overwhelm them, and who nevertheless were given new hope by the prophecies of Isaiah: 'Look to me and be saved, all the ends of the earth; for I am God and there is none else' (Isa. 45:22); 'I am the Lord, your Holy one, the creator of Israel . . . Behold I will do a new thing' (Isa. 43:15, 19). So they remembered the creative acts of God in their own history, in the very formation of their own nation, which had been called out of nothing to be the people of God. And they saw God's ordering, saving power reflected in the world around them. This, then, is the vision which underlies the first chapter of Genesis. It is not too distant a step from this to see that same ordering, saving power at work in evolution. Temple wrote: 'He did not make the things, we may say; no, but He made them make themselves'.[5]

It was not all plain sailing, though. For one thing, Darwin had destroyed the popular form of the argument from design for God's existence. The famous analogy of the watch needing a watchmaker was undercut when the marvellous adaptations of living organisms were seen to belong to a tiny, select and successful minority. The appearance of design arises because, as organisms adapt progressively to specific circumstances, only the well-adapted survive. Temple accepted this. Nevertheless, he said, these creative adaptations could not have taken place unless the materials of the universe were such as to make evolution possible. Design is simply pushed one stage further back. Not every set of initial conditions could have produced a world as complex as ours; so design still enters into it, though at a more fundamental level. Temple's argument has reappeared in a different form today in the appeal to the so-called anthropic principle – based on the discovery of the extraordinarily fine balance in the most basic properties of matter and the physical constants of the universe – a balance which was necessary for there to be a world at all.

But perhaps the most convincing form of a modern argument from design rests on the fact that the universe is intelligible to human minds. Scientists have progressively revealed the degree to which it makes sense. And reflecting on the surprising correspondence between our own minds and whatever the reality is 'out there', raises huge questions about its ultimate meaning and purpose. It is not enough to retort that there is nothing odd about this, because human minds have evolved specifically to enable us find to our way around the universe. There *is* something odd about an apparently mindless, purposeless universe learning how to understand itself.

To pursue this argument would bring us back full circle to an appreciation of scientific discovery, and to the consequent awareness of ultimate unity as in its own way revelatory of the mind of God. This is the exact opposite of clinging to what we do not know, as if God could only be found in miracles and mysteries and incomprehension. Temple hovered on the edge of this understanding. He was still firmly convinced that life itself was the direct creation of God. But he also saw that it was on this deep level of wonder at the intelligibility of the universe that a theory which at last began to provide a coherent framework for biology could also be theologically welcome.

He also toyed with the notion of progress. It appeared in his discussion of the problem of suffering, to which I shall return later. Meanwhile I want to look briefly at the theological significance of the fact that the Darwinian concept of order included progress – not progress in the sense of movement towards a fixed goal, but progress in the sense of progressive adaptation and, frequently, progressive complexity and differentiation. Theologically this could be both liberating and threatening.

It was liberating because it took seriously the dimension of time within the purposes of God. Christians no longer had to see themselves as the guardians of an eternal, unchangeable order of things, but could see God at work in the world of nature as the Bible sees him on the stage of history, within the processes of change. Creation no longer had to be thought of as a single, immutable event, but could be experienced as a continuous divine activity in which human beings could themselves find a new freedom to create. It is easy now to mock the heady dreams of progress which marked the latter half of the nineteenth century, and which only began to crumble in the face of our twentieth century disasters. But there is a real and proper excitement in knowing that the universe is open-ended, that we are part of a world in the making, and that human choice is a significant factor in what our world becomes. It is also true that, whether or not we believe in progress, our human world continues to move in the direction of greater and greater complexity, and in that sense it matches the movement characteristic of biological evolution, though clearly not by the same means. Cultural evolution is not genetic, but there may nevertheless be a kind of cultural natural selection.

Evolution, randomness and God

The effect of Darwin was to set the seal on a historical dimension of science, which has proved to be enormously important. For some, it vitiated the claim of evolutionary theory to be scientific. A process dependent on chance and accident, and whose outcome is unpredictable, doesn't fulfil the criteria of testability and repeatability which form the backbone of the exact sciences. It is all very well to map connections between different organisms, say the critics, but how do you prove with any degree of scientific rigour that a development which is essentially unrepeatable actually took place?

If that is the way you want to define science, runs the reply, so much the worse for science. In the real world, events cannot be totally captured in repeatable laboratory experiments. The biological world is a hugely complex and constantly changing interconnected system, which has to be understood as a system in its wholeness, and not as a set of isolable and independent parts. The kind of reductionism which may work well in physics and chemistry fails when applied to biological evolution. What is special about biology at every level is that it investigates the way in which materials and entities are organised, rather than their properties or behaviour in isolation. Indeed, organisation is the key to life.

Evolutionary theory has thus inevitably pushed science in the direction of holism, and in curious ways can be seen to link up with similar holistic tendencies in nuclear physics. The world today seems a much more mysterious, interconnected whole, with a much more open future, than in the heyday of mechanistic and reductionist science. And there are new sciences to illustrate this. Ecology, a holistic science *par excellence*, is an offshoot of evolutionary theory. In the last decade or so the gropings towards a science of complexity constitute a major effort to come to terms with the fact that the whole is greater than the sum of its parts, that new properties emerge at different levels of organisation, and that what happens in complex systems may be by its very nature unpredictable.

All this is to run a long way ahead of Darwin and Temple, but the seed is there in the words 'progress' and 'development', the injection of the dimensions of time and chance into scientific understanding. And it could be theologically liberating for those who grasped the point that the time dimension is central to Christianity as well, that creation and revelation are not static, once-for-all, events but part of a continuing process, in which God is at work through all time.

But it could also be threatening. An open-ended process is by definition not working towards a fixed goal. The unpalatable conclusion reached by Darwin and his supporters was that evolution simply goes the way it goes. There is no purpose or direction in it, and to suppose that developing creatures are working towards something, rather than simply adapting to competition and environmental change, is to falsify the basis of natural selection. Temple, and many who have followed him, smoothed over this point. To speak of God 'making things make themselves' subtly intrudes a hint of purpose and direction, while seeming to acknowledge that the process goes its own way.

Countless Christian apologists since then have described evolution as God's way of creating. There has been talk of God 'guiding' evolution. Process theologians use the idea of God 'luring' creation towards an ordered future. It has been claimed that Darwinists are the victims of a mechanistic interpretation of nature; a science which excludes purpose as a causative factor in natural processes leads to a world-vision in which the human experience of purposiveness can have no place. It is not there, because it has been deliberately left out. There is some truth in this. But at the root of such objections is a revolt against the idea that chance and accident can somehow serve the creative purposes of God.

I believe that these objections rest on a false assumption that a process fuelled, as it were, by chance must necessarily be nothing more than the result of chance in its outcome. On the contrary: the kind of instability with which we associate chance and accident can be highly creative; but what is actually created depends on the rules of the game in which the instability occurs.

Think of the difference between three different types of game – roulette, Monopoly and chess. Roulette is a game of pure chance, and nothing else. I do not know enough about it to be able to say whether there is any skill in the placing of bets, but I suspect not. The only meaning which emerges from the game is whether a player's luck is in or out.

Monopoly is fuelled by chance. The throw of the dice creates the opportunities to which the players have to respond – to pass Go and collect £200, to buy a property, or build a house; and there are other elements of chance in the picking up of cards, from Chance and Community Chest, corresponding to the accidents and opportunities of everyday life. But nevertheless it is a game in which skill counts for something, and in which it is possible to develop strategies, to read your opponents' minds, to play offensively or defensively. Chance, as it were, drives the engine; but where the game goes depends on a host of other factors, including deliberate choice.

Chess, supposedly, contains no element of chance at all, except the chance of a player making a mistake. But in a game in which there is an almost infinite number of possible scenarios, the limits of rationality are set by the limits of prediction. Even the most logical moves have fuzzy edges as one thinks about their long-term implications. In practice, therefore, this open-endedness leads to the development of certain well-known strategies and patterns which the successful player instinctively learns to recognise. Though theoretically limitless, the game is actually constrained within some fairly well-defined parameters.

I suspect that nature is a bit like a mixture of Monopoly and chess. Natural selection fits the pattern of Monopoly. Chance and accident drive it – random mutations, environmental changes, sheer coincidences. But the effect of these depends on the interactions between an immense variety of players, each trying in its own way to win, responding to each other, stimulating each other, devouring each other. Whether or not their strategies are successful depends – as in Monopoly – in part on themselves, in part on the circumstances, and in part on the rules of the game. While the input may be random, therefore, the output is not. It is the best response possible within those particular parameters.

The chess-like features of nature are only just beginning to be understood. One fairly recent observation, made possible by the development of computers, is that a few simple rules applied successively to simple entities can give rise to huge complexity. The rules of chess can be set down in a few sentences. The actual game of chess can fill libraries. But within this complexity there are patterns, there are winning strategies; and these depend, not on anybody's conscious decision, but on the rules and character of the game itself.

So in the world of nature, it may be that the rules of organisation are comparatively simple, if only we knew what they were. We see them operating in living organisms every time a set of genes gives rise to the enormously complex finished product. But it seems that, as with computers, standard patterns also emerge at a more abstract level in the interaction between different entities of whatever kind, simply through the operation of repetitive processes in appropriate conditions. The growing of crystals is the most elementary example of this ordering principle. In other words, it seems that, built into the way things are, there are not only vast possibilities for freedom and creativity, but also certain inherent rules and structures which channel this creativity away from relapsing into chaos, and towards greater complexity and order.

Put these two together – chess and Monopoly, deep structures of ordered creativity, and a dynamic process which allows chance to create options for appropriate response – and I think we have not only an abstract model of how evolution actually works, but one which theologians might happily live with. God, as it were, wills and upholds the conditions for the process. And since the world, in so far as we understand it, is made up of processes of various kinds, then whatever or whoever prescribes the conditions for them is the ultimate basis of reality. That is not far, in philosophical terms, from what we mean by God.

I have telescoped a long argument. My concern has been to show that there are ways of understanding evolution as God's creative activity which do not involve fudging, as if God had rigged the answer beforehand. The fact is that a free, creative process could have produced many alternative forms of life quite different from those we see today. The creatures capable of understanding and commenting on the process might have been quite different from ourselves. But that there would be creatures of high complexity, able to accumulate and transmit knowledge, with a capacity to know themselves and ultimately to transcend themselves in their relationship with God, seems to me to be built into the nature of things.

Perhaps the game of roulette can help us to see why there is this inbuilt drive towards complexity. I dismissed it earlier as a game of pure chance – and while that is true, it is not the whole truth. There is one player in roulette who in the long run always stands to win – the banker. The other players act as separate individuals, but the banker has connections with them all. His multiple connections give him a more complex role, and spread the risks. And this is what gives him an advantage. Whoever wins or loses, the banker can almost always come out on top. In a game of pure chance, the key to winning is diversity of connections. The same seems to be true in the game of life. Multiple connectedness, and the complexity which goes with it, are evolutionary winners. So it is not religious prejudice which makes me say that complex systems tend to ramify in the direction of ever greater complexity, and that self-conscious intelligence is not an accident. We might have had bodies like little green men from outer space, but on any reasonable interpretation of evolution we would still have had brains. In fact, it is no coincidence that those who speculate scientifically about creatures from outer space implicitly assume that they have an intelligence something like ours, and that communication with them is thus theoretically possible.

The sufferings of creation

I mentioned earlier that Temple introduced the idea of evolutionary progress into his discussion of suffering, and it is to suffering that I now turn in the final part of this chapter. I have made the point that we must be grateful to Darwin for his unifying vision of the natural world. We must be grateful too for the sense of dynamism which evolutionary ideas have injected into contemporary thought, including theology, and we must welcome the long-term implications for science in having to take time, history and development seriously. I could have dwelt on the fears engendered in Darwin's day about the demotion of human beings to the level of animals – and it is noteworthy that even Temple tried to wriggle away from this. In fact, he advanced a highly dubious argument about the human branch of the tree of life having separated from the remainder at an extremely early stage. It is only in this century that we have seen positive advantages in acknowledging our cousinship with the animals, and our role as part of nature rather than as lords over it.

But it is the fact of suffering, both in animals and humans, which has for some always constituted the greatest obstacle to Christian belief; and that obstacle seemed all the greater when suffering and death were demonstrated to be an essential part of the machinery of evolution.

Temple made the familiar point that creation is incomplete, and that evolution makes clear its present imperfection. He did not actually quote St Paul, but might easily have pointed to the famous passage in Romans 8 about 'creation groaning and travailing in pain together until now . . . waiting for the redemption of the body'. In other words, the answer lies not in what we experience now, but in what will be, when God's purpose of love and justice is fulfilled.

That is a sort of answer, but it leaves a vague unease. Temple tried to expand it with a further, very odd argument linked to the notion of progress, discussed earlier. 'Survival of the fittest', he said, 'implies a perpetual diminution of pain and increase of enjoyment for all creatures that feel. If they are fitter for their surroundings, most certainly they will find life easier to live.' He went on to paint a quite extraordinary picture of the whole animal world becoming happier as the unfit are weeded out. Remember that this was the time when the colonial powers were busy scrambling for Africa, and then consider these words: 'Many species of animals perish as man fills and subjugates the globe, but those that remain have far greater happiness in their lives'.[6] Tell that to the elephants.

The fact is that we perpetually deceive ourselves over suffering, and clergy are often the worst offenders. We feel that, unless we can somehow fit suffering into a rational scheme of things, it is impossible to believe in the goodness of God. We tend to forget that suffering has always been part of human experience, and that religions have arisen out of it and in the face of it, because they have provided a practical answer to suffering even if they cannot provide a theoretical one. Darwinism did not add to the total of human and animal suffering, but simply put it in a different context. And while that may, in some ways, have made it more difficult to accept as an agent of God's creative purpose, in other ways it actually eased the problem.

Natural selection provided a rationale for waste. Intolerable problems confront a theology which ascribes all that happens in the world to the direct, unmediated intention of God. But a world which is allowed to make itself, in order to develop the freedom to be itself, at least contains some explanation of why fragility and vulnerability are an essential component of it. A complex mixture of competition and co-operation are the conditions for free creativity – and free creativity is the basis of life. I stress co-operation as well as competition, because the natural world is not just a chaotic jungle of competing interests. It contains a massive interplay of forces in which living organisms depend on one another, and learn from one another, and urge one another up towards further levels of complex adaptation to their environment. I shall return to the point about co-operation in Chapter 3, but let me here recall what I was saying about roulette, where it is multiple connectedness which counts. The picture which emerges is much more subtle than the old horror story of 'nature red in tooth and claw', in which each struggles against all. There are still horrors, but there is also a connectedness which gives life.

To see the roots of vulnerability in this kind of creative ferment is not to explain away, still less to excuse, suffering. But it is to see it not merely as pointless waste. There can be no freedom without clash of interests. There can be no creation without destruction. There can be no life without death.

I said earlier that Temple might have quoted St Paul's words about 'creation groaning and travailing', to make the point that we only see part of the picture. But the deeper meaning of those words is that God himself groans and travails, as the one who takes the world's vulnerability on himself and redeems it. Our Victorian forefathers were shy of speaking about the vulnerability of God. The twentieth century has taught us to think differently. But we can, I believe, be grateful to Darwin for beginning to show us, in ways which I am sure he did not suspect, how better to make the connection between redemption and creation; to see that the God who upholds the creative process is also the God who bears its weight in suffering.

3

Evolution and ethics

In the previous chapter I suggested reasons why theologians could feel grateful to Darwin for helping to set some of their problems in a fresh and illuminating perspective. I used Frederick Temple's 1884 Bampton Lectures, written at a time when the most intense period of religious controversy was over, as a guide to the reactions of a prominent churchman. In this chapter, I want to continue that approach, centring on a topic which has proved to be peculiarly ambivalent. I have in mind the idea that religion itself, and especially morality, can be understood in evolutionary terms.

Morality – revealed or evolved?

Temple was firm in his belief that the 'moral law', as he called it, was not itself part of our ordinary scientific knowledge of the natural world. Scientific knowledge is at best partial, he said, and in any case gives us no mandate for identifying justice, goodness and holiness. The moral law is known by faith and conscience, and rests ultimately on the revelation of God in Christ. But this does not mean that science has no place in illuminating it; nor does it follow that the moral law itself has been revealed once-for-all, complete and perfect. In fact, although Temple did not put it quite like this, many of the problems which had been worrying biblical scholars – the barbarities recorded in some parts of the Old Testament, crude concepts of religion, claims which flew in the face of contemporary science – could be eased by using the analogy of evolution.[1] This is how Temple describes it:

> The Christian Religion does not profess to be wrapped up in one divine communication made to one man and admitting thereafter

of no modifications. [He had in mind Islam.] Though resting on divine revelation it is professedly a development, and is thus in harmony with the Creator's operations in nature.[2]

He goes on to spell out how moral laws are progressively superseded. The role and dignity of women, polygamy, divorce, slavery, the sense of individual responsibility, attitudes to children – all undergo profound changes within the pages of the Bible. But these changes are not arbitrary. Moral ideas are subjected again and again to the test of universality:

> The pivots of all the prophetical teaching are the incessant inculcation of justice and mercy; justice which requires us to recognise the rights of others side by side with our own; mercy which demands our sympathy with the feelings of other creatures that can feel.[3]

In other words, there is an evolution, a progressive extension of moral feeling, into wider and more demanding environments. But at each stage the moral demand had the force of revelation. People in past ages spoke truly of God, but partially. And even the New Testament is morally incomplete: despite the perfection of its basic teaching, it gives no clear guidance, says Temple, on such contemporary issues as patriotism, or the right use of wealth, or the moral principles of government. We might say the same today in thinking of such topics as genetic engineering or vegetarianism or minority rights.

Thus far Temple. He gladly embraces the idea of progressive revelation. He uses it as a basis for filtering out some of the more embarrassing aspects of biblical teaching. The infamous slaughter of the Amalekites recounted in 1 Samuel 15, for instance, could safely be relegated to an ignorant past. And he legitimises this by an appeal to the principle of evolution. What he does not do, however, is give any credence to the view that evolution could by itself provide an explanation of the basis of morality, or guidance as to its contents.

Social Darwinism

Darwin, meanwhile, had gone much further. He saw no reason why morality itself should not have evolved. He was also aware of, and disturbed by, the way in which belief in natural selection could be used in moral and political arguments. Racism, for instance, was already beginning to become an issue in the 1850s. In Britain the self-esteem of the gentry required them to believe in an unbridgeable gulf between themselves and what most of them regarded as black savages. A proof of common ancestry was thus deeply unsettling. Yet Darwin was also aware of other implications – of how, in a world driven by competition, the so-called inferior races were in danger of dying out. Years ago, on the voyage of the *Beagle*, he had noted in his diary the gradual near-extinction of the Maoris in New Zealand through European expansion.

Evolutionary theory, in fact, could both interpret social change, as in the case of the Maoris, and could also accelerate change by seeming to legitimise it. One of the most militant of the accelerators was Ernst Haeckel, a Prussian zoologist and disciple of Darwin, who preached the gospel of Darwinism with revolutionary fervour. He saw it as an all-embracing philosophy with profound social and political implications. His gospel was violently anti-clerical and nationalistic. Bismarck's successes in uniting Germany were hailed by him as a great Darwinian leap forward, the birth of a new evolutionary phylum, a higher group – the *Volk* – whose racial integrity was explained by natural selection. He saw this privileged *Volk* as having developed through the same process of struggle and selection as the new Prussian state. The old order in Germany regarded this social Darwinism (as it came to be called) as so threatening that the teaching of biology in the upper forms of schools was forbidden for three decades. The educationally excluded, however, took up the ideas enthusiastically, and the first phase of social Darwinism in Germany was an attack on the flabby morality of compassion inherited from Christianity and the Enlightenment. It was to be replaced by an ethic in which self-preservation and self-assertion were the primary values.

However, by the turn of the century there was less confidence that this ruthless kind of competitiveness was automatically beneficial. It was obvious too that purely biological principles of selection could not be applied to the much more complex and intentional processes of cultural change. Attention therefore shifted, in the second phase of social Darwinism, to the much more conscious manipulation of society through racial hygiene. Fears were expressed about social degeneration, given the fact that those deemed socially inadequate –

most of whom would probably not have survived without the advances of modern medicine – bred many more children than those deemed socially superior. The professor of racial hygiene in the University of Munich declared in 1930: 'The question of the genetic quality of the coming generations is a hundred times more important than the struggle of capitalism versus socialism'.[4] From there it is but a short step to this statement about programmes of eugenics by a leading German anthropologist in 1934, the year after Hitler came to power:

Many worthy and well-meaning people will be harshly and cruelly affected. But can any sacrifice be too great when it is a question of saving a whole nation? Was it not particularly this nation that lost infinitely more of its most valuable genetic stock in the war? Ethnical renewal, deliberate racial care, pulls a nation back from the abyss to which the so-called culture of the last few decades has brought it.

The third phase of social Darwinism in Germany was Auschwitz.

I have concentrated on Germany because it provided the most startling and horrific evidence of what can go wrong. It is a familiar story, but still relevant at a time when there is much talk about the possibilities of genetic improvement, in the light of the major work being done on mapping the entire human genetic structure. One can understand present-day German fears in the whole area of genetic manipulation.

Social Darwinism had its heyday in Britain too, most notably in *laissez-faire* economics. There were also the same fears of genetic degeneration through the overriding of natural selection, and these persisted until well after the second world war. It is perhaps significant that Sir Peter Medawar thought it worthwhile to devote the whole of his 1959 Reith Lectures to combating such mistaken ideas about how genetic inheritance actually works. In so doing, he roundly rejected all the assumptions of social Darwinism:

We can jettison all reasoning based upon the idea that changes in society happen in the style and under the pressures of ordinary genetic evolution; abandon any idea that the direction of social change is governed by laws other than laws which have at some time been the subject of human decisions and acts of mind. That competition between one man and another is a necessary part of the texture of society; that societies are organisms which grow and must inevitably die; that divisions of labour in society are akin to what we can see in colonies of insects; that the laws of genetics have an overriding authority; that social evolution has a direction imposed upon it by agencies beyond man's control – all these are biological judgements; but, I do assure you, bad judgements based upon a bad biology ... It is a profound truth – realised in the nineteenth century by only a handful of astute biologists, and by philosophers hardly at all – a profound truth that nature does *not* know best; that genetical evolution, if we choose to look at it liverishly instead of with fatuous good humour, is a story of waste, makeshift, compromise and blunder.[5]

Interestingly, T. H. Huxley, despite his fierce championship of Darwin and his vicious critique of religion, would have agreed. In his famous Romanes Lecture of 1893, he gave his final testimony on the subject which had worried him for most of his working life – the relationship between evolution and ethics:

Let us understand once for all that the ethical progress of society depends, not on imitating the cosmic process, still less in running away from it, but in combating it ... The one supreme hegemonic faculty, which constitutes the essential 'nature' of man ... holds up the ideal of the supreme good, and demands absolute submission of the will to its behests. It is this which commands all men to love one another, to return good for evil, to regard one another as citizens of one great state.[6]

In other words, Huxley, for all his agnosticism, still believed essentially what Frederick Temple believed about the independence and authority of the moral law. Evolution can tell us what we are, but not what we should be. His grandson Julian Huxley, himself a Romanes lecturer 50 years later, had no such doubts about evolutionary progress or the belief that it could furnish moral insight. This was not social Darwinism: it was a more subtle attempt to look at the whole sweep of evolutionary history, and to deduce from it how humanity, as now the manager of the process, should guide it towards the future. Openness, flexibility, integration, individuation – these are the qualities to be

45

developed in what he called 'Evolutionary humanism'. 'Anything which permits or promotes open development is right', he wrote in 1953. 'Anything which restricts or frustrates development is wrong. It is a morality of evolutionary direction.'[7]

It is significant that Julian Huxley wrote the introduction to the Jesuit Teilhard de Chardin's *The Phenomenon of Man* – at the time of its publication a much-praised attempt to set this vision of evolutionary progress in a Christian context. This was in 1959, the centenary year of *The Origin of Species*, and I have vivid memories of taking part in a television discussion programme with Julian Huxley, who was clearly enormously excited by his discovery of de Chardin. As in his grandfather, there was real religious feeling buried under an apparently hard scientific exterior. I mentioned in Chapter 2 that similar ideas about the inevitability of evolutionary progress have emerged in recent years through the study of complexity. Given the right conditions and a few straightforward rules of operation, simple systems do seem to develop into complex ones – at least in computer simulations. But it is a far cry from this to saying that such growth or development in complexity can or should be the basis for moral guidance. And even on a purely practical level, can we really imagine anybody deciding, say, whether or not adultery is wrong on the basis of whether it points in the right evolutionary direction? Or how, for example, are we to judge the case increasingly being made against Western civilisation that our open, developing, increasingly differentiated, pluralistic, uncommitted kind of culture is in fact a runaway world heading for disaster? I am not saying whether it is, or is not. The question is, how are we to judge whether the direction in which our world is moving is good, simply on the basis of a theory of development? We are back with Frederick Temple again, and his belief that, although history and evolution can tell us much about what *has* developed and about *how* it has developed, the basic moral law somehow stands outside these, as simply *given*.

But may it not be given to us in what T. H. Huxley called the 'essential nature of man'? And may not a study of evolution help us to discern what this is?

Morality and human nature

The great Anglican moralist, Joseph Butler, set out his moral teaching in a famous series of sermons on human nature. They are full of acute observation; in fact Butler might be called the father of moral psychology. They are also very eighteenth century in their flavour, and on first reading give the impression that they belong to a vanished world. 'Nothing can possibly be more contrary to nature than vice', he wrote. He stressed the importance of actively pursuing human interests through what he called 'cool self-love'. And he saw the various affections and appetites brought into harmony through rational reflection, the voice of conscience, Temple's moral law within.

All this may seem impossibly remote from twentieth-century experience. Yet Butler remains important precisely because he does not have some overriding theory of morality which subsumes everything else. He encourages us to look at the actual complexities of human experience, to be aware of the powers of self-deception, to see that morality is about being human, and to recognise that there are limits beyond which we become self-destructive. Furthermore, the moral law within is not simply imposed on us. Conscience is not the name of some esoteric faculty. Interpreted as rational reflection, it is the capacity for self-judgement, for being honest with ourselves, for weighing up before God what we are, and what we might and should become.

Writing in 1729, Butler is not likely to have taken much notice of Roman Catholic writings on natural law. It is worth pausing for a moment, though, to reflect on the difference between these two ways of trying to root morality in human nature. Butler's method was empirical: look at what human beings are actually like, and what enables them to find fulfilment both individually and socially. This is not to say that morality merely reflects what human beings want. As he was never tired of saying, human beings are adept at deceiving themselves. But Butler insists that we take stock of human nature as we find it, and there is thus always the possibility of discovering more about ourselves and our obligations.

For St Thomas Aquinas, and those who followed in that tradition, natural law was not primarily empirical but teleological. In other words, it looks at human nature in terms of its ends, as understood within the purposes of God. Each natural function has a purpose, and to discern that purpose is to discover how it should be used. The purpose of sex is reproduction: any sexual activity, therefore, which does not serve the purposes of reproduction is against natural law.

As purposes become more strictly and more authoritatively defined, it is difficult for such a system to change. Indeed, Pope John Paul II's encyclical, *Veritatis Splendor* (1993), with its emphasis on intrinsically evil actions, reveals just how firmly set against development such a system can become.

Butler's empiricism, by contrast, positively invites development and change, and therein lies an opposite danger. One of the consequences of evolution has been to fluidise the concept of human nature. The nature of things is not given once-for-all: the world is a flux of events, a torrent of innovation, creation in the making. Obviously there are more or less enduring patterns and stabilities within this overall dynamism, but our understanding of human nature is no more fixed than anything else. Think, for example, of the strong contemporary emphasis on personal autonomy. This is a fairly modern insight, but it has already had profound consequences in education, medical practice and many other aspects of public life, including citizens' charters. Within the memory-span of many of us, it has made us think differently about ourselves: self-fulfilment has taken the place of duty. The question therefore arises: if we are to look to human nature for moral guidance, where are the fixed points?

There are some who have tried to give an evolutionary answer. The fixed points, they say, are those dispositions and characteristics which our evolutionary history has already implanted in our genes. It is because we have evolved to be social creatures that we need to take seriously insights into our nature, which the comparative study of animal social behaviour can provide for us. This is not a return to a discredited social Darwinism. The attempt to found a morality solely on the basis of the struggle for existence is now well recognised as a contradiction in terms: morality is precisely what rescues us from such a struggle. But suppose it is possible to give an evolutionary explanation of altruism, then it is no longer absurd to think of moral attitudes as having a genetic component. This is the basic message of sociobiology which, in the last 20 years, has uncovered a wealth of altruistic behaviour in animals, and has made some high claims about the significance of this for the understanding of human nature.

Altruism and sociobiology

The biological explanation of altruism is in terms of kin-selection. If animals were only isolated individuals, so the argument goes, they could only act selfishly, to secure their own survival. But in fact they are not. They belong to groups, families, herds – and share much of their genetic inheritance with their kin. It may not be to an individual's advantage to sacrifice itself on behalf of those related to it – but it may be an advantage to those who share the same pool of genes. A larger proportion of the genes of the sacrificed individual may be preserved for future breeding, as a result of the sacrifice, than if the individuals had simply acted in self-preservation. In other words, one set of genes dies in order that a greater number of closely related sets of genes may live. Natural selection thus works to the advantage of families and groups which develop altruistic tendencies of this rather limited kind.

There is an obvious difficulty in trying to construct a morality on such a basis, precisely because the altruism is so limited. Indeed, if that were all, there would be no escape from family selfishness – still less from the other tribalisms which bedevil today's world. The supreme test of a moral system is whether it can apply universally; and by this test, kin-selected altruism fails miserably.

E. O. Wilson, the main protagonist of sociobiology, was well aware of this difficulty, and acknowledged that he could only account for wider forms of altruism in terms of cultural evolution.[8] It is an admission which effectively undercuts sociobiology's claim to provide a genetic foundation for morality. But there is still plenty of scope for argument about the extent to which studies of animal behaviour can legitimately be applied to human beings, and how far it makes sense to think of complex human behaviour-patterns as being under strong genetic influence.

There are questions to be asked, for instance, about the central role given by sociobiologists to altruism. The biological case for it, as I have presented it, slides over a crucial distinction. It is assumed that, if altruism can be identified in animals, then it means roughly the same as when we speak about altruism in human beings. A blackbird which gives a warning to other blackbirds that there is an owl in the vicinity is not behaving ethically. It is simply reacting. So are worker bees, which maintain the hive but have no chance of breeding. But altruism in human beings is intentional, and is not morally significant unless it *is* intentional. There may be predispositions to associate with other human beings, even to love them. But moral behaviour begins when we choose to do these things. Therefore to locate the essence of morality in an interpretation of altruism which exploits the ambivalence between altruistic behaviour and altruistic intentions is to indulge in sleight-of-hand. The two meanings of altruism, in a biological and in a human context, are simply not the same.

Estimates of the value of sociobiology are also related to larger questions about the size and significance of the genetic component in human behaviour. There are not likely to be any firm answers to such questions for a very long time, if ever. It is hard enough trying to disentangle the degree to which relatively straightforward conditions, such as heart failure, may be genetically predisposed. To try to do the same in any rigorous fashion for complex social behaviour would seem to me to involve so many imponderables as to be largely wasted effort.

As a source of suggestive comparisons, though – and as a reminder that we have an evolutionary past – sociobiology has a lot to offer. Nobody who has seen the famous films of the domestic life of gorillas in the wild can doubt that we are related to them not only biologically, but also in terms of social behaviour. Biological studies can indeed tell us a great deal about human nature. But if we want to study what is characteristically and essentially human, we have to look elsewhere. And among other things that means refusing to explain away morality in terms of something else. In fact, one could say that moral awareness is central to human self-understanding.

All of which brings us back to Frederick Temple with his consciousness of the moral law; and to Butler with his assertion of the supremacy of conscience; and to many of the great Victorian doubters like Huxley, who could no longer believe in religion, but could not let go of morality. Such a belief – that goodness is not simply a matter of our likes and dislikes, and is not to be explained away by evolution or any other natural process, and is not to be located arbitrarily in some heady vision emerging out of contemporary science – still haunts those who want to be morally serious. My own belief is that it cannot in the end be detached from religious faith. But I also believe that there may be intermediate stages, half-way houses as it were, in which certain fundamental moral principles may be seen to have become established through a process of trial and error. And these form the basis of a kind of common morality, and of what are now almost universally recognised as human rights.

In the previous chapter I used the analogy of certain games to illustrate how evolution could be driven by random events without being random in its results. Here is a moral game, known as the prisoners' dilemma.

Imagine two prisoners in separate cells, both suspected of complicity in the same crime. The only way they can be convicted is by giving evidence against each other. Each is promised that if he gives evidence against the other, he will be set free and given a large reward. What are the prisoners to do? If neither gives evidence, both will go free. But can they trust each other? If only one of them gives evidence, he will win everything and the other lose everything. If both are motivated only by fear and self-interest, the likelihood is that both will give evidence, and both will therefore suffer the worst possible consequence.

The question is, given that this is the human situation in an amoral world, how do we escape disaster?

But suppose you set this dilemma up as a game, and allow the two players to play it, not once but, say, 100 times, some strategies will emerge. The best strategy turns out to be tit-for-tat – in other words, be nice, but tough. Learn to trust, but punish breaches of trust severely. Given such a policy applied consistently, the most frequent outcome of repeated games is that both prisoners will stay silent, and thus achieve the best possible consequence for both of them. To a limited extent, mistrust has been replaced by co-operation.

Morality learned from experience?

The final sense, therefore, in which I want to consider evolution and ethics is this rather weak sense in which ethical attitudes can be said to evolve through being repeatedly put to the test in practice. This has nothing directly to do with biological evolution; nor is it about making large-scale historical generalisations. But it is the acknowledgement that human beings can, and do, learn morally from cumulative experience.

Temple, in accepting that a historical process is to be found in the Bible, used evolution as an analogy for the gradual growth in religious and moral sensitivity. Others pursued the same ideas more radically and comprehensively. There was a time when evolutionary interpretations of Scripture were seen as the key to critical understanding. The steady progression from lower to higher religion provided the framework in which beliefs and practices could be located, and even dated. Furthermore, the framework could accommodate not just biblical religion but a wide range of other religious cultures. It was a way of thinking given considerable impetus not long after Temple's lectures by an essay called 'Incarnation and development' in the liberal Anglican Catholic manifesto of 1889, *Lux Mundi*. The essay was an evolutionary interpretation of the incarnation – not in any crude biological sense, but as the culmination of a process which included other faiths besides Christianity. Teilhard de Chardin, had he read it, would have approved. But as a key to biblical criticism the whole approach soon proved to be far too simplistic, and is now well out of favour.

Nevertheless there is a real insight here. Religion and morality can indeed be seen to develop through a historical process. Inspiration can pass on from generation to generation, and adapt itself to different circumstances; it can grow and deepen in the face of experience. Think of the gradual growth of the sense of personal responsibility in Old Testament religion. Key insights may be lost and rediscovered. Explosive material may lie buried like a time-bomb, and shake the world when the time is ripe. It is not a simple matter of onward and upward, but there is real and significant change.

A. N. Whitehead asked himself why it had taken so long for slavery to be abolished, when the ideas which were to do so were already present in ancient Greece, in Judaism, and in New Testament Christianity. His answer was that ideas may have to mature through many generations, and that major moral changes can only be implemented when the social and political conditions are right for them. Those who actually implement them are not necessarily morally superior to those who contributed much earlier in the process. It is just that 'what is possible now may not have been possible then'.[9]

Nor can we be sure that the process does not work the other way too. We might in our day be losing moral insights which are vital to our humanity. I think we are right to be alarmed, for instance, by the new possibilities for manipulating and commercialising human life opened up by genetic engineering. I have already commented on the new emphasis laid on human autonomy which could dangerously weaken our sense of ourselves as fundamentally social beings. And we have seen only too sharply in recent years how brutal, vengeful instincts can lie buried, perhaps for generations, to revive in full force when the opportunity is there, and overwhelm civilised decencies.

Despite the ups and downs, though, I believe it is possible to identify a very broad consensus about some necessary conditions for being human. Without such a consensus I do not see how it could be possible to communicate meaningfully about moral issues across the boundaries of different religions and cultures. Yet to a limited extent we can, and the human rights movement is evidence for it. Part of the consensus may come from our evolutionary history, when our remote ancestors discovered painfully how human beings could live and thrive together. Some of it undoubtedly stems from quite recent cultural history, as we have been forced to accept the implications of living in one world. But major advances in moral understanding have usually come through individuals or groups who draw inspiration from outside the consensus, and go beyond it.

We thus find what might be called a basic human morality which is common to most peoples and cultures, and which has developed over millennia through a gradual process of learning from experience. But this has constantly been refined, supplemented and criticised from another level of moral experience and inspiration, usually religious. The basic morality may in some very general sense be said to have evolved. The leading edge of moral discovery, though, has generally been formed by outstanding leaders, teachers, prophets and thinkers, and by crucially significant events. We can see this happening in the biblical tradition. It was the prophets who awoke a new sense of moral seriousness. It was belief in the holiness and transcendence of God which hugely enlarged the area of obligation, leading to what Iris Murdoch has called the awareness of 'irreducible incompleteness', of being on an endless pilgrimage. It was the death and resurrection of Christ which gave a whole new meaning to faith, hope and love, and set the scene for a distinctively Christian morality.

I have been looking at ethics as it were from below, as a human phenomenon. But just as I ended the last chapter by pointing to the relevance of what I was saying to belief in God as creative power and suffering love, so let me complete the Trinity by underlining what I have just been saying about inspiration. The moral law, as Temple knew, is indeed given to us: given by history; given by culture; but also, and most characteristically, given by the Spirit, working through events, inspiring individuals, decisively for Christians opening our eyes to the significance of Christ, and writing the moral law in our hearts.

4

The sacramentality of the natural world

In exploring the common ground between science and theology in previous chapters, my main emphasis has been on the impact of scientific discovery. I turn now to a more specifically theological interpretation of science, and to some of the practical implications of this, taking as my starting-point the work of an Orthodox theologian, Alexander Schmemann, in his book *The World as Sacrament*.[1]

The transformation of the ordinary

Schmemann wanted to relate the sacraments to the life of the whole world. The first, the basic definition of *Homo sapiens*, he wrote, is that he is the priest:

> He stands at the centre of the world and unifies it in his act of blessing God, of both receiving the world from God and offering it to God . . . The world was created as the 'matter', the material of one all-embracing Eucharist, and man was created as the priest of this cosmic sacrament.

Human beings, he went on to say, are hungry for God and, cut off from God, can only eat dead food. 'Man is what he eats. So the question is, What does he eat and why?' Within the Christian mystery, life is given back to us in Christ, dead food is transformed into living presence. Indeed, the world itself only has meaning and value when seen as the sacrament of God's living presence. The secular vision of the world is a lie: it tells of emptiness and meaninglessness. Christianity declares precisely the opposite – the possibility of living in the world and 'seeing everything in it as the revelation of God, a sign of

55

his presence, the joy of his coming, the call to communion with him, the hope of fulfilment in him'.

Thus far Schmemann, writing in 1965. One can recognise the same vision set out a few years earlier by Teilhard de Chardin in his *Mass on the World*. It comes from a different scientific perspective and is rooted in a different theological tradition, but has the same sacramental focus.

> Like a pagan I worship a God who can be touched; and I do indeed touch him – this God – over the whole surface and in the depths of that world of matter which confines me: but to take hold of him as I would wish . . . I must go always on and on, through and beyond each undertaking, unable to rest in anything, borne onwards at each moment by creatures and at each moment going beyond them, in a continuing welcoming of them and a continuing detachment from them.[2]

Here Teilhard is not just contemplating a world but wrestling with it, acting in it, constructing a new, unified vision of it, conscious that it is no mere passive object. Implicit in his approach are questions about what we actually mean by such a simple phrase as 'the natural world'. Is it simply *there*, or is it in some sense a human construct? But more of that later. For the present, see how Teilhard deals with the idea of the world being given back to us sacramentally in Christ:

> Do you now, therefore, speaking through my lips, pronounce over this earthly travail your twofold efficacious word: the word without which all that our wisdom and our experience have built up must totter and crumble – the word through which all our most far-reaching speculations and our encounter with the universe are come together into a unity. Over every living thing which is to spring up, to grow, to flower, to ripen during this day, say again the words: This is my Body. And over every death-force which waits in readiness to corrode, to wither, to cut down, speak again your commanding words which express the supreme mystery of faith: This is my Blood.[3]

The sacramentality of the natural world lies in its possibility of being thus transformed. Writing at about the same time, but in a much more prosaic style, I myself tried to express something of the same sacramental vision in terms of making sense of the world by relating it to God. In a book published in 1993 I quoted a passage I had originally written 30 years earlier, and I intend to quote it again. I am sorry if this sounds a bit like theological environmentalism – a continuous recycling of old material – but at least I can claim a certain consistency:

> The characteristic method of Christian worship is to take bits of the ordinary stuff of life, bread and wine and water, and raise them to a new level of significance. The action is not arbitrary; the sacraments are what they are because they stem from Christ; they are 'given'. But once given, the sacramental principle can be extended to the whole of nature. Natural things can be clothed with new meaning by relating them to Christ. The world which would be meaningless by itself, becomes a purposeful place as men make it so; and they are enabled to do this because they themselves find a purpose for their lives in the man whose life was wholly one with God. A Christian who thinks like this can then see his vocation as an active process of 'making sense' of the world. This is different from the passive attempt to make sense of things, i.e. to understand them. The Christian attitude is to ask what sense we ought to make of them, what their possibilities are in a world responsible to God, and how far they can be made the grounds of worship and thanksgiving.[4]

By exploiting the passive and active meanings of the phrase 'making sense', I was trying to embrace the dual thrust of sacramental action – as a change in our perceptions, and a change in actuality. Sacramentalism is about perceiving a deeper meaning in things through the transforming presence of Christ. But it is also about the conveyance of grace, about the active work of God in enabling human beings to become what we truly are in him. And this duality runs through much of our experience.

I have already mentioned the difficulty of knowing precisely what we mean by the simple phrase 'natural world'. One part of the difficulty is that what we now call the natural world is, to a large extent, our own creation. The very fact that we now tend to use the word 'environment' in preference to 'nature' underlines the way in which we have come to regard what is 'out there' as closely relating to us. It is what is around us, environs us. Moreover this is an astonishingly recent concept. Don Cupitt has pointed out that there was a gap of only 14 years between the first unmistakably modern use of the word 'environment' and the appointment of the first government minister for the environment. Certainly in a country like Britain it is hard to find anything which has not, to a greater or lesser extent, been dependent on or influenced by human contrivance. We have shaped the landscape, the soil, the vegetation, much of the animal life. The American author of a recent book called *The End of Nature* lamented that the real tragedy of the greenhouse effect is that we have now irreversibly changed the earth's atmosphere, and with it every other aspect of nature which used to be its own wild self – even the weather.[5]

The idea of the natural world also gives rise to much deeper philosophical difficulties – questions about knowledge itself, and the degree to which it is conditioned by culture and language. It is a platitude nowadays that we cannot wholly escape from the business of creating a world, even in the process of studying it as objectively as possible. My main point, though, is that for good or ill, in trying to understand the world of nature we are never merely detached observers. Inevitably we activate some of its potential, and maybe also destroy some of its potential. To know something is also to change it, and what we now know is conditioned by what previous generations have bequeathed to us through their own thoughts and language, as well as through their more explicit actions in shaping the world. Our task in making sense of the world is thus inextricably bound up with this history and this potential for further change.

If our culture and our history convey to us a purely secular vision of the world, emptied of divine meaning, the likelihood is that we shall think of it as mere material, available for manipulation and exploitation. If, on the other hand, in trying to make sense of it, we begin with the presupposition that material things are capable of bearing the image of the divine, then we are likely to be more respectful. And we are more likely too to be receptive to the energy and grace released through encounter with God, whether through church-based sacraments or through those aspects of nature which most readily lend themselves to a sacramental interpretation.

I am conscious that this is all rather abstract. It may help if I earth it in terms of a familiar offertory prayer. It is a prayer which ought to have been in the Alternative Service Book (ASB) – but it is not there because some members of General Synod felt that it was too dangerously Catholic. So it hovers on the fringes of the ASB as a kind of ghost, with only the response to it – 'Blessed be God for ever' – actually printed in the text. As was said at the time, the responses are there, like the smile of the Cheshire cat, to remind those who know about these things of what is missing. The prayer is: 'Blessed are you, Lord God of all creation. Through your goodness we have this bread to offer, which earth has given and human hands have made. It will become for us the bread of life.' And there is a similar prayer over the wine.

I find it a profound and satisfying prayer. It contains a subtle balance between recognising God's gift, acknowledging our human role in developing and using it rightly, and accepting its potential as a conveyer of God's own reality. Bread, at once the most basic and ancient of foods, is also the human product that perhaps more than anything else made possible the civilised world. The development of civilisation in Egypt depended on corn. So all the ambiguities I have described are contained in bread. It is both a product of nature and culture, and a prime former of culture. This fundamental support of life, says the prayer, will reveal a new level of meaning, made possible and actual by God's own involvement in material reality through Christ. It will become for us the bread of life – echoing the words of John 6 with all their overtones of manna in the wilderness, bread for the hungry, and eternal life in Christ himself.

What is true of bread can be true of anything else. Bread as used in the Eucharist locates us in the given, historical actuality of revelation in and through the life of Jesus. But just as all the books in the world are not sufficient to contain the things which might be written about him, so all the splendour and variety of the material world is available to disclose him. Nature in all its abundance can be clothed with the divine, as in Thomas Traherne's vision of 'orient and immortal wheat which never should be reaped nor was ever sown'. Perhaps it is no coincidence that these are the opening words of his description of a glorified world. In another passage, he describes waking up in the world as if in our Father's palace:

You never enjoy the world aright, till the sea itself floweth in your veins, till you are clothed with the heavens, and crowned with the stars: and perceive yourself to be sole heir of the whole world, and more than so, because men are in it who are every one sole heirs as well as you. Till you can sing and rejoice and delight in God, as misers do in gold, and kings in sceptres, you never enjoy the world.[6]

That may seem a bit too heady. At a much lower level of awareness, a sense of the goodness or meaningfulness or value of the world can form part of many people's basic religious awareness – even if it is only glimpsed in fleeting moments. Sadly such experiences are frequently never integrated into any coherent pattern of thought or symbolism, and therefore can remain isolated, unproductive, or even rejected. Again and again one hears of frustrated spiritual awareness or longings, which may have arisen from some kind of nature mysticism and which remain stuck there. There is no language for them in a secularised culture. They lack the complex interplay between what is given, and what human beings must do, and the illumination that comes from setting individual experience within a developed and subtle religious tradition. A sacramental approach to the natural world, as I have tried to describe it, seems to me to provide such a tradition.

I want now to spell out in more concrete terms what such sacramentality might mean in practice. In doing this I shall draw rather heavily on an essay I wrote in 1990 for an American book on ecology, which I suspect has not been much seen in this country.[7] I shall do it in three sections: the first on the notion of the recognition and activation of potential; secondly on the need for co-operation; and thirdly a few words in conclusion about transformation by redemption.

1   The recognition of potential

What might it mean in practice to live as if anything or everything might become a vehicle of divine grace?

Perhaps it is easier to start by imagining the opposite – a universe in which anything or everything is ripe for exploitation. The essence of such a regime is that human needs and desires are sovereign, and the stuff of the world can be bent to human purposes with no respect paid to what it is in itself, or to what it might become within the purposes of God. Numerous tragic pictures of ravaged countrysides, polluted seas and rivers, waters depleted of their fish, animals subjected to abominable treatment, squalid shanty towns, and so forth, make the point that this God-forsaken view of the natural world is no mere supposition. This contrasts vividly with the sacramental vision of a world created by God, owned by God, and ultimately finding its fulfilment in God.

But this simple contrast, though I believe it to be valid, does not tell the whole story.

Paradoxically, the practical consequences of these two opposed visions might not always be so very different. Rubbish, for example, might be seen as a resource by the sacramentalist who is concerned not to dismiss anything as mere waste, and may equally well be seen as a resource by the commercially-minded entrepreneur who dreams up a way of making money from it. Deep motivation may be one thing, but the ability to see a problem as an opportunity is not confined to those who share a particular philosophy of life; and this needs to be acknowledged if a sacramental approach is to engage with political realities.

Equally, there may be different motives for wishing to preserve, say, a forest or an animal species. Long-term prudential considerations can provide reasons for holding back, even within a general philosophy of exploitation. The destruction of forests, or of biological diversity, could be seen as foolish even on purely selfish grounds. Recognition and respect for divine potential might provide a less selfish, and therefore less vulnerable, motive – which might be based, for instance, on respect for the evolutionary process, recognising this as the means whereby most of the potential within the living matter of the universe has so far been released. To let a forest be, or to protect a species, is to acknowledge that they have within them a still greater potential for life, growth, and development, and that their development may therefore form part of the larger purposes of God in using evolution as a means of creation. But the recognition of divine potential does not provide an unambiguous answer to the question: What should be done?

This philosophy – of giving things the respect due to them for what they can reveal of God through being themselves – is difficult to carry through into practical programmes. To let everything be, to respect its right to be itself, to allow it to develop in its own way, would, if carried to extremes, make human life impossible, and negate our own creativeness. Forests also have a potential to become fuel, or furniture, or agricultural land – and some of the greatest human achievements have resulted from seeing the potential in things and developing it rather than letting them be. Human beings have interfered decisively and irreversibly in many kinds of animal breeding, often bringing out latent potentials that have been hugely to our benefit. We are now well into a genetic revolution which greatly enhances these creative powers, and we face enormously difficult decisions now – and even more so in the future – about how far this process can rightly be taken, while holding on to a proper respect for the wisdom of nature as it has evolved under the guidance of God.

There are no easy answers. The key religious insight seems to be that, whether things are left alone or whether they are developed by human ingenuity for human purposes, they belong to God and not to us. There is a respect due to them, an awareness of human limitations, a fine balance to be struck between penitence for what we have done to God's world in the past, and hopeful creativeness for the future.

Sacramentally such an attitude also seems appropriate towards inanimate things – at least, towards things of a certain complexity. A flowing stream, a clear sea teeming with life, a mountain landscape, surely deserve respect and care despite the large subjective element that enters into our appreciation of them. They can be treated in specific ways that still further reveal their potential. The great eighteenth-century creator of English landscapes, Capability Brown, earned his nickname for his skill, not in imposing his will on a recalcitrant nature, but in drawing out its aesthetic capabilities. A sculptor carving a particular stone or block of wood may describe his work in similar ways: the finished object is somehow seen as being already there in the natural formation of the raw material, waiting only to be revealed. An engineer may see a valley as waiting to be dammed, a chasm as waiting to be bridged, an ugly and unhealthy swamp as a place of potential beauty and usefulness. Such actions may become in their own way secular sacraments – an enhancement, a liberation of what is already there, a transformation which does not violate a thing's essential nature.

I fully admit that such a way of speaking creates acute difficulties for those who are more used to seeing the universe as a torrent of change. 'Essential natures' do not have much place in evolution. Clearly by itself the recognition of potential is not enough. It is too vague a concept and can lead us in too many different directions. Sacramentalism is also about God's work in complementing and giving substance to our human work in a world still in process of creation.

2 The need for co-operation

The offertory prayer speaks of bread 'which earth has given and human hands have made'. Co-operation with natural processes, working with the grain of nature rather than against it, is now part of the conventional wisdom among conservationists. Can the sacramental context add anything significant to this already familiar idea?

The Eucharist is a symbolic act of giving and receiving, in which the worshippers are both givers and receivers – as is God. At its highest it is a mutual exchange of love. But all this is set within the context of what God has already done. Despite the mutuality, therefore, the key word is *response*. In the exchange of love, 'we love because he first loved us'. Sacramental action is thus essentially a matter of responsive co-operation rather than co-creation. As human beings we share a role with God in drawing out the divine potential of the world – but only because God himself has already taken the decisive steps.

The theme of co-operation receives further emphasis in communion. There can be no true giving and receiving with God unless others form part of it. As those who are themselves loved by God, worshippers caught up in the eucharistic action are commanded and enabled to love their fellow human beings. And the action spreads outward to include 'angels and archangels and all the company of heaven'. Heaven and earth praise God in mutual embrace.

But how far should this mutuality spread? Should it, for instance, include battery hens? There is an evolutionary case for including battery hens in some kind of relationship with human beings as very distant cousins – and this common membership of the community of life constitutes some kind of moral claim, even if not a very strong one. If the sense of community goes further than this, and if it is possible to hold that at a very rudimentary level there can and should be a co-operative relationship between human beings and hens, then the moral claim is strengthened. If, to put the point more strongly, God gives hens a being of their own, and values them prior to their usefulness as a cheap source of food, then the hen's point of view as a partner in this larger communion begins to assume some importance.

Admittedly it is not easy to know what a hen's point of view is – but in the case of battery hens there would seem to be a fairly simple test. In a battery, the human element in the relationship with hens so dominates the conditions of life that the possibility of co-operation virtually disappears altogether. The hen is reduced as far as possible to a machine-like operation. And that would seem to me to fly in the face of morality and of good animal husbandry, as well as of communion.

Even when a relationship ends in death, it can be marked by respect for the life taken. The ritual surrounding animal sacrifice, in cultures where sacrifice was the almost inevitable preliminary to eating meat, witnessed to the seriousness of taking life, unpleasant though some of the rituals were. I recall a vivid picture of an African Bushman apologising to an impala he was about to kill. Here again, the theme of communion with the life sacrificed can perhaps help modern Westernised consciousness to develop a different feel for the products of industrialised scientific agriculture. One doesn't see anybody apologising in a twentieth-century abattoir. Organic farming, to take another example, almost certainly does not fulfil the quasi-scientific claims made for it, but it may have moral and spiritual benefits for societies which see the need to develop a more sensitive relationship with the natural world.

The limits of co-operation become all too evident, however, when there is a mosquito in the bedroom. I am reminded of the story of the mosquito in the nudist camp which complained, 'So much to do that it is impossible to know where to begin'. We could echo the same thought in trying to make sense of the multitude of natural evils. Letting things be themselves, discerning their point of view and looking for their divine potentiality, cannot be allowed to become a recipe for the passive acceptance of whatever befalls us. Our human place in God's purposes is to co-operate with him in the process of creative change. Sacramental thinking points to a world which has to be redeemed before it can truly reveal the face of God. There is an inescapable element of struggle, discrimination, suffering and tragedy in the process – and any theological approach to the natural world that belittles or ignores these is hopelessly unrealistic. Hence my third and final heading.

3 Transformation by redemption

The sacraments are sacraments of Christ's death and resurrection. Suffering, and the transformation of suffering, belong to their very essence. Sacramental theology, therefore, has no excuse for under-rating the extent to which the divine potential of the world is denied, frustrated, distorted, defaced and ignored. Nor need we shrink from accepting that the very means of creation through evolution entails conflict and suffering. Sacramental awareness is not at all the same as sentimentality. The perceptions of divine glory in a world capable of bearing God's image have to be matched by the belief that God bears the weight of the suffering of his own creation on the cross.

All this is basic Christianity. Interpreting the cross in the light of a sacramental understanding of the natural world can help to strengthen the bridge between the redemption of human sin and suffering, and the redemption of the rest of creation. St Paul's language (in Romans 8) about creation groaning and suffering and waiting for the redemption of the Son of God expresses the same link. To allow the doctrines of creation and redemption to exist, as it were, in separate compartments is to fall into ways of thinking about the natural world which make any sensible containment of its ambivalences impossible. It seems to me that this link is present in the Old Testament too. I find myself increasingly attracted by the idea that it was Israel's consciousness of being a redeemed community, created, as it were, 'out of nothing', which provided the context for Isaiah's great vision of God as creator: 'Look to me, and be saved, all the ends of the earth; for I am God, and there is none else'.[8] To believe in creation is to believe in an ultimate security, an ultimate order, a place and a responsibility for humanity, within the saving purposes of God.

And part of that responsibility is in fulfilling what Schmemann called our human priestly role – to offer back to God in penitence and thanksgiving our broken and ambivalent world, shot through with so much good and evil, that it may by his grace be consecrated and transformed. The evil and the ambivalences are not ignored. They may have to be located intellectually in the mystery of God's inscrutability. But a sacramental approach to nature allows us to do this, without becoming disheartened or debilitated by all that does not reflect the glory and goodness of God. We can still say, in the sacramental experience, 'He is here', and accept it as a foretaste of what is yet to come.

As part of the natural world which is to be offered and transformed, we have no room for arrogance, or for the exploitative mentality which assumes that creation is 'ours'. But we – who are called by God to our priestly role, and who dare to describe ourselves as made in the image of God – we have a responsibility not simply to accept the world as it is, but to recognise and pursue its possibilities for revealing God's glory more fully. Christian thinking has to move between these two poles of acceptance and transformation, humility and creative power. And one of the great strengths of sacramentalism is that it provides a sufficient richness and diversity of imagery for this movement to take place.

5

The word made flesh

'And the word was made flesh . . .' St John uses a very earthy concept – 'flesh' – or, as we might put it, 'flesh and blood', a real human person, grounded in ordinary things.

I reflected on this word 'flesh' after reading in the Press a curious little pre-Christmas story about the occult society in the University of Leeds. The students had appointed a witch as their chaplain. It wasn't a joke. It seems to have been a serious attempt to provide for those who want to be pagans.

But why on earth would anybody want to be a self-consciously religious pagan nearly two millennia after the coming of Christ? Wasn't it Christ's coming which eventually exposed the emptiness of the follies of paganism in the classical world? What has gone wrong?

I come back to the word 'flesh'. Paganism is a very earthy religion. It is about our rootedness in the world of nature. It is about the tides and the seasons, and the natural forces which flow through us. It is about emotion and sex and the manipulation of mysterious powers. It is about our humanness. It resonates with the image of the flesh. One can see the attraction – particularly in times when people feel oppressed by the artificialities of much modern life, and when we are worried about the environment, and when there is a deep sense of things having gone wrong with our technological society.

Go into almost any bookshop these days and you will see shelf after shelf of 'New Age' literature. People must buy them by the million. Here is our modern paganism – books purporting to explain the mysteries of our human nature, to release new power in us, and to give us new ways of getting in touch with our emotions. They take us back to the kind of world seething with strange ideas and empty nostrums into which Christ was born.

And the word was made flesh. This whole world of human longing, this earthy expression of human hopes and needs, was satisfied in a single human life which pointed uniquely to God.

Put it another way: how are we to know God? Pagans throughout the ages have generally answered, 'By rooting ourselves more firmly in the world of nature'. The Jews answered, 'By attending to what God has done to us through our history'. Christians answered, 'By uniting ourselves with the life of a human person in whom all nature and all history are summed up'. The word became flesh . . . and the word St John is writing about is not only the word of God in history – as understood in the Old Testament – but also the ordering principle of the world of nature – as understood in pagan Greece. Our modern sciences carry the same thought: biology, zoology, psychology . . . the 'ology' part simply means 'word', the ordering principle that was in the beginning with God. And this word, says St John, was finally and fully expressed in a person.

That, in a nutshell, is what the Christian faith is about, and what Christmas Day is about; and it is why Christianity converted what was best in paganism, and why the present-day return to a modern form of paganism is so misguided and pointless.

But one can see why it happened. Christians tended to forget that the word of God was also the word that spoke through nature. Sometimes they so concentrated on the awesome reality of God in Christ that they forgot the flesh and blood. But not always: look at some of the baroque churches in southern Europe and there is the whole world of the flesh brought into the service of Christ in a kind of cultic exhibitionism. There is sex and gold-leaf and cherubs and miracles and ecstasy all tumbling over one another. We don't do that kind of thing in England. But look closely at the windows around you in York Minster, and you will find a modest form of it: stories human and divine; and humour; and monkeys round the edge; and even a dragon high above you, who has lost his St George.

All this has seemed very shocking in some periods of Church history. There have always been movements within Christianity wanting to clean the whole thing up, to reduce it to something lean and austere and cerebral, to swing the pendulum back from flesh to word. The poet Edwin Muir wrote this about his native Scotland:

> The word made flesh is here made word again . . .
> God, three angry letters in a book.

A not-very-effective-sounding witch in Leeds is only a small straw in the wind. But perhaps she can remind us that Christmas is about earth as well as about heaven, that the world of nature belongs within God's purposes, and that the ox and the ass at the manger are not mere casual visitors.

Nor is it just the nice, David Attenborough world of nature which is somehow redeemed and transformed by the coming of the Son of Man. It is the dark and chaotic forces, the violence, the untamed energies – as much in our own hearts as in the world around us – which Christ can enter, and where the word made flesh can dwell. The first Christians, struggling with paganism, came to realise that the saved world was not only the good world, but the whole world.

Christmas is a day for taking up that vision, for seeing the whole world – with its pains and pleasures, its tragedies and its wonders, its mess and muddle, its confusion and self-indulgence, and its deep longing for something more – as the place where God's grace and glory and truth can be found.

And we focus it here, in the offering of bread and wine; in the bringing of our whole selves with all our ambivalences to the Christ who gives himself to us; and in the story of an innocent child who carries the hopes of all the ages.

6

Life on Mars?

Shortly after the recent announcement that there might once have been life on Mars, I was rung up by a national newspaper and asked to comment by a journalist who gleefully supposed that this spelt the end of God. I expressed some surprise, and reminded my caller that it was not so long ago that one of the favourite arguments for atheism was the apparent emptiness and wastefulness of the universe. Whether the universe is teeming with life, or whether we are alone, does not seem to me to have much bearing on whether God exists. Nevertheless there are some theological implications worth exploring.

But first it is as well to be cautious about the evidence. As the scientists have made plain, this is by no means conclusive. And even if what have been observed really are fossilised micro-organisms from Mars, it does not follow that they represent a separate origin of life from that on earth. Professor Fred Hoyle has for many years contended that life on earth came from organic materials in outer space. His ideas were once ridiculed, but are now taken more seriously – and the possibility cannot be ruled out that both planets were fertilised from a single source.

Suppose, however, we take the evidence at its face-value: it is then hard to resist the implication that there must be millions of inhabited worlds in the universe. Nobody has yet come up with a fully convincing scientific account of how life might have arisen, but the study of the evolution of self-replicating mechanisms is now well advanced, and there are some plausible guesses about how it might have happened spontaneously. It follows that, if this happened on earth, then it is overwhelmingly likely that it has also happened on other planets where the conditions were right for it. If we accept the principle, inherent in a theological interpretation of evolution, that God makes things make themselves, this vision of life emerging all over the place should not cause too many theological headaches. The fact that this is the kind of universe where such development can take place still leaves room for a meaningful doctrine of creation.

The issue is not new. In 1866, Bishop Westcott began one of his books – *The Gospel of the Resurrection* – with a vision of a traveller in the universe complaining, 'I am lonely in creation . . . The full world is great, but Vacancy is greater'. And the answer came, 'In the sight of God there is no Vacancy'. Then his eyes were opened and 'suns and planets were seen to float as mere specks in the vast ocean of life which was revealed to him'. And through the immense galaxy of stars, he eventually recognised earth, and cosmic life streaming from the risen Christ.

Thirty years later a certain Mrs Hamilton King, in a long poem called *The Disciples*, wrote some lines which much impressed William Temple:

> When God formed in the hollow of His hand
> This ball of Earth among his other balls,
> And set it in the shining firmament
> Between the greater and the lesser lights,
> He chose it for the Star of Suffering . . .
> For God has other words for other worlds,
> But for this world the Word of God is Christ.

Some of the wording might be more felicitous, but the theology, both in Westcott and in Mrs King, is not only evidence that Christians were prepared to think positively about other worlds at a time when science was offering considerable challenges to faith, but it was also remarkably perceptive. Life is indeed the ultimate reality of the universe for those who believe in resurrection. Furthermore it is possible to think about God's relationship with other worlds without losing hold of the centrality of Christ.

Let me expand that last point. As earthbound Christians we know God's revelation through a particular series of historical events, and in the life, death and resurrection of a particular person. Because we believe that these were the saving acts of the God who made the universe, we see in them a universal significance. The New Testament uses language about Christ which sets out this cosmic role. The underlying assumption is that there is only one series of events which is historically significant, and only one world to which it is relevant.

As human horizons have expanded, it has become necessary to think in broader terms. The familiar difficulties concerning other faiths – whether, and in what sense, God might also have revealed something of himself through these – provide a foretaste of the issues which might have to be faced if contact is ever made with other worlds. The doctrine of the Trinity makes it easier to handle this kind of question, by distinguishing between the second person of the Trinity – God in his outgoing activity – and the particular form of his activity in Jesus Christ. Given this distinction, it is possible to say of other faiths that God as Son may in some sense be discerned in these, though not so explicitly as in Jesus.

The same could be true of other worlds – in fact, this is what Mrs King was suggesting in the two last lines of my quotation. God as second person of the Trinity may be present in other worlds in ways appropriate to whatever life-forms there might be. But because he is the same God we, though not they, would know him as Christ. Similarly they, but not we, would recognise in Christ whatever for them represented the saving presence of God.

These are deep waters, and everything I have written needs to be hedged around with lots of ifs and buts. My sole purpose in indulging in some rather wild speculation is to show that it is possible to think coherently about such matters, and that theology is flexible enough to adapt to them. In the mean time we can await with some interest the next chapter in this dramatic story.

7

Is there reliable knowledge about God?

The key word in my title is 'reliable'. It is a word which falls short of
certainty. To claim certain knowledge about God would be impious.
But reliable knowledge is knowledge adequate for the practical purposes of living; it is knowledge to which it is both possible and sensible
to commit oneself.

This practical slant to the word is important to my meaning. I am
not keen on the modern use of the word praxis, but at least it serves as
a reminder that theory and practice are inseparable. Belief in God is
not an idea which may or may not make a difference; it has no
substance unless it makes a difference. Knowledge about God belongs
within a total context of life, a total environment of doing, willing,
thinking, feeling, relating, responding, and historical conditioning –
and if extracted from this context it becomes arid speculation.

Furthermore, reliability is not some kind of bonus within the
religious life, but belongs to the heart of it. Religion *is* relying: the two
words come from the same root. The phrase 'reliable knowledge' can
therefore carry some faint religious overtones, even when used in a
thoroughly secular context. It opens up the possibility that faith may
have something to do with it. In fact, the phrase can act as a kind of
bridge between faith on the one hand and a hopelessly impracticable
ideal of total objectivity on the other. And it is a flexible bridge:
there can be degrees of reliability; there can be questions about when
knowledge is reliable enough.

Knowing and knowing about

The chapter title refers to reliable knowledge *about* God – and before I
plunge into the main subject let me spell out the significance of that
word 'about'. In some ways it is easier to defend knowledge *of* God

rather than knowledge *about* him – because knowledge of him, where it exists, is mostly interior and incommunicable; and hence difficult to test or refute. It can be profound and wordless as in the mystics, or no more than a vague feeling as in the lady from East Barnet who was overheard saying, 'I don't actually believe in the resurrection, but I do think that there's something going on up there'.[1]

If there is certainty at all in religion it seems to belong at this level of ineffability, at the point where philosophy and theology run out into silence. To try to express it can be to destroy it – or at least to distort it so seriously that all expressions of it become controversial. That, at any rate, is what it feels like, and why talking about God can seem so problematic in comparison with interior knowledge of him. There is a plausible view of religion which sees it as a response to an inexpressible something, articulated in a variety of forms which are bound to differ from one another – not just because the subject-matter is difficult and the basis of knowledge contested, but because description itself always, to a greater or lesser extent, falsifies what it is attempting to encapsulate.[2]

But how is this 'something' known, even inarticulately, unless there is some prior framework of understanding, some rudimentary language of thought, within which it can be recognised? Without language it is doubtful whether we could think at all. In saying this, I do not want to deny the immediacy of religious experience. I believe that all our knowledge of God depends upon our having a prior relationship with God – a relationship in which God himself takes the initiative in making himself present to us. But we cannot know his presence as presence – indeed, cannot even acknowledge a religious awareness – without a language and without thought-forms in which to identify it. And a language always belongs to a historically conditioned culture and to a particular mode of rationality.

Thus, despite the incommunicable nature of claims to know God directly, there is no escape from trying to articulate knowledge about him. In this chapter I want to concentrate on these articulate claims, while recognising that, precisely because they emerge from a struggle to say something which cannot in the end be said, they are bound to be different from one another, and controversial. In what sense can such diverse and fragmentary knowledge claim to be reliable? The more we talk, the more we become aware of the multiplicity of answers.

The evolution of reliable knowledge

There is plenty of evidence of unreliable knowledge of what God is like. Who now believes in Baal? Perhaps there are nature-worshippers who respond in their own idiom to the same sort of reality as Baal-worshippers once responded to in theirs. But Baal as a concept is dead – and so are hundreds of other gods who once formed the centres of cults, who exacted sacrifice and devotion, who engendered a theology, however rudimentary, and who were believed to be powerful. As H. L. Mencken said of them, in his memorial service for the gods in which he listed 100 or more now-forgotten names, 'They ranked 5,000–6,000 years ago with Jahveh himself . . . yet they have all gone down the chute'.[3]

This mass-extinction is a vivid reminder that religions are not closed, immutable systems. They can lose their plausibility, die, be defeated; or they can develop, adapt to circumstances, reinterpret their basic tenets, and be radically transformed. It makes sense, therefore, to ask how far the knowledge of God can be seen to conform to some kind of empirical model. Do gods die because they no longer relate effectively to the world as it is perceived to be? And if so, is the corollary also true – that where perceptions of God have survived through many millennia and many transformations, there must be something in the nature of things which continues to make belief in them a plausible option? We can press the point further. If scientific knowledge evolves through a process of trial and error, is it possible to identify the same process at work in theology? After making allowance for very different subject-matters, is there a valid analogy between scientific and theological knowledge?

I turn first to the character of scientific knowledge, and I do so deliberately through the work of a practising scientist rather than the philosophy of science. John Ziman is a physicist whose book, *Reliable Knowledge*, gave me the title of this chapter.[4] He sets out extraordinarily well what most ordinary scientists see themselves as actually doing and aiming for. Scientists can be curiously unreflective in philosophical terms, and some of the excesses of scientism spring from this lack of critical awareness. But most, I believe, would acknowledge the goal of reliable knowledge – the consensus of rational opinion, the idea of public knowledge which is in principle accessible to all who go through the requisite procedures.

In what, then, does its reliability consist? Apart from the process of trial and error to which I have already referred, Ziman spells out the need for unambiguous language – language which is universally translatable, language stripped of all its overtones and historical associations, language which carries its full meaning on its surface. The language of science need not always be mathematically precise, but it must be clear. Great moments of scientific advance have usually been linked with the forging of some new concept – like force, or mass, or charge – with sufficient clarity for it to become an organising principle around which numerous ideas and observations can then fall into place.

Scientists cannot, however, avoid metaphor and analogy in the process of theorising and pushing out the boundaries of knowledge, because these are usually the only means available for describing what cannot be directly observed. Indeed, the function of scientific models is to explore ways of understanding which 'look right', and a certain imprecision may be positively helpful in stimulating the imagination and pointing up the limits of the analogy. Underneath the idea of 'looking right' lie unwritten assumptions or agreements about what counts as an explanation – and such assumptions may, in their turn, be developed further by the stimulus of good, analogical thinking. Interacting particles, for example, do not behave like billiard balls; in fact (as I discovered when asking a foolish question on a visit to CERN – *Conseil Européen pour la Recherche Nucléaire* – a few years ago), it becomes progressively more difficult to know what a particle is. But the billiard table is a marvellous place to begin.

Unambiguous language operating within potentially fruitful models can build up a network of concepts and interpretations which reinforce each other. Ziman uses the familiar metaphor of a map. Criss-crossing fields of study can, over time, produce a reliable map of a major area of knowledge. It is the cross-checking – the ability to approach a subject from many different angles, and to travel round it intellectually by many different routes – which creates confidence. This is one reason why science can never be a solitary exercise. Maps are created by consensus. They are put together from innumerable travellers' tales. And they do not have to be final and perfect to be useful.

This is a deliberately modest account of what natural scientists are trying to do, seen from the perspective of a physicist. But even by these standards, says Ziman, the behavioural sciences fall at almost every hurdle. Sciences like sociology and economics, for instance, lack clear, unambiguous and universally recognised theoretical concepts. This is not due to any inadequacy in the researchers themselves: the idea that there could be a Newton of the social sciences, who could identify such concepts and unify the whole field, is fantasy. The irreducible difficulty is that, if human beings are to take account of the significance of their own actions, they cannot do it in language which has been stripped of all its human associations. Metaphors, analogies and models exist in abundance, but for the most part they are limited in their application and fail to coalesce into the kind of large-scale map which gives such strength and reliability to the natural sciences.

Ziman questions whether behavioural maps are any more reliable than conventional wisdom. Perhaps we learn more about ourselves from novels, plays, poems and traditional rules-of-thumb, which are in many ways better suited than abstract analyses to handle the actual complexities and ambiguities of human living. I am reminded of the plea made by Howard Root, in a seminal essay written in 1962, that natural theology should 'begin all over again' by attending to 'the disturbing visions of human nature which find expression in serious modern literature'.[5] Does this mean, then, that in such fields the process of building up consensus towards the goal of reliability has to be abandoned?

Thus far Ziman. I have used him at some length because he gives convincing expression to a widely held and basically pragmatic view of science, which gives content to the word 'reliable', which pinpoints some of the difficulties in the behavioural sciences, and which (by implication) leaves theology firmly at the unreliable end of the spectrum of knowledge.

Knowledge and hermeneutics

Suppose, however, we take up his hint about literature and traditional wisdom, and ask how we understand and learn from these. We then find ourselves engaged in a very different critique of knowledge, which in turn throws back some awkward questions to the natural sciences. I refer, of course, to hermeneutics and to the huge intellectual industry which has grown up around seemingly simple questions about how to read books intelligently, and how to grasp the meaning of what other people are saying. It rests on the insight that all knowledge is interpretation – which may seem fairly obvious. But its implications are dizzying.

At this point, I merely want to note that hermeneutics began with the attempt to systematise interpretation of the Bible. Some months ago, when I mentioned the title of this chapter to a clerical colleague, his immediate response was, 'So you're going to write about revelation'. In a sense, yes. But not in the sense that there is a given store of reliable knowledge about God in the Bible, which can be painlessly extracted without difficult enquiry into how the Bible is to be understood and evaluated.

Gadamer, a key figure in the development of hermeneutics, on whom I am relying in this section, does indeed talk about truth as a kind of revelation, a disclosure.[6] Great art, or literature, or significant events, can exercise a claim on us. They can uncover some part of our world or our lives which was previously hidden from us. But the claim is not a simple one. The disclosure depends also on ourselves – who we are and where we stand, our historical conditioning, our prejudices.

For Gadamer the starting-point is prejudice – not in the pejorative sense, but in the sense that none of us starts with a clean slate. Prejudice forms the perspectives from which alone the growth of knowledge is possible. We build on what is already there – but not uncritically. The so-called hermeneutic circle is a constant process of re-evaluation. To the interpretation, say, of a classic text, the interpreter brings his own traditions and assumptions, and first projects these on to the text in order to begin to understand it. He may, for example, approach a particular biblical passage as theology, or history, or mythology, or liturgy, or fantasy, or whatever – but he must also allow the text itself to modify and correct that original projection. So begins a kind of dialogue between the text itself and the developing understanding of the interpreter as initial apprehensions and assumptions are challenged and refined. There is no simple, objective, ultimately true meaning of a text abstracted from a particular place and time. A text belongs within its own time, and has to be interpreted in our time. But it does not follow from this that anything goes. There can be what Gadamer calls 'a fusion of horizons' by the integration of different perspectives. This demands a long process of dialogue, a continuing conversation. The goal of this conversation, whether between text and interpreters or between interpreters themselves, is understanding. The method is self-criticism and willingness to learn, together with openness to the subject-matter, and the defining and testing of prejudices in relation to its claims. The validation of understanding is agreement.

I am bowdlerising a complex story. My purpose in telling it is to make two simple points: first that the study of literature, or of any meaningful human communication, can be as serious and self-critical as any other intellectual activity, including science; secondly, that there are partial ways of escape from the subjectivist trap in which mere prejudice, mere private opinion, have the last word. To acknowledge the conditioned character of all human thought and perception is not to be set loose on a sea of uninformed opinion. It may not be possible to substantiate claims to some ideal of total objectivity, always assuming that to be desirable. But there remain ways of being rational, of growing in understanding, and of acquiring more reliable knowledge. The heart of the process is dialogue. This is not a return to Hegelian dialectic because it does not presuppose, as Hegel did, that there is some point of absolute knowledge beyond which no further advance is possible. The process remains open. There is no escape from the possibility of being wrong, and the willingness to go on listening to others always threatens whatever interim conclusions may have been reached. But the process as a whole does lead on to a richer, more developed rationality.

Gadamer's approach says more about the behavioural sciences than about the natural sciences. This is because the behavioural sciences, like the humanities, entail what has been called a double hermeneutic: not only are they constituted by their own traditions of interpretation (like any other rational enquiry), but their subject-matter also includes the meanings which people ascribe to their own actions, and hence the traditions or prejudices by which they interpret these. There are thus two layers of tradition, one belonging to the science and the other belonging to its subject-matter – and the interactions between these can be extraordinarily complex. So it is with theology. It is not a science in the same sense as the natural sciences, whose goal – however remote, unattainable and, in Gadamer's terms, inadmissible – is complete objectivity. The subject-matter of theology is meaning. Theology claims not only to be meaningful as an intellectual tradition, but also to characterise God as himself the focus of meaning – a meaning which can only be known by identifying with it and living by it.

At this level, the practical dimension of hermeneutics becomes crucial. Knowledge about God is never simply book-knowledge, though there are elements of book-knowledge within it. There is a rational study of religion at the first level of hermeneutics which may or may not yield agreed public knowledge. At the second level of hermeneutics, where communities and individuals have to face the meaning of their own existence, reliability takes a different shape. It relates more to what I described earlier as an interior certainty, glimpsed in whatever forms of expression are available. Yet even at this level such certainty needs to be tempered by continuing openness, dialogue and self-criticism.

The limitations of language

This idea of a double hermeneutic helpfully distinguishes between theology, the humanities and the behavioural sciences on the one hand, and the natural sciences on the other. But it is important to grasp that all claims to knowledge, including those of the natural sciences, are subject to at least one kind of hermeneutic process. The sustained philosophical critiques of science throughout this century have led to the growing recognition that scientific data are not detachable from theory, and that theories are not detachable from the historical contexts in which they are formulated. *All* knowledge, in other words, is interpretation. Furthermore, the language in which the interpretation is given determines the character of the result. I made the point earlier that successful scientific language is clear, unambiguous and universal. For the study of many phenomena this is a *sine qua non*; and for the study of some phenomena the clearest, totally unambiguous and most universal language of all, namely mathematics, is almost wholly sufficient. Ziman describes physics as 'the science devoted to discovering, developing and refining those aspects of reality that are amenable to mathematical analysis'.[7] Physics, in other words, is a mathematical fishing-net for capturing mathematical relationships.

As an ideal of language, though, and as a determinant (by implication) of what counts as reliable knowledge, clarity, precision and universality can be disastrous, as the recent history of British philosophy has revealed only too obviously. Alasdair MacIntyre has described part of the heritage of the Enlightenment as precisely such a modernised, sanitised language which achieves universality at the cost of uprooting itself from the cultural traditions in which different languages had hitherto grown. In his book *Whose Justice? Which Rationality?* he makes the point, very much in the spirit of Gadamer, that it is not only moral concepts like justice, but also concepts of rationality itself, which have been embodied in long intellectual and social traditions, and which cannot be fully understood apart from these.[8] The Enlightenment thinkers, in deliberately cutting loose from such traditions, deprived rationality of its history − of that long process of refinement through constant debate which had given the criteria of rationality their stability. Bereft of such traditions, we are left with the illusion that all which can be said significantly can be said within the confines of a modern, universal language which uproots profound ideas from their contexts, and puts them on display in a market-place of opinions. Customer preference rules.

The word 'God' is a case in point. Part of the theological crisis of modernity lies in the difficulty of giving any actual content to the word. To attempt to describe God in purely conceptual terms is to be reduced to incoherence or banality. Martin Buber, when challenged by a friend saying that all the evil which had been done in the name of God had ruined the word, replied:

Yes, it is the most heavy-laden of all human words. None has become so soiled, so mutilated. Just for this reason I may not abandon it. Generations of men have laid the burden of their anxious lives upon this word and weighed it to the ground; it lies in the dust and bears their whole burden. The races of men with their religious factions have torn the word to pieces; they have killed for it and died for it, and it bears their fingermarks and their blood. Where might I find a word like it to describe the highest? If I took the purest, most sparkling concept from the inner treasure-chamber of the philosopher, I could only capture thereby an unbinding product of thought. I could not capture the presence of Him whom the generations of men have honoured and degraded with their awesome living and dying. I do indeed mean Him whom the hell-tormented and heaven-storming generations of men mean. Certainly they draw caricatures and write 'God' underneath; they murder one another and say 'in God's name'. But when all madness and delusion fall to dust, when they stand over against Him in the loneliest darkness and no longer say 'He', but rather sigh 'Thou', shout 'Thou', . . . and when they then add 'God', is it not the real God whom they implore?[9]

It is a word with a history – and the meaning has to include the history. Reliable knowledge about this God cannot be abstracted from the anxious debates and the blood-stained controversies which have shaped the ascription of his name. The report of the Church of England Doctrine Commission, entitled *We Believe in God*, referred to 'well-winnowed traditions'.[10] Reliability has a time-factor built into it. All traditions, including scientific ones, remain 'provisional, corrigible and incomplete', but to have become traditions at all they have to have achieved a certain stability over time. And in their time they can be adequate.

In a sense, what I have been saying in these last few paragraphs is what any Bible-based Christian should know instinctively. The God whom Christians worship can only be known through immersion in the whole biblical tradition. Nothing less than the whole Bible will do, and nothing less than a constant return to it and renewal by it. And for a mature understanding there has to be some sense of the way in which biblical themes have been interpreted and elaborated throughout Christian history. It is not a fossilised tradition, but a living one in which criticism and development are the signs of vitality. Christianity is particularly resilient to this kind of treatment, as Pannenberg explains:

In Christianity the history of religious experiences and their changing forms has itself become the theme of religion, the sphere of divine self-revelation. This is the source of the ability of the biblical religions to survive the experience of their own historical change. Whereas religions which are dominated by the idea of an allegedly unsurpassable, mythical Golden Age and a corresponding world-order are swept away by the changes produced in them in the course of history, the Jewish and Christian religion, because it is a religion of history, can integrate changes in itself and see them as divine guidance.[11]

Evaluation through dialogue

Nevertheless the problem remains of sustaining this constant process of re-evaluation, of growth in understanding through dialogue, in a world where religious and intellectual traditions have become attenuated. Attenuation and distortion are inevitable when by reason of the fact that the only language on offer for cross-cultural exchange is the neutral language of a pluralist society, which tends to reduce basic religious insights to their secular counterparts. I have already fallen into this trap earlier in this chapter in referring obscurely to God, through a bloodless abstract concept, as 'a focus of meaning'. I now want to suggest that perhaps one way of strengthening the sense of belonging to a tradition, while at the same time exposing it to questioning from a coherent alternative tradition, is through inter-faith dialogue. My hope is that such dialogue may in time provide us with just that kind of cross-checking, that complex network of interrelated experiences and interpretations, which gives strength and stability to scientific thought. Could a more comprehensive religious map help us to find our bearings? I speak here from very little experience, but it seems to me that inter-faith dialogue has rightly been moving centre-stage, not just for social or missiological reasons, but because theologians have begun to perceive that the integrity and credibility of Christian faith depends in part on its ability to define itself in relation to other faiths.[12]

Dialogue is more than talking. It is about the meeting of minds and people in their total cultural context. It entails the learning of the other's language in the broadest sense, to the point at which it is possible to think and feel in and through the other's language. McIntyre writes about 'second first languages', which imply much more than the ability to translate one sentence into another. He asks us to imagine, by contrast, a dialogue conducted solely in sentences from phrase-books – a recipe for farce. Inter-faith dialogue entails an openness and a willingness to learn of the kind which Gadamer described as essential to his hermeneutics. It is very demanding and threatening. At first sight it also seems to undermine the very notion of reliability which I have tried to locate within the experience of belonging to a mature and tested tradition. How can we assert the reliability of our own knowledge when faced with an alternative mature and tested tradition?

I am told, however, that the experience can be just the opposite of what might be feared. In a minor classic written nearly 30 years ago, Klaus Klostermaier described his own deeper conversion to Christ through dialogue with Hindu friends.[13] He began for the first time to see Christ in India, not as a stranger who had come from Europe, but as one who had been there from the beginning.

This was a discovery of oneness and reinforcement. But even when dialogue only serves to expose differences, there can be a kind of reinforcement through the recognition of a certain commonality in difference. Surely the most dramatic encounter between different faiths took place in 1519, when Cortez anchored off the Mexican coast and two religious traditions – which had been isolated from one another since the dawn of human history – met for the first time, like aliens from outer space. There are records of the meeting from both sides, and though Aztec religion was terrifyingly different from Spanish Christianity even as it was then, in its most bloodthirsty phase, these aliens recognised religion as religion. Cortez knew where to set up his first images of the saints – on sites which were already religiously significant.[14]

It is not wise to conclude too much from the apparent universality of religion – though again and again there is fresh evidence of it, even in our own country, as the opinion polls demonstrate. Gods, as Mencken said, can die. But while the questions, the feelings, the hopes, the needs, which seek religious expression may be frustrated and distorted when there is no adequate vehicle to carry them, nevertheless they do not seem to disappear. The religious impulses of humankind have an astonishing record for reliability. And the fact that, over thousands of years, only a small number of great traditions have survived, and are now finding it possible to talk with one another to their mutual benefit, is at least an indication that these religions are responses to some coherent, though ultimately hidden, reality.

Beyond that we can only rely on our traditions and see them as containing within themselves the roots of an understanding which goes deeper than present-day secularisms. And we can go on talking, as Gifford lecturers have talked for over 100 years; and we can go on acting together for the world's good, as increasingly it is possible to do across the barriers of different beliefs. And who knows – one day we might find each other closer than we imagined, in the place where the world's suffering is most fully exposed. As Brunner said in commenting on the text, 'I, if I be lifted up, will draw all men to myself': 'Christ crucified draws us to himself that there we might meet each other'.

II

THE COMMON GOOD

8

What can Japanese industry teach Britain?

Some years ago I attended an international conference at Maryknoll in New York State. Maryknoll is well-known as the home of a radically minded Roman Catholic religious order, originally set up to send missionaries to the Far East. It now focuses a good deal of its concern on radical social policies in the USA. One morning at breakfast, I was approached by one of the monks who sat down beside me and asked me what I thought was the greatest force for peace in the modern world.

I do not like being questioned at breakfast and I knew the sort of answer he was expecting anyway – prayer, or the pope, or nuclear disarmament, or whatever. So I wickedly replied, 'Wall Street'. The effect was explosive. 'Wall Street?', he said, '*Wall Street*!' – and he went off muttering. The idea that international finance or international trade could be a force for peace may seem outrageous to those who see most of the evils of the modern world stemming from capitalism, consumerism and unbridled competitiveness. I did not live it down for the rest of the conference.

Yet it is actually trade which in the past has forged many links between nations, to the point at which war between them becomes unthinkable. This is part of the vision underlying the European Community. It is the reality underlying those many parts of the world where frontiers no longer have to be protected. For some years I was part of an annual consultation between Christians, Muslims and Jews, set up in the hope of finding common humanitarian grounds on which the three religions could co-operate. Interestingly, the consultation quickly focused on business ethics as an area in which some of the then intractable problems of the Middle East could begin to be tackled, and cultural differences explored, without getting too bogged down in politics or theology.

The idea of the global workplace, therefore, is a potentially unifying concept, which might have repercussions far beyond the particular fields of industry and commerce. There is also a down-side to all this. Global commerce may put very damaging pressures on national economies. Fierce and unrestrained international competition may be good for the strong but disastrous for the weak – and in a debt-ridden world, we have to ask how and when the weak are going to be given a chance to pull themselves up. There are plenty of people in this country who deplore the loss of control and protection which comes from exposure to world markets – the grief felt in Newcastle over the demise of Swan Hunter is only one example of this attitude. It is important to remember this down-side, even while we celebrate the opportunities which globalisation brings.

I have begun with these personal reflections because I am very conscious of not being well-versed in industrial or commercial matters, and therefore find myself in the familiar but uncomfortable position of being an amateur commentator in a highly complex field. It is important, though, not to leave the discussion of such matters solely to experts, and I believe there is much to be learnt, even by non-experts, in comparing the values and assumptions which under-gird Japanese and British business enterprises.

Values and assumptions

There is a little-known report called *Changing Britain*, published by the Church of England's Board for Social Responsibility in 1987, which received an undeservedly hostile reception. As chairman of the working party which produced it, I felt that we had opened up some issues about values in a pluralist society which needed attention, but which were dismissed as not being sufficiently theological. In particular we spent some time exploring differences between British and Japanese culture, and their significance for industry, because we felt that this was one possible route to greater self-understanding. It is really on the basis of that experience that I make these reflections. Things have, of course, moved on both in Britain and in Japan in the intervening years. It is going to be particularly interesting to see how Japan responds to the much tighter economic environment in which its industry now has to work – but I suspect that the changes in underlying values have not been all that great in either country.

Let me start by listing three of those aspects of the Japanese cultural framework which are perceived to underlie its industrial strength.

1 The sense of community within business enterprises. Unlike the normal pattern in Britain, businesses in Japan are regarded mainly as communities of employees – managers and workers together – with strong organisational loyalties rooted in a shared sense of long-term commitment. The guarantee of permanence may not be as strong as it once was, and may increasingly apply only to a minority of larger firms. Nevertheless this sense of being a stable community does seem to be to some extent institutionalised in the relative importance given to employees over shareholders.

2 A highly developed educational system, with a strong emphasis on the recognition of merit. This seems to have been achieved without the kind of envy or false egalitarianism which has been such a feature of British, or perhaps especially English, education. There is an unashamed acknowledgement of an educational elite, who form the managerial class both in industry and in national life, and there does not seem to be the kind of resentment found in Britain where even an educational elite based on merit is so often equated with unfair privilege.

3 Japanese culture seems to have retained a sense of the common good, so that people can easily identify themselves with what is felt to be good for the whole nation and not just good for themselves or for their particular interest. A specific example of this, which was brought to our attention when we were writing our report, is the system of wage-bargaining which takes place as a synchronised exercise once a year, and which thus allows consideration of the total national income – rather than a system which involves pitting one sectional interest against another.

All three of these characteristics – the community view of industry, educational elitism, and the common good – are regarded with deep suspicion in Britain. In some people's minds they seem to epitomise the worst characteristics of a conformist society. To speak or write about community in Britain these days, as I frequently do, is to evoke the immediate response that one of the great advances since the 1960s has been precisely to escape from the stifling narrowness and conformism of traditional communities. In the 1980s, 'community' tended to be identified with the dead hand of a collectivism which assumed that 'nanny knows best'. A healthy entrepreneurial individualism is still claimed to be the foundation for true prosperity.

Educationally there has been some return to the concept of merit, but this is against the background of a system which has been so predominantly child-centred that it has narrowed the whole notion of achievement to mean just achieving one's personal best. This may be fine for building up self-esteem, but does not actually encourage respect for those with high academic attainments. In fact the Western world has been developing a culture in which expertise is regarded as a purely relative matter, to be treated with suspicion – and certainly not as the gateway to widely respected positions of leadership.

As for the notion of the common good, we remember Rousseau and all that flowed from him in terms of collectivism, bureaucracy and the tyranny of the state. Wage-bargaining geared to the national interest, for instance, would seem to many of those involved to smack of the worst excesses of government interference.

I have been drawing caricatures, but I hope that what I have just said about typical British reactions to the Japanese style of doing things is enough to make the point that we are culturally very different. When we ask *why* our industrial cultures are so different, we need to look partly to history, and partly to basic philosophy and religion. History is perhaps the easier starting-point.

The historical perspective: starting from scratch

In the late 1940s I used to share a research laboratory with a French student with the somewhat disconcerting name of Karl Marx. We talked much about the differences between our two countries, and I remember how he constantly used to say, 'Of course the trouble with you British is that you were not invaded'. In a sense he was right. In the years after the second world war we did not have to start again. Having been the first nation to embark on industrialisation – for many decades without government involvement or even regulation – for a century we had gained all the advantages of being pioneers. By the end of the nineteenth century, and in the years between the wars and since 1945, we have been suffering all the disadvantages of having made the initial mistakes, and having been stuck in patterns of behaviour which over the past two generations have become less and less appropriate. We accept the confrontational view of industrial relations as if it were normal, whereas in fact it is an absurdity – and in Japan it is seen to be an absurdity. But it was not an absurdity at the time of the Industrial Revolution – nor were *laissez-faire* economics, and the ruthless exploitation of those who had no means of protecting themselves.

However, that is not our world as it need be today. Progress in any field entails both learning and unlearning – and of these unlearning is far the harder part, especially when it entails the emotional unlearning of a long and bitter history. This is why big, well-established industries tend to be less innovative than small, new ones which have nothing to unlearn. To be able to start with a clean slate, learning from the experience of the past but not bound to it, is a huge advantage; and those who have to lead our Churches know that this is just as true in church life as in industry.

Japan's great advantage was that, starting from scratch, it could embark on the process of modernisation in the 1870s and then, after 1945, undertake its national economic recovery on its own terms. The great skill of the Japanese is the discrimination with which they have transformed themselves from a closed, self-contained society into one which has been able to absorb external influences and internalise them, but adapt them to traditional Japanese patterns of thought and procedure. They have avoided the kind of pluralistic and individual-istic chaos which is now increasingly characteristic of the West. By preserving many of its traditional cultural values and incorporating them into its business ethos, Japan has retained a stability and a cohesion which the West now lacks. In consequence, Japan has been able to develop rational processes for organising its industry and con-trolling its economy, on the assumption that the nation genuinely shares some common values and purposes.

The state has played a much larger part in all this than would now be tolerable in Britain – but in Japan's industrial revolution this could be accepted as inevitable given the nature of the stimulus that goaded Japan, first into modernisation, and then into the effort of national recovery following total defeat. Ronald Dore, on whose writings I am heavily relying, reports a question asked at a business seminar: 'When shall we in Britain come to accept the need for a positive role for the state?' 'When', came the answer, 'the British wake up to the humiliating realisation that our standard of living has fallen below Italy's.' I am reminded of my friend Karl Marx: our difficulties stem from the fact that we have not had to start again. We have not been humiliated – yet.

The cultural perspective: criticism and co-operation

I turn to the more difficult question of philosophical and religious differences, and here I mainly want to consider some of the things which I believe have gone wrong in our own Western culture. I must leave those who know Japanese culture from within to say what, if anything, has gone wrong in that. All I will say, by way of introduction, is that Japanese culture seems to depend upon a degree of trust, and of respect for authority, which are becoming increasingly threadbare in the West. Ours is a culture which has to a large extent been shaped by the spirit of criticism, and particularly by the Enlightenment's radical questioning of all forms of tradition and unexamined authority.

I am not one of those who deplores the Enlightenment, or who would want to undo its consequences. The spirit of criticism lies at the very heart of science and of much modern achievement – in Japan as well as in the West. Although romantics sometimes dream about going back to a pre-scientific world, I strongly suspect that most of them, if they actually got it, would hate it. The spirit of criticism and the questioning of authority are also closely related to our Christian and Western concern for the dignity and freedom of individuals. Whether we identify the basis of human rights in Christian – particularly Protestant – theology, or in Enlightenment rationalism, most of us would not want to renege on the concept of such rights, and would want to see them extended to cultures which, from our perspective, still seem unnecessarily subservient.

But there is also a negative side to the spirit of criticism and the repudiation of authority; and we are becoming increasingly conscious of the heavy price that our culture has been paying for them.

At the level of philosophy and religion we have reached a state of self-questioning which has become obsessive and destructive. Our culture seems to have lost confidence in itself – to feel guilty about its past, uncertain about its future, and to take delight in a kind of cultural iconoclasm, or even nihilism, in which what is novel or extreme or bizarre is valued more highly than what is established or traditional – a process which has gone even further in the USA.

I have referred elsewhere to what a writer in *The Tablet* called 'the culture of contempt'. He related it particularly to the contempt which some politicians express towards others; the contempt which government has expressed towards such groups as doctors, teachers and university dons, in overriding their professional judgements; and the contempt reflected back towards the institutions of society by those contemptuously excluded from them.

This is an extreme diagnosis. In rather less dramatic form, we see that much of our political and social life is rooted in the idea of the inevitability of conflict – from the ritual and increasingly tedious jousts which go on in parliament, to the equally ritual and tedious jousts which have divided industries against themselves, and which have exalted a kind of machismo increasingly irrelevant to the actual conditions of modern industry. The cries of 'No surrender' on both sides of the 1994 rail dispute, were, alas, all too typical.

Even theologians have absorbed something of the same spirit, and nowadays write approvingly about what they call 'the hermeneutics of suspicion'. The basic idea seems to be to distrust your sources, to interpret what is said in a suspicious frame of mind, and always to look for the hidden snags. The media also work on the basis of a hermeneutics of suspicion – though I don't think they would call it that.

I am not decrying such criticism. Not all of this need be deplored, and some of it can be applauded. What lies behind it, I suppose, is one of the great lessons our age has slowly begun to learn – namely, the extent to which power can be abused, and the distortions which different power-relationships can exert over our human affairs. Furthermore, as human beings we have a huge capacity for self-deception, and a measure of criticism, challenge and suspicion is one of the best-proven means of exposing falsehood and undermining dominance. Our problem is that we do not know how to control these powerful weapons, to use them within reasonable limits, and to prevent them from destroying us. That is why exposure to some other culture, in which benevolence is assumed and trust is a starting-point, can at first be disorientating, but perhaps in the long run refreshing and challenging.

We need to be aware, however, that even in a culture of trust there is a sense in which the business world itself tends to undermine its own moral foundations. I pose the question, therefore, of how well in the long run Japanese culture will itself withstand these influences.

I have in mind a book, by an American economist called Hirschman, with the engaging title *Exit, Voice and Loyalty*. In a word or two, his thesis is that a strongly market-orientated economy, with an emphasis on choice, encourages people to move away from districts, schools, shops, products, etc., which they find unsatisfactory, rather than to protest, argue or work for change. It is easier simply to migrate to a different supermarket then to get your nearest one to stock different items. In other words, exit predominates over voice. Traditional, static communities have usually engaged in intense internal discussion to find ways to overcome problems – and it is still the case that those who are stuck in a particular community have to work from within to improve it. Freedom of choice, on the other hand, encourages individualism, and by allowing easy exit erodes loyalty. The market, therefore, inevitably undermines community, which has to be rooted in loyalty if it is to be more than skin-deep; and since community is the context in which moral education takes place, the market can also undermine its own moral foundations.

This is a grossly oversimplified argument. There is a sense in which those involved in the market try to encourage loyalty – at least to their own brand. There is a sense, too, in which a community from which exit is difficult can be stifling and oppressive. And there are important senses in which the market, and the spirit of enterprise which undergirds it, can form the basis of a new set of values concerned with freedom, creativity and the flexibility to cope with an unknown future. But Hirschman, I believe, still has a point. A civilised society needs moral communities, within which values are formed and tested. It needs stable relationships without the kind of oppressiveness which is rightly rejected as the undesirable concomitant of traditional communities. It needs loyalties which are neither blind nor self-seeking, but which can withstand the attractions of individualistic freedom and the corrosive effect of relentless criticism. But there are real doubts about whether a society in which freedom of choice is the central value can actually develop or maintain such communities; about whether our present weak sense of community loyalty can actually inculcate the moral values of promise-keeping, truth-telling and personal integrity; and about whether, without these, the market itself can flourish.

It is not surprising that the subject of moral education is high on our present political agenda – but it needs to be stated very clearly that moral education does not happen just through propounding moral principles. It happens through a largely subconscious absorption of values and standards from within the kind of community where those principles are actually lived out. In a word, a good society needs good people; and this is true even, or perhaps especially, in a technological age. I recall the remark of a Japanese industrialist on the aims of education: 'What we need are good people; we can make anyone an engineer'.

The best of both worlds?

Co-operation with Japan is welcome, not least because a sympathetic study of Japanese culture might help Westerners to look in a constructively critical way at our own culture, which many of us see as being in deep crisis. I think there are already hopeful signs, through the presence of Japanese industries in this country, that some of their insights and practices can be assimilated into our own way of life. They may help us to recover that proper sense of community, loyalty and trust which are an important part of our Christian inheritance, but which all too often are submerged under those elements within our Christian tradition which are more sceptical about human nature. Life need not be a power struggle. We are persons in community, who need each other and can build each other up, and there is an urgent need to translate what may seem platitudinous in the life of the Church into political, social and industrial realities. The search for consensus has not been a primary aim in Britain of late, and there is much food for thought about its highly significant role in Japanese success.

I hope also that our Japanese friends may learn something from us, about how to survive in a context in which most of the traditional conventions and securities are under attack, and in which an all-pervasive pluralism is being foisted upon us by social and economic forces beyond our control – a pluralism which seems to threaten the sense that we share a common humanity.

I am intrigued by the suggestion that Japan may resist consumerism but that, if it does develop, it is not likely to be along Western lines, because society still operates on what is basically a village model. I suspect this was true of Britain in the early stages of the Industrial Revolution when, despite the movement of huge numbers of people into the new industrial cities, there still remained a very strong local culture in the communities in which they settled – just as today, in Britain, the ethnic communities maintain their cohesion by living as far as possible in the same areas. It will be interesting and important to see how long Japanese culture resists the pressures of individualism, or whether out of the encounter between our different cultures it is going to be possible to produce something which combines the best of both.

It is in this sense that I see the Japanese firms in our midst as important experimental laboratories; and I hope that management, in particular, can show the way, by exhibiting virtues which we too value as part of our Western Christian culture, but which all too often are not much in evidence. I end with some words by Ronald Dore about the costs and advantages of trying to develop the kind of trust and good-will which ought to exist between responsible human beings in a co-operative enterprise, and in a culture which places an increasing premium on specialist expertise. He is writing about the increasing need for such expertise:

> The more we have to take expertise on trust, the more important it becomes for our economic efficiency that the people who have expertise can actually get on with using it instead of having to defend their claims to authority every inch of the way, so the more important become the tokens of assurance that they are using that expertise and dedicated authority benevolently, in good faith. And what are those tokens of assurance? Putting, and being seen to put, serious effort into the work itself and into achieving and retaining competence in it; transparency of the reward structure; abstention from claiming privileges which do not accord with current perceptions of what are fair principles for matching rewards to contributions; sufficient confidence willingly to admit ignorance when necessary; and, if managers can manage all that, abstention, then, from the arrogance of righteousness.[1]

These may seem like modest aims in face of the large historical and cultural issues on which I have been touching. But history and culture are changed, not by talking about them, but by actually doing a few small things differently. We should not therefore despise modest beginnings.

9

The Church in society

While Japan may be able to show us some of what is wrong with Britain, there are other problems which need the sharp eyes of an insider – and which may properly be addressed by an organisation such as Affirming Catholicism. I was startled not long ago to be introduced to one in which I have some personal interest. It is the concept of Habgoodism, and it appears in an article by Clifford Longley who identifies it as, if not the cause, at least one of the underlying factors in the current British malaise. In brief, his argument is that there is a deep unreality at the heart of English culture – the theory of what he calls 'an Anglican state'. It is the belief that it is the duty of the Church of England to be providing the 'public religion' of the English. And he concludes that, since all is not well with English society, this must imply that something is seriously wrong with the religious and moral pillars which ought to be upholding it – pillars of which he sees me as a chief upholder and defender. Hence Habgoodism.

In part, this is a familiar complaint. Clifford Longley has for years had an obsession with establishment, and I do not propose to rehearse familiar arguments about it, nor to comment on his drastic over-simplification of my actual views. But I am interested in the contrast he draws between the veterans who marched to celebrate VE Day and for whom decent, 'Anglican' values are still a reality and a token of what they fought for, and the under-40s who live in a different world. There are serious questions about the kind of society we are now, and the kind of society we are likely to become. I quote from Longley's article:

England is a depressed nation, unsure of its own future, increasingly fractious. The English are among the most pessimistic in Europe.

Facing the European Union, they sense how fragile their institutions are, how uncertain is the definition of Englishness and how vulnerable it seems, therefore, to foreign absorption. This is not the attitude of a self-confident people. A lot of this self-doubt is not primarily about Europe. It is a fear of change, fear of the different; fear, above all, of the future.[1]

Is this true? Whether true or not, it seems to me a useful starting-point for an exploration of where we are as a Church and as a society in the context of a forward-looking faith, as it seeks to evangelise in both the Roman Catholic and the Evangelical senses of that word. I want to examine it from three perspectives: sociological, theological and European.

1   The sociological perspective

For the sociology, I turn to Grace Davie's book, *Religion in Britain since 1945*, with the telling subtitle, *Believing without Belonging*. The subtitle points to a phenomenon which is familiar to us all: not, as was once predicted, a wholesale shift to a secular society, but a persistence of interest in moral and spiritual matters, allied with a rejection of institutional life, both in the Churches and in secular life as well. The shift is most marked in the younger generation, though disillusionment with the major institutions of our society is certainly not confined to the young. For the Churches, one disturbing consequence of this distancing from institutions is that belief tends to become more and more detached from any of the traditional forms, and thus more personal and idiosyncratic. In this sense Clifford Longley is right to say that public faith is much less of a reality to the under-40s than to earlier generations, for whom the institutional links were stronger and folk religion was closer to something vaguely resembling orthodoxy.

But this is not the whole picture. Older people have always been more religious than the young. It is possible that we are experiencing a marked generational shift with respect to religious understanding and behaviour, but we cannot yet be certain of this. If, as seems to be happening, there is a growing demand for good religious education in schools, a growing popularity of Church schools, and growing competition from other faiths, it is possible that more of the basic elements of religion may be conveyed to the next generation than has been conveyed in the recent past.

On top of this generational problem, we have to recognise the widespread change in consciousness in the direction of post-modernism: the shift from duty to self-fulfilment, from truth to opinion, from community to individual, from the understanding of a comprehensive tradition to transitory insights. These shifts are not just the prerogative of the chattering classes. They have permeated our culture more deeply than that, partly through the political climate of recent years, but also as one of the consequences of the information explosion. There are simply too many things for us to react to, to assimilate – things which challenge our own ideas, and disorientate us. Saturation by the media encourages a kaleidoscopic kind of con-sciousness. The idea that there may be public and unassailable truths and values becomes hard to entertain. And with this loss comes, not so much a failure of nerve, as the loss of a sense of shared landmarks and of direction.

Yet the longing for something more enduring persists. Jonathan Sacks, in his writings about the importance of the moral law as the basis for community and family life, has won plaudits from people (including Clifford Longley himself) who, in varying degrees, sense the dangers of becoming locked into the kind of culture I have just described. He reinforces the point that, even if the sketch I have given is a fair description of what has been happening to our society, this is not the moment to abandon the attempt to build up a public faith and morality, but the moment to try even harder. Grace Davie quotes a moving passage from David Martin describing the role of the Church in such a culture:

We in England live in the chill religious vapours of northern Europe, where moribund religious establishments loom over popu-lations that mostly do not enter churches for active worship even if they entertain inchoate beliefs. Yet these establishments guard and maintain thousands of houses of God, which are markers of space and time. Not only are they markers and anchors, but also the only repositories of all-embracing meanings pointing beyond the immediate to the ultimate. They are the only institutions that deal in tears and concern themselves with the breaking points of human existence. They provide frames and narratives and signs to live by, and offer persistent points of reference. They are repositories of signs about miraculous birth and redemptive sacrifice, shared tables and gift-giving; and they offer moral codes and exemplars for the creation of communal solidarity and the nourishment of virtue. They are places from which to launch initiatives which help sustain the kind of networks found, for example, in the inner city; they welcome schools and regiments and rotary clubs; they celebrate and commemorate; they are islands of quietness; they are places in which unique gestures occur of blessing, distribution and obeisance; they offer spaces in which solemnly to gather, to sing, to lay flowers, and light candles. They are – in Philip Larkin's phrase – serious places on serious earth.[2]

2 The theological perspective

That quotation brings me to what I want to say from a theological perspective. I begin with the familiar description of the Church as sign, instrument and foretaste of the Kingdom of God. To think of the Church simply as a kind of social cement, an undergirding for the values on which public life depends, is to miss all the subtlety of that description. It is to lose the sense of fundamental tension between Church and society which is inherent in the message of the cross.

The Church, as a sign of meaning in a bleak and unfriendly world, is all that David Martin says it is. It should affirm an ultimate hope, in the light of the cross and resurrection, and thus provide an environment in which many lesser hopes can flourish, and many otherwise struggling human endeavours can be affirmed. A large part of an archbishop's job, for instance, is to go round giving encouragement – not by vacuous back-slapping, but by setting good things in their divine context.

But the Church should also be a sign of contradiction, a critic, an awkward customer, an exposer of evil and injustice, a reminder of judgement. I am conscious that Anglicanism is on the whole better at affirming than at criticising, and this is one reason why I am a passionate ecumaniac. We actually need a variety of witnesses, a variety of experiences, if the diverse forms of Christian social witness, and the tensions within such witness, are to be expressed. It is essential, though, that this variety should exist within a single Christian fellowship, and not simply in the differences between separate Churches. My experience of ecumenical working is that it enables the Church to be a sign of affirmation and a sign of contradiction simultaneously, both pointing to that which lies beyond the Church – the Kingdom of God which is, and is to be.

The Church should also be an instrument of the Kingdom, and that must surely mean involvement in the ambivalences of social and political action. Charles Davis, in his book *Religion and the Making of Society*, goes so far as to claim that social and political action is now the sole, valid means of expressing the Christian gospel.[3] He distinguishes between what he calls the three worlds of modern culture: the objective world of human knowledge, the social world of practice with its norms, and the subjective world of self-awareness. Our apprehensions of transcendence relate to all three, in terms of cosmic religion, political religion and contemplative religion. Nowadays, he says, knowledge is too fragmented to provide any standing-ground for the kind of cosmic synthesis which sustained medieval faith. By the same token, we now have other ways of exploring the depths of human consciousness, and there is not necessarily anything peculiarly religious about inwardness, vital though inwardness can be in enabling religious experience. By contrast, the Christian religion has always been concerned with action, and it is much more characteristic of Christianity to find God in our neighbour than to find him in our inner consciousness, or in the cosmos.

I have compressed what is already a compressed argument, and Davis would be the first to admit that he overstates his case. Actual Christian experience contains all three of the elements I have been describing. But Davis may well be right in giving a central place to action – not as part of a desperate attempt to be relevant, but in recognition of the truth that Christianity has always been political, just as the acts of God have always been, in the broadest sense, political. What has so often gone wrong with Christian political action is not that it has been political, but that it has been inept, and has lost touch with the basic Christian imperatives.

Thus far Charles Davis. I have dwelt on him because there is a case here to be answered by critics who want to take Christianity out of the public sphere, or who despair of trying to articulate a publicly relevant faith. Our culture may be exerting powerful pressures in the direction of privatisation, but I do not see how this could possibly be condoned by those who see the Church as an instrument of the Kingdom, or by any who call themselves Catholic.

On the Church as a foretaste of the Kingdom of God, I will only say that this leads us straight to the much-discussed topic of community. It is fundamental to our understanding of Catholic Christianity that human fulfilment is not found in individualism, but in our relationship with each other and with God. I always recall the story of the somewhat over-zealous saint who was greeted at the gates of heaven with the question, 'Where are the others?' To stress community is not in itself an argument for the public dimension of faith. There are communities quite happy to keep themselves to themselves. But the call to community points us in the direction of public faith, if 'the others' are those who flounder in our society because it seems to lack sense and purpose.

Let me repeat that I strongly believe it to be an important task of the Church to undergird that search for sense and purpose in a society – unless the society is itself so rotten that it has to be abandoned. And the Church does this through the affirmation of what is good; through the identification of, and opposition to, what is wrong; through social and political action; and through the quality of its own life as a community. All this remains its responsibility, even though the particular culture in which we now live may be unreceptive.

3 The European perspective

I come thirdly to the European context in which our present English culture needs to be understood. The most obvious retort to Clifford Longley's identification of a peculiar English malaise is that it is by no means unique. There is enough evidence in the European Value Systems Study to show that the social changes which afflict us in Britain are common to Western Europe as a whole. David Martin, lecturing recently to the Northern Church Leaders, spoke about a strongly secular belt running diagonally across Europe from Berlin to Birmingham, through the most highly fragmented and individualised regions of European society, and drawing no distinction between Catholic and Protestant areas.

My own contacts with the European churches, particularly in relation to the European Community, have revealed a similar picture.

Britain may differ from other European countries in its political attitudes, but socially and culturally we all face much the same problems.

Chapter 15 began life as a lecture to a group of university dons and politicians in Leuven on the subject of the Anglican Church and the unification of Europe. I think they were somewhat bemused by my exploration of different models of unity, from the Commonwealth and the Anglican Communion to the Council of Churches for Britain and Ireland. They were in no doubt about their own relatively uncomplicated approach to European union, and it was not hard to see why. I had a longish conversation, for instance, with a German living in Luxemburg who works in Belgium: frontiers, languages and currencies meant nothing to him. Most of the central European countries have had constant changes in their borders. Belgium itself is a fairly recent invention, with such a weak sense of national identity that the Belgians to whom I have spoken seem to contemplate with equanimity its possible division into two separate countries. Many Germans, despite their social and economic successes, still suffer from huge self-doubt, and see European union as in part a protection against themselves. Geographically and historically the contrast with Britain could not be greater – and I find it much more plausible to link differing political perceptions of Europe to these factors, rather than to some unique English malaise.

I wonder, for instance, what the artistic gimmick of wrapping up the Reichstag in polythene sheeting says about the respect for political institutions in Germany – a country where obedience to authority is much more highly rated than in Britain. Indeed, political life in most Western European countries seems at a lower ebb, and in some of them much more dangerously unstable, than in Britain. The Germans have been far more generous in their treatment of refugees than we have, but much less generous in giving them citizenship. In probing the reason why, it became obvious that, at the root of it, is a deep problem about German national identity.

My purpose in giving these examples is not to enter into the argument about European union, but simply to make the point that Western European society as a whole is suffering from contradictions and uncertainties, though these may take different forms in different countries. And because in many parts the Churches have been closely bound up with the societies within which they belong, these Churches have suffered self-questioning decline along with the other institutions. This may be an argument against getting too close to the sources of power. It also raises questions about how power has traditionally been distributed. The Church of England may have more of the trappings of power than many continental Churches, but we have not for a long time had a total monopoly of the kind which emerged when continental countries defined themselves at the Reformation by their religious allegiance. The tension between establishment and dissent in England has saved us from the worst excesses of intolerance and anticlericalism, and has ensured that the national Church has always had vigorous critics – from without and also, healthily, from within. This is a further reason why I believe that ecumenism should nowadays be central to our thinking about Church and society.

The question remains, though, why Western Europe has suffered such a catastrophic decline in church membership and in institutional life in general. The fact that it is common to the whole of Europe should make us look for deeper causes than the failings of a particular Church. Europe as the home of the Enlightenment, and as the generator of the acids of modernity and the even more corrosive acids of post-modernity, is frequently described as having eroded its own philosophical and moral basis. Too much criticism and too little faith has brought us to the brink of nihilism. Authority has been undermined – in principle during the eighteenth century, and in practice in the twentieth. Increasing ease of access to information in our own day means that nobody is an authority any more, except individuals with their modems and their computers, and with the Internet to supply their needs.

Anti-Enlightenment thinking has been much explored by the Gospel and Our Culture Movement. I remain unconvinced, though, that one can or should try to undo the main achievements of the Enlightenment, and I am sufficiently old-fashioned to believe that faith should be reasonable, and that there are still traditional and well-tested authorities worth trusting. Nevertheless, it is true that there have been, and still are, destructively critical forces at work in European society, and that there is real evidence of a *trahison des clercs* among the guardians of tradition. A relentless search for the new, the shocking, the pin which bursts the bubble, and the fashionable radicalism which grabs the headlines, has penetrated beyond the

Sunday supplements deep into the intellectual life of Europe – and to some extent into the Churches as well.

My hunch is that all this has had more effect on Western culture than on other cultures for two reasons, both closely bound up with European history. Europe since Christendom has always had a missionary stance. It has been concerned with universal truths and with universal power. Greek philosophy was believed to have laid down principles of reason and logic which were of universal application, and which still remain essential to science in whatever culture it is practised. The Christian influence on Europe reinforced this sense of a universal mission. Christ transcends all cultures and breaks down all barriers. The gospel is true for everybody. Whether or not this is expressed in actual missionary endeavour, the perception of universality remains the same – and must surely remain a fundamental Catholic principle.

But the sense of mission is not confined to philosophy, science and religion. We have been missionaries in the broadest sense. We have exported Western ways of life to almost every part of the world: African natives in the bush, more likely than not, wear trousers; Papuans listen to transistor radios. I shall never forget going into a Palestinian refugee camp in Beirut in 1981, and finding the children reading Shakespeare.

The claim to universal truth has in the past been uncomfortably close to the exercise of universal power, including fire-power. I do not want in any way to denigrate the century of missionary expansion – but one has only, for example, to read the history of Africa to confirm that it depended on guns as well as Bibles. There was a degree of arrogance in the assumption that Africa was virgin land waiting to be exploited. We think differently now. We have renounced this kind of power, militarily if not economically. There are profound undercurrents of guilt about some of the abuses of power. There is a growing sense that what Europe has exported to the world, though life-giving in many respects, has also been uncomfortably ambivalent.

In other words, two important assumptions at the heart of European self-consciousness – assumptions about truth and about power – have both been at least partially eroded. Add to this the undermining of authority and the growing spirit of destructive criticism, and I think we can see why Western Europe as a whole lacks self-confidence and shares a common sense of disorientation. The malaise has deep roots in the history that we share with other European countries, and in the very achievements of our common culture.

Affirming Catholic hope

So far I have been trying in a roundabout way to pinpoint some of the factors in our present situation – sociological, theological, and broadly cultural – which all Churches must recognise if they are to relate meaningfully to their social environment. Running through the chapter is a subtext about the need for public faith – a faith not exclusive to the Churches themselves, but able to inform, and to some extent guide and sustain, public life. I come finally to the question, what has this to do with attempts to restore a more outward-looking Catholic Anglicanism?

The intention of Catholic Christianity is to be all-embracing. How can we give expression to this in a society which may need us, but by and large does not want us? How can we, with our sense of the universal, communicate effectively in a society which no longer believes in universals? And how can we sustain our own Catholic identity without falling into the trap of rooting it in peculiar practices, in marks of distinction, a self-chosen Catholic style, which in earlier generations indirectly marked out Catholics as being separate and odd – i.e., not Catholics at all.

I am reminded of a cartoon in which a wife is showing a friend her husband's observatory, where he sits with his eye glued to an enormous telescope. The caption reads: 'This is my husband. He lives in a little world of his own.'

It seems to me that our all-embracingness as Catholics depends more on what we are looking at than on precisely where we stand in relation to all the distinctions and controversies which can occupy us so much in our small, ecclesiastical world. What we have to offer is a vision, a hope, and a means of expressing these in worship.

This vision is of an ultimate unity which can contain our present fragmentations because it is itself many-sided and dynamic. Let me try to unpack that as part of the significance of the doctrine of the Trinity. For me one of the theological excitements of our age has been the turning of what has often in the past seemed a dry static formula, designed to make the best of contradictory historical claims about the nature of God, into the rediscovery of the doctrine which holds within it the living heart of Christian faith. It can give us profound insights into the nature of reality, into our own nature as persons, and into our dependence as persons on our relationship with others.

Though we have a long way to go before we can translate these insights into the clues needed to interpret our present culture, I believe that the possibility is there. Just to give one example – it seems to me that the doctrine of the Trinity provides the most promising way of tackling issues about the uniqueness of Christianity in relation to other faiths. This is an explosive issue which raises all the hard questions about universal claims made in a pluralist culture. But if we ask what it means that the Spirit proceeds from the Father as well as from the Son, we might be able to identify works of the Spirit which, though ultimately centred on the incarnation, are not exclusively linked to it. And this leads on to a further question: can we recognise the Spirit of God even where Christ is not named? The doctrine of the Trinity opens up a range of subtleties in talking about God which may be hugely valuable in an age when we tend to be overwhelmed by the variety and contradictoriness of human experience.

We need, in other words, to take more seriously the widespread consciousness of a transcendent dimension to life, the search for some kind of spirituality among people who reject traditional religion. A grasp of the complex dynamism of Trinitarian faith, of the nearness and the mystery of God, of his presence beyond us and within us, can save us from the simplistic images which are instantly and rightly dismissed. Catholicism tells us of a big God who is present in unexpected places.

Hope is needed, perhaps even more than vision, in an age when vision is all too frequently derided, or all too quickly overtaken by the next fashion. In 1995 I was slightly put out by numerous headlines proclaiming 'Hope for York', as if it were in particularly short supply in my diocese. But I am comforted by the thought that, since Moltmann, hope is now one of our key theological categories. I believe it is also central to the understanding of Catholicism.

I have always seen catholicity more as a goal for the future than as a gift from the past. I rather doubt whether there ever was a complete Catholic past, any more than there was a time when the Church was completely united. Christianity was an explosion of new life and new ideas, flowing out in all directions, gradually creating forms of unity, then losing them and rediscovering them – but always conscious of differences, and finding it hard to let go of traditions once they had become the vehicles of this life. The very fact that the need for unity is so constantly stressed in the New Testament is evidence that from the beginning it was hard to achieve. To my mind it is quite impossible to read the New Testament as if the gospel were a carefully designed package handed over by Jesus, and simply needing to be passed on. There was variety and dissension from day one. Though in one sense everything had happened in the cross and the resurrection, the disciples also knew that it was simply a beginning, and that in some sense the Body of Christ still had to be fashioned. So they looked forward in hope.

To see the Church in this way is not to underrate the classic marks of catholicity. These emerged out of history, and they are not to be ignored. They define the road – but they are not some sort of ticket, nor do they define the destination. Difficulties and deviations on the journey need not invalidate the ultimate hope. Every time we read the Psalms we are reminded that the Jews lived primarily by hope: they experienced the destruction of almost all they valued, yet they went on in hope. Though as Christians we say that their hope was fulfilled in Christ, we recognise that we too have to live in hope, until Christ is all in all. In hope we can face the fact that we live in lean times. In hope it is possible to accept and work with the fragmentariness and transitoriness of much of today's social scene, because we do not have to claim a unity and a certainty which human beings will not possess, this side of the end.

We do, however, possess a means – and this is why I want to end with a brief word about the significance of Catholic sacramentalism in the context I have been attempting to describe. As sacramentalists we have it laid upon us to take the whole created order seriously. It is basic to our faith that creation contains within itself the possibilities of revealing and conveying the divine. But we actually see this happening only on a small scale – in individual lives, in particular acts of worship, in elements set aside for this particular purpose. I have written elsewhere about 'making sense' as being at the same time both an act of discovery and an act of creation. When it is hard for us to make our universal claims through analysing the ways things are, and in times when we are more conscious of fragmentation than of unity, it is still possible for us, by the grace of God, to create islands of meaning and tokens of God's presence – to make sense even on a limited scale. By seeing God in a transformed life, in sanctified bread and wine, in a good deed performed in love, in steps taken to relieve human distress, we are renewed in hope. And it is not foolish to say, this is reality; and this is for everyone.

10

The family and the new social order

The strains within our present society are nowhere more clearly seen than in the frequently expressed worries about what is happening to family life. In this chapter, written before the Board for Social Responsibility's report, *Something to Celebrate*, my aim has been to explore the mutual interaction between the character of a society and the character of the families which make it up, and which it helps to form.

The need for families?

I begin 20 years ago when I visited a kibbutz on the shore of the Sea of Galilee. It was impressive to encounter a community in which family distinctions had almost been abolished. Though married couples lived together, their children for the most part lived communally, only staying with their parents for limited periods during the day. They were looked after by people who had been specially trained for the job; they appeared happy and well-adjusted, and there was obviously a high degree of socialisation. There were interesting signs, though, even among what was still a first or second generation of kibbutz-dwellers, that the pattern was not totally satisfying. Parents were increasingly concerned to have their children sleeping with them at night, and one sensed that before very long the parents' sleeping huts would come to be regarded as home.

The psychologist Bruno Bettelheim, writing about the kibbutz experience at about the same time, in his book *The Children of the Dream*, noted similar signs.[1] He described how the inspiration for kibbutz-living came out of the experience of Jews in central and eastern Europe – frequently confined to ghettos, oppressed by tight-knit family structures, and wanting to escape into a new social order in which the demands of child-rearing and the dominance of parents would no longer overshadow their lives. It was the pursuit of an ideal in which an open community life could break down barriers, and create a new sense of belonging.

But it had its costs. What Bettelheim particularly observed was the loss of individuality and intimacy. If everything is public, communal, well-ordered, and rationally planned, then the times and places when one can simply be oneself disappear or become constrained. 'Being oneself' is what we do at home. But if 'home' is a hut visited by children from 5 pm to 7 pm, then it does not provide the kind of emotional security or depth of relationship that children need. Parental care is controlled by the hands of the clock. Security lies in the kibbutz as a whole, not in a set of intimate relationships; and this makes it extremely hard for individuals to stand out over against the community, or to have ideas of their own.

I have started with this experience because it is the major example of social engineering, as applied to family life, in the last 50 years. It seems to illustrate how different patterns of family life tend to produce different kinds of people. Discussions about the family, therefore, have much wider implications than on the family itself: they concern the sort of society we are creating for ourselves. To the extent to which this is true, our contemporary concern in Britain about the family is, or should be, central to social policy. The kibbutz experience also illustrates the tension between communitarian ideals and individualism; it reveals that, behind differences of opinion about different patterns of family life, there may be deeper ideological issues.

In the new social order which has been emerging in Britain (and much of the Western world) over the past quarter-century or so, we have been witnessing what some interpret as the deconstruction of the family. The statistics are all too familiar: there is one divorce for every two marriages; 32 per cent of all births are outside marriage; 19 per cent of families with dependent children have lone parents; there are 120,000 abortions a year among unmarried women; cohabitation is on the increase, whether as a prelude to marriage or as an alternative to it. We all know such figures, and they generate a sense of crisis, particularly when linked in people's minds with the crime statistics, the overwhelming proportion of which relate to young men between the ages of 15 and 25. Something seems to have gone wrong with the process of socialisation – more so in men than in women, perhaps because men are more in need of the maturing effect of family responsibility. Thus, growing uncertainties about the viability of traditional patterns of family life are seen by some as a causal factor in some of the most obvious ills in our present society.

Others take a more sanguine view. Marriage is still enormously popular. Most people get married eventually, and the fact that an increasing proportion do it several times is an ironic reminder of its continuing importance, even to those who have experienced repeated failures. Furthermore, though the social conditions under which marriages exist may change, the bonding between husband and wife, and the sense of responsibility for children, are as old as humanity itself. They tend to reassert themselves even when, as in the kibbutzim, social engineering presses strongly in the opposite direction. The notion that the nuclear family is a recent phenomenon, and underlies many of the present strains in family life, is firmly discounted by those who see it as just one more way in which this fundamental bonding adapts itself to a more fragmented society. Indeed, it is hard to read the Bible and not to see there, in a very different cultural milieu, things which we can immediately recognise as belonging to our own experience of family life. The description in some of the Pauline epistles of the relationship between husband and wife implies an intimacy which belies the notion that romantic love was a much later invention.

But some things *have* changed – in particular, there have been three developments: the emancipation of women; the growing economic independence of the sexes; and the cultural and ideological changes which have given increasing importance to personal self-fulfilment. The conjunction of these three factors means that the crisis in marriage today is to some extent a crisis about the role of men. With changing patterns of employment, the diminution in what has traditionally been 'men's work', and the apparently limitless opportunities for sexual encounters without responsibility, there is a growing body of men who feel that they have no particular stake in society, and who by and large are regarded by women as not worth marrying. It is this group of young men who now form the most visible manifestation of a society under strain and who, at least in part, are the victims of social changes outside their control. Their plight is made worse by their having to exist on the fringes of a culture which judges success in terms of self-gratification. I mention them at this stage because they are, as it were, the fall-out from the processes of change which some see as having fatally and irreversibly weakened family life, but which others (including myself) believe can be surmounted.

Meeting children's needs

If it is true, as I suggested earlier, that different patterns of family life tend to produce different kinds of people, then the right starting-point for assessing the value of different patterns must be the basic needs of children, if they are to grow up capable of living responsible and fulfilled lives in a free society.

The children of the kibbutz enjoyed the security all children need, but they had little exposure to intimate relationships. Their emotional lives were mainly focused on the group. This may at first sight seem like a return to the much-praised concept of the extended family. But there is a subtle difference. An extended family has a structure, a hierarchy. Its members are bound together in organic relationships which themselves constitute a kind of intimacy, even though it may not be a strongly emotional one. In fact, there are grounds for seeing the development of more strongly emotional relationships, not as a consequence of the reducing size of the family, but as one of the consequences of declining infant mortality. This is not to suppose that parents in earlier ages did not love their children – clearly many of them did. But with high infant mortality they had to safeguard themselves against investing too much of themselves in children, most of whom were likely to die young.

When greater personal investment in the lives of children became less likely to have traumatic consequences, the family could become more close-knit, more geared to the needs of individuals – and in some instances more oppressive. The sturdy entrepreneurial individualism, which flourished from the 1850s onwards, owes something to this shift – as did the claustrophobic closeness against which the ghetto Jews reacted.

In our own day, the death of a child is regarded as the ultimate tragedy – and understandably so. When one reads about the huge newspaper campaigns and money-raising efforts to send some hopelessly sick child to America or Russia for treatment, one realises how far the pendulum has swung. Indeed, might it perhaps in some cases have swung too far: can one always be sure that the efforts are being undertaken for the child's sake, rather than the parents'?

There is a proper balance between the deep attachment to individuals, and the acceptance that individuals need to exist in a multiplicity of relationships. No other person is ever wholly ours, not even our child. We need community as well as intimacy; intimacy as well as community. And when we look in adults for strength of character and sensitive awareness of others, for a right blend of freedom and responsibility, it is in the balance between intimacy and community in childhood that we may hope to find its origins.

But if it is difficult to get this right with young children, it becomes much harder as they grow up. I suspect most of us are conscious of widespread bewilderment among parents about how to do the best for their children – and I am thinking here of conscientious parents, not those who have given up the struggle already. One factor in this bewilderment is the extent to which parents may feel de-skilled by the professional services available to their children from an early age. The family somehow seems less important than when most of the life-skills acquired by children had to be learnt within it. Furthermore, in a rapidly changing society, the children may grow up in a world largely unfamiliar to their parents, under the influence of a powerful and class-transcending youth culture reinforced by the media. There is thus a rapid loss of authority, and an increasing dependence on residual emotional attachments which may have become stuck at a particular stage of development. When parents complain that they have no control over their children, it may not be the result of weakness or fecklessness, but simply the end-product of a long process of growing away from each other in an increasingly differentiated kind of society.

In describing this scenario, I have in mind basically good and fairly traditional families – the families one would expect to be strong formers of character. If it is difficult in these, how much more difficult must it be in families with deep internal divisions, the families of serial marriages, and families which lack stability, mutuality and trust. There are unresolved arguments about the long-term consequences of divorce on the lives of the children involved. Scientifically it may be difficult to establish precise connections between the behaviour of parents and the emotional problems of their children. But I doubt whether most teachers need convincing that there *is* a connection. And while some children may become more self-reliant in the long term, as a result of troubles at home, it is equally plain that others may suffer directly or indirectly for much of their lives.

Privacy and community

I shall return to the question of divorce later, and to other patterns of family life as they have developed in recent decades. But still concentrating on what promotes the balanced development of children, I want to say a word about privacy. There is a nice architectural illustration of changing ideas about privacy in the historical growth of the house where I used to live as Archbishop of York. It began in the thirteenth century as a great hall and a chapel. That was all. Everything except worship happened in the great hall or in the basement underneath it. Life was totally public: people ate, worked, slept and played together. By the fourteenth century ideas were beginning to change, and two small rooms were built on the end of the hall for the use of the archbishop. In the late fifteenth century this accommodation was enormously expanded, and it seems likely that members of the household, except servants, had their own bedrooms. But the house itself still retained a very open character, with no division between work areas and domestic areas until the mid-twentieth century. Nowadays even archbishops demand some domestic privacy, but it was only about 25 years ago that a private entrance was built for the archbishop and his family.

Like the children of the kibbutz, all of us need a place where we can be ourselves, and this has become more important as the pace and the demands of life have increased. As with the balance between intimacy and community, the balance between private life and public life is important, and there are dangers for those whose private lives are constantly open to public scrutiny. I am not just thinking of shocking goings-on, but of the need I have referred to earlier for a home where it is possible for a certain inwardness to be developed, a deeper sense of individuality.

There are strong overtones in this about the need for prayer and silence, for pausing in life, as the remedy against simply being trapped in other people's demands and expectations. Translating this into family terms, it seems to me that all of us — and perhaps particularly young people — need the kind of living space in which there is somewhere which is especially our own. The fact that this is impracticable for all too many families is maybe a further reason why the development of a strong, responsible individuality is fraught with such difficulties.

There are plenty of ways in which the socialisation process I have been describing can go wrong. Emotional attachment can easily become oppressive and self-regarding. Intimacy can become exploitation, and may be but a short step from abuse. Privacy can cloak selfishness, and can seem to justify possessiveness. We have seen the fruits of some of these in the kind of individualism which lacks moral direction, and is seen solely as a means to personal fulfilment. A family life which is exclusively about emotional attachment, intimacy and privacy, lacks the very qualities of openness which gave the individualism of the nineteenth and early twentieth centuries its strength. It lacks the sense of being part of a larger whole, and sharing a moral purpose. No wonder the kibbutz alternative looks attractive, and one can see its counterpart in other societies in the reaction against 'family values' – 'tawdry secrets', as they were once memorably described – and through experiments in communal living, and involvement in movements of various kinds, from veal protesters to house churches.

But community values are also, or can be, fostered *within* families themselves. People sometimes speak as if the relational aspects of marriage can be entirely separated from the procreation and nurturing of children. Contraceptively they can – but psychologically it is not so easy. A *pas de deux* which systematically avoids the possibility of children runs the risk of self-absorption. I underline the word 'systematically'. Couples who desperately want children, and are denied them, can sometimes marvellously turn this longing into generosity towards others. But a fear of children, who might place a strain on a 'good relationship', is more likely to be a sign of immaturity.

If children can help a parental relationship to mature, then equally the quality of that relationship can be of vital importance to children. I like the description of family life as a 'school of charity'. A family is a tiny, differentiated society, each member of which has a distinct role and individuality. If it can actually do its work as a school of charity, the chances are that it will lay the foundations for an individual's sense of stable identity in a meaningful society, an increasingly rare and valuable commodity in the world for which its members are being prepared.

This is the concern which underlies doubts, which I have expressed in the past, about one-parent families. I know that most one-parent families are not so by choice, and it is clear that many single parents do an excellent job in bringing up their children, and should be given all possible support in doing so. A deliberate choice of single parenthood, however, seems to me to convey a very different message. It is about an unwillingness to enter a mature, reciprocal relationship, and it must therefore fail to provide that schooling in charity – especially charity between the sexes – which helps to balance intimacy and community.

The role of families within the larger society is another aspect of this community dimension in family life. I acknowledge that cohabitation is an increasingly popular alternative to marriage. In 1991–2, almost 30 per cent of those in the 25–34 age-group were cohabiting. When the General Synod of the Church of England debated the subject in July 1992, it adopted a surprisingly relaxed attitude towards cohabitation as a prelude to marriage. But most Christians, I suspect, find it hard to countenance cohabitation as an alternative to marriage, despite the fact that our present marriage regulations are not yet 250 years old. The commonly heard claim, that marriage is 'only a bit of paper', misses the central point. Though the registration of marriages is comparatively recent, and though forms of marriage may have changed, marriage itself has for many centuries been regarded as a fundamental social institution, and as such it has been able to carry meanings which transcend the couple concerned.

To reduce the family to a temporary liaison, or to think of marriage merely as a contract which can be broken as easily as it is made, is to empty it of much of its social meaning, and fatally to weaken it as a social support for love and fidelity. It is also to ignore the reality of the new, organic relationships to which the bearing of children necessarily gives rise. Children are not contractually related to their parents; they organically belong to them, and they need to be able to trust that organic relationship as a constituent part of their own identity. The enduring social meaning of marriage ought to be able to provide a publicly recognised framework for that trust, independent of the particular state of personal relationships.

You will notice that, despite the obvious difficulties, I have been moving towards a very traditional view of marriage and family life. I have done so on the grounds that this is what children need, because it seems to me that the value of the traditional family is as the optimum setting within which the emotional and developmental needs of children can be met. And I believe it important that Christians at least, and I hope others alongside them, will not be deflected from this central insight.

Family life and the life of faith

I have stressed the traditional family also because this is the direction in which a Christian understanding of marriage inescapably points. It is true that the Old Testament is not as strong on monogamy as it might have been – but it is quite clear on the subject of fidelity. It is also true that Jesus said some dismissive things about his own family. 'Who is my mother? who are my brethren and sisters? . . . Whosoever shall do the will of God, the same is my brother and sister and mother.' Families are not the be-all and end-all of existence. Families may misunderstand and frustrate us. No one can be a prophet in his own country. Conversely, there are dangers in any family that love and generosity may be concentrated entirely within the family itself, in a form of higher selfishness, rather than extending to those outside.

Such a religious critique of family life has nothing in common, however, with contemporary efforts to deconstruct the family. The fact that obedience to God may override family loyalties, and spell trouble at home, does not devalue all that is associated with home and family. It merely puts it in a larger context. For Jesus, home and family had to be transcended – just as, early in the life of the Church, Judaism, rooted as it was in the idea of descent, had to be transcended if Christianity was to become a universal faith. But as we see in the Epistles, this was not the whole story. Marriage is a covenant relationship. It is about the God-given possibilities of love and faithfulness which are seen, both in the Old Testament and in the New, as in some way mirroring the relationship of love and faithfulness between God and his people. The gospel message for families is that the love and faithfulness, and indeed the forgiveness, on which they depend, are not ours alone, but God's. The Epistle to the Ephesians – which develops the analogy between husband and wife, and Christ and the Church – is the high-point of this interpretation of marriage as profoundly rooted in the idea of God's initiative in covenanting with us. And this in turn is what, for Christians, gives stability and purpose to life. Both the attitude of Jesus towards family life, therefore, and the theology developed around family relationships elsewhere in the

121

Bible, point beyond themselves to the God who encompasses, transcends and gives meaning to these relationships, together with the grace to sustain them.

I have taken this brief theological tour because my argument so far has been based on the needs of children, and on the need for certain qualities of character if people are to live freely, responsibly and creatively together. But the question as to why couples without children, or with no possibility of having children, should take marriage seriously, is more difficult. A preliminary theological answer is that as human beings we need, and must practise, love and fidelity because that is how God expresses himself towards us – and that is therefore how we shall find our deepest fulfilment. I have also hinted earlier that creating a small school of charity is not only important for children, but is good for adults too. Neither of these answers may carry much conviction, though, with those who see human relationships as essentially transitory, and who look for short-term gratification rather than for enduring love. They may discover that, whatever the attractions of transitoriness, there is a heavy price to pay. Nevertheless, if changing social expectations make the prospect of permanent faithfulness seem less and less plausible, transitory happiness may not seem such a bad option.

There is, however, a further non-theological argument in favour of traditional marriage, even for the childless, which takes us back to the nature of marriage as a social institution, rather than just a personal contract. The point about social institutions is that they provide a context to enable us to understand and shape our experience without our having to start from scratch. We 'enter into marriage' as a state of life already thoroughly explored by others. Within that state of life we have to create our own marriage; and our chances of creating something worthwhile are, at least in theory, greatly enhanced because we are not simply dependent on our own resources. This is why lovers read love-poetry and buy roses. But I add 'at least in theory', because norms, expectations and institutions can be destructive as well as creative. Unrealistic expectations and bad role-models can frustrate good intentions. An over-romanticised view of marriage can make actual marriage more difficult. Soap operas, in which marital quarrels and infidelity are a main source of dramatic interest, subtly change perceptions of what should be regarded as normal. The same is true within each marriage, if individuals behave in ways which cumulatively weaken or strengthen the institutional supports of family life. This is why the quality of a particular marriage is not just the concern of that particular family. In so far as we all depend on institutional norms, we also contribute to them – and if we undermine them, we may be decreasing the life-possibilities of others.

Not long ago I aroused considerable media interest by an off-the-cuff remark about fiscal incentives to marriage. Changes in the tax system in recent years have gradually eroded distinctions between married and cohabiting couples, and in some instances married couples actually fare worse in terms of tax than cohabitees. Predictably, many people interpreted my remarks as a bid to attract more marriages back to the churches; there were angry responses from the single, the divorced, and those who I suspect would describe themselves as liberated; and there were a surprising number of morally superior comments from those whose love was untainted by money. But all these missed the main point, which was simply that, if marriage is a socially important institution, then there need to be some socially significant distinctions between the married and those who adopt alternative forms of relationship. This is not bribery. It entails the recognition that some things go with the grain of a particular society, and some things go against it – and that if we want to encourage certain forms of behaviour, then we need to make sure that the grain of our society goes in that direction. To use the jargon, it is about 'social markers'.

I feel the same about the current use of the word 'partner'. I know it is intended as a neutral and unembarrassing way of acknowledging different types of relationship – but what it also does is to prescribe a new norm. It is saying, in effect, that there is nothing particularly distinctive about being a husband or a wife. Is that what we want to say? The language not only hides the truth of relationships, but also provides a further impetus to think in purely contractual terms. Partnerships can dissolve at the drop of a hat; marriages can't.

I come therefore finally to the issue of divorce. Much of what I have been saying so far may have seemed impossibly idealistic and abstract. The reality of many marriages is not at all as I have described it. It is all very well to defend a traditional view of marriage and family, say the realists, but these were never as ideal as they were supposed to be – and now, in a more open society, our forms of relationship can be less hypocritical.

I grant that realism is essential – but not, surely, a realism which has lost hold of ideals and has no vision of what it wants to strive for. Nor is what I have been saying *mere* idealism, because plenty of people achieve something like it, and I have argued that it is vital for the future health of our society. But there has to be room for failure, and that is why I have also argued in recent years for better divorce laws, and for a more understanding approach by the Church of England towards those whose marriages have broken.

In particular, I strongly supported from the start the Lord Chancellor's attempts to define a more satisfactory basis for recognising marriage breakdown without using the concept of fault. This is not to claim that fault plays no part in the reasons why marriages break down. Frequently all too many people are at fault. The point is, though, that if fault is made the basis of the divorce, then the whole issue becomes confrontational as soon as divorce proceedings are initiated. This entails increased trauma for the couple and their children, a probable legacy of bitterness, and a denial of the possibility of reconciliation before the full implications of divorce have been explored. By contrast, there is a human dignity which can be preserved, even in the face of failure, and, without going into further details, I believe that the Family Law Act can help to achieve this. I believe that more civilised divorce procedures – not necessarily easier ones, but less confrontational ones – will encourage married couples to feel that the law is on their side, enabling them to face up to the full implications of what they are doing and to work through their problems. And I believe that better procedures could, paradoxically, strengthen marriage itself, and perhaps in some cases save it.

Family life in our new social order is clearly under strain. We can accept the new patterns which are emerging, with all their unknown consequences. Or we can seek to strengthen and support family life as it has developed in our culture, so that it provides a stable, humanly attractive and, I believe, much-needed foundation for the formation of future generations. The choice is ours.

11

Religion and democracy

One of the tests of a healthy society is the quality of its democratic credentials. Individual freedom and responsibility, it is claimed, find their clearest political expression in Western-style democracy. Even those who are suspicious of democracy, but support it on the grounds that every other political system is worse, recognise that freedom and responsibility are desirable ends. In Western society, at least, they have become primary secular virtues.

But does democracy also have a religious basis, and does Christianity in particular have any contribution to make in keeping it on course? I recall an occasion some years ago when I was chairman of a panel of European theologians, meeting in Brussels on matters to do with the European Community. At one stage the panel was asked by a member of the audience to give an account of the Christian basis of democracy. The answers given by these distinguished men and women were extraordinarily, even shamingly, weak. Most went no further than reminding the audience of human sinfulness. I felt challenged, therefore, to try to get a little nearer the root of the matter.

I believe we have to start by acknowledging that the origins of democracy were not religious; that democracy has frequently been resisted by religious traditions; that religious bodies, though they may have democratic elements, are usually reluctant to think of themselves as democracies because they are conscious of being under a higher authority; but that nevertheless, some of the ideas drawn on by democracies have profound religious connections and implications.

The beginnings of democracy in ancient Greece seem to have been based on expediency. Kleisthenes, who started it all, enlisted the ordinary citizens of Athens in a highly participatory form of democracy in order to stave off political defeat. What developed out of this was a remarkable system of citizen self-rule, rooted in ideals of freedom, responsibility and collective solidarity. The freedom was unfortunately not extended to slaves, or women, or those on the margins of Athenian society. Nor did it provide a leadership strong enough to cope with external political threats, and it eventually succumbed to military defeat. Meanwhile, both Plato and Aristotle had been highly suspicious of it, on the grounds that it left no room for the exercise of authority based on superior knowledge and excellence. In that earliest experiment in participatory democracy, therefore, we can already see the kind of weaknesses and criticisms which recur in the much more sophisticated democracies of our own day. Who has a right to participate democratically? Is democracy really compatible with order, strength, firmness of direction, and the promotion of the highest human or religious qualities? Are democracies vulnerable to those who are more single-minded in the pursuit of power?

As in ancient Greece, democracy in our own day has arisen out of a mixture of necessity and idealism. The necessity for it has been dramatically revealed by the collapse of its alternatives. No other system can cope with the sheer complexity of the modern state. No central command-structure, and no state bureaucracy, can process the mass of information now available to decision-makers. Some form of dispersed decision-making, backed by freedom of choice, becomes inevitable. And the democratic system seems the only way of holding this together, by making decisions on the basis of majority preferences. It is thus possible to argue that democracy is a necessity, if fully developed societies are to remain stable and in touch with reality.

The balance of order and freedom

Behind all this lie ideals which were vigorously fought over by religious thinkers, and which are still very much part of contemporary political debate. I want to illustrate this by picking out a few historical landmarks, and by trying to relate them to the basic conceptual framework which Christians have usually brought to the subject. All Christians, for a start, would want to assert the basic dignity and responsibility of each human being. We would also want to claim that, though each of us is an individual, we are also essentially communal beings. We belong to one another, depend on one another, and must be sensitive to each other's needs and respectful of each other's freedom. On the other hand, the Christian faith also declares that life is not simply what we make it, but that there is a divine purpose for humanity, and that our well-being depends on our discernment of this, and our conformity to it. Freedom therefore is not absolute, but is only known in its fullness as we freely become what God wills us to be. There is thus an inherent tension in Christian thought between ideals of order, seen most fully in the holy community dedicated to living according to God's purposes, and ideals of freedom, based on the belief that God's ultimate purpose for humankind is to elicit the free response of human love to divine love.

This tension has its political counterparts. In its most extreme form, stress on a given order of things can lead to tyranny. And this is true also of religions. Some theocracies based on a rigid belief in divine prescription have in effect been tyrannies. At the other extreme, an exclusive emphasis on human freedom of choice can lead to anarchy, or the *de facto* tyranny of the strong over the weak: unrestrained capitalism, for instance, can appear tyrannical to those at the bottom of the economic ladder. It is also noticeable how sectarian religion, which often begins with an assertion of freedom against some oppressive religious structure, frequently ends up either by dissipating its energies, or by itself becoming highly authoritarian.

In medieval Christendom the balance was tipped heavily in favour of order – and this strand of thinking still runs very strongly through Roman Catholic social thought. The concept of social order is not empirically discerned, but based on divinely given principles. These can take a democratic form, when set in an empirical context. In his encyclical *Centissimus Annus*, Pope John Paul II wrote:

> The Church values the democratic system inasmuch as it ensures the participation of citizens in making political choices, and guarantees the governed the possibility of both electing and holding accountable those who govern them, and of replacing them through peaceful means when appropriate.

But in the very next encyclical *Veritatis Splendor*, he warned against 'an alliance between democracy and ethical relativism which would remove any sure moral reference-points from political and social life' – and even in *Centissimus Annus* he had claimed that, 'as history demonstrates, a democracy without values easily turns into open and thinly disguised totalitarianism'. There are, in other words, firm moral limits set on human freedom, and as we have seen in *Veritatis Splendor*, these are in the end imposed by authority. The questions which troubled Plato and Aristotle continue to trouble their modern heirs.

Nor did the Reformers do much better. Many of them certainly had ideas about self-government, but in the sixteenth century these were firmly subordinated to belief in the sovereignty of God and the divine authority of rulers.

The first really modern democratic ideas were spelt out by the Levellers in the mid-seventeenth century, during the political vacuum between the end of the English Civil War and Cromwell's assumption of power. They only survived for three or four years, and were soon dispatched by Cromwell. But their writings had it all – citizens' rights, representative government, freedom of debate, equality before the law. This was not mob-rule democracy, as it was accused of being, but a principled attempt to create a kind of political equality which took seriously the corruptions of power. It was not a specifically Christian movement, but its leaders were rooted in the tradition of religious dissent. Dissent formed the background, too, of the basic ideas of individual freedom and responsibility, which drew their inspiration from a Protestant theology of individual salvation, and the assertion of the rights of individual conscience against an authoritarian Church. The Levellers, however, were felt to be too anarchic, too subversive of established order. But they could not be completely crushed. By that time a new factor had emerged: the power of the written word. Ideas went on circulating far away from the direct influence of those who first propagated them. It is worth reflecting in passing on how much the growth of democracy has depended, and still depends, on literacy.

The *third* landmark, which I find enduringly fascinating, is the controversy between the parliamentarian, Edmund Burke, and the republican, Tom Paine, at the time of the French Revolution. Burke stood for conservative order, a balanced constitution, rule by those best fitted to rule – but he knew enough about human corruptibility to realise the vital importance of setting checks on unbridled power. He saw the implications of a sudden access to new freedoms and popular rule, and accurately predicted the course of the French Revolution from liberty to anarchy, terror and dictatorship. Tom Paine vehemently opposed Burke, and wrote *The Rights of Man* to rebut Burke's thesis in his *Reflections on the French Revolution*. Paine was an active revolutionary: in America during the War of Independence, and subsequently in France, he had a strong following among religious dissenters. Burke was more popular in the Church of England. The whole period is a wonderful illustration of the tensions in religious thought and between different religious traditions, finding their counterpart in political tensions.

This absurdly rapid historical sketch leads me to think, therefore, that perhaps the best Christian contribution to democracy is the constant reminder to democratic governments of precisely these tensions, showing how deeply they are rooted in our nature as human beings under God. For government to be effective there has to be a focus of authority and order, not solely dependent on the concentration of power, but also relying on the presence of something or somebody people can look up to, and obey in loyalty and affection. When rulers were believed to have divine authority, they could, if they were wise, be less dependent on the sheer exercise of power. But if democratic institutions no longer generate this sense of majesty, of something admirable to be saluted and cherished, then the balance can easily tip from order to anarchy, and back to a more ruthless order. A Roman Catholic writer recently coined the phrase, 'a culture of contempt', to describe our own society, starting from the manifest contempt in which some politicians in recent years have held each other. If he is right, then I believe we are facing dangerous instabilities.

The priestly and the prophetic strands

The tension between order and freedom has often been analysed in Judaeo-Christian thought in terms of the tension between priestly and prophetic religion. The priests represented, as it were, the settled order; they validated the authority of kings and spelt out the implications of the moral law. The prophetic strand in religion is, by contrast, highly critical of the identification of divine power with political authority. The prophet is the outsider, the opposition, the individual who, like Luther, declares 'Here I stand. I can do no other.' The prophet insists that each of us, and all of us together, must answer for what we do before God. If the prophetic element in democracy is to be safeguarded, perhaps the most important single feature of any democratic system is its ability to embody the principle of resistance to government within the system of government itself. The mere right to vote loses much of its meaning unless it is possible to express opposition without incurring a charge of disloyalty – and it seems to me that many attempts to set up modern democracies fail precisely here. But the difficulty is that loyalty in opposition requires the acceptance of at least some common moral ground between contending parties. It presupposes a moral climate in which the rights of minorities can be safeguarded by the forbearance of the majority. And this leads us back to the need for the priestly strand, with its emphasis on order and continuity, and the importance of the implicit religious order which sustains and inspires this – an order constantly enlivened and challenged by the prophetic spirit. Maintaining this tension is thus a prime contribution which religions can make to democracies.

The Christian faith ought also to have important and distinctive things to say about the nature and exercise of power. To believe in a crucified God ought to turn upside-down all normal assumptions about where true power resides. Liberation theologians have attempted to write a political agenda, starting from the needs and perceptions of the poorest and weakest of people, in the belief that it is among them that Christ is most characteristically to be found. Where this has happened there has been a new upsurge of radically participatory democracy – but it seems to me that this can fall foul of the corruptions of power like any other political system unless democratic checks and balances are built into it. And because it is essentially local, it cannot tackle global political issues in an increasingly complex and interdependent world.

This strand in Christian thinking – the paradoxical emphasis on weakness – cannot in my view translate directly into a political programme. But it can provide a corrective. It can remind us of those whom democracy is supposed to serve. It can undergird the principle that the quality of a society is judged by its attitude towards its most vulnerable members. A democracy which seriously accepted this as a basic principle would no longer be at the mercy of conflicting self-interests. But modern pluralist, democratic societies do not work like that. They are highly suspicious of basic principles which seem to derive from a particular religious tradition. And this inevitably sets limits on what any religion can contribute to a democratic system out of its central beliefs, rather than from general moral and religious insights which are more widely shared.

12

Paradoxes of freedom

Freedom has become so entrenched as an ideal in the modern world that it is easy to overlook the difficulties which underlie it as a concept, and the disputes to which these give rise. Loose talk of freedom begs many questions, both practical and theoretical, and it is primarily the latter which this chapter explores.

When politicians discuss freedom, the practical questions may be intractable but at least they seem to be clear-cut. Is this or that behaviour likely to be so harmful to others that legislation is needed to prevent it? Will the proposed legislation work? How do we balance the loss of one person's freedom against the need to protect another? In the prolonged debates on the Family Law Bill recently, the question of harm was prominent whenever the effects of divorce on children was under consideration; hence the discussion of how to protect children was not about principles, but mostly about ways and means. Many people, however, also had strong feelings about the undesirability of divorce itself, and the much more general and unquantifiable consequences for the whole social fabric if the tide of divorces was not stemmed. Such discussions are much more difficult and controversial – and theoretical. We were uncomfortably aware that all our good intentions were quite irrelevant to the growing number of people who have settled the question for themselves by living together without being married. The underlying questions were only indirectly about harm, and much more about the kind of society people wanted. Behind them lay more general questions about the nature and limits of freedom. How far does a society have the right to set limits on people's freedom to do what they want, and to impose its institutional arrangements on individuals? These questions seem to lead inevitably in the direction of paradox.

The obvious starting-point in considering the paradoxes of freedom is Isaiah Berlin's justly famous lectures on liberty, in which he drew a distinction between what he called negative freedom and positive freedom.[1] Negative freedom is essentially about non-interference. It is the preservation of an area of individual choice, seen as being central to the value and dignity of human beings. The boundaries are different in different societies, but they are not simply internal to particular cultures. Human rights are an attempt to lay down universal standards. This, according to Berlin, is the most defensible form of freedom, and underlies John Stuart Mill's definition of freedom as 'pursuing our own good in our own way', with a minimum of interference. It is closely related to what I have already referred to as the prevention of harm.

Positive freedom is much more controversial. It begins with the forward-looking question, 'What shall I do or be?' But this quickly leads on to the question, 'Who is to say what I am, or what I am not, to do or be?' – and from there to the question, 'By whom am I ruled?' Berlin goes on to expound with passionate intensity how such questions invite the imposition of all-inclusive answers, which then become the seedbed of tyranny. To draw a distinction between what I am and what I might be, between my empirical self and my true or ideal self, and to see the distinction as having some kind of universal validity, provides the impetus for trying to create an ideal society, and for forcing everybody to conform to it. Monogamy, Berlin might have said, may be the ideal for some – but do they have the right to insist on it as the only norm?

He was writing at a time when totalitarian regimes were still very much in evidence, and his argument hinged more on what he saw as false claims about there being only one supposedly rational solution to questions about how human beings should live, than on a rejection of social ideals as such. But he issued a much-needed warning against the danger of high-minded aspirations to freedom resulting in bondage. It is a paradox to which I shall return later. Meanwhile I simply want to add two comments. The first is that we have grown much more used to the idea of living in a pluralist society, for which single solutions are not possible, than we were when Berlin was writing in 1958. Secondly I note that the distinction between myself and my true self – which, in the context of politics, was the target for his critique of positive freedom – is fundamental to most forms of spirituality, and certainly to Christian spirituality, finding classic expression in the doctrine of original sin. Ideals for oneself and others, as a basis for social reform, start from the perception that human life falls short of what it could be. Christians, therefore, have a strong motive for not accepting Berlin's argument at its face value.

Ernest Gellner, writing 36 years later about civil society as the basis for liberty, avoided sliding so easily from personal aspiration to civic imposition. 'Virtue as the aim of state or public policy is probably disastrous for liberty. Virtue, freely practised between consenting adults, may be a great boon to Civil Society, or even its essential pre-condition.'[2] Unlike Berlin, he was writing against the background of a widely accepted cultural pluralism, and he saw that a certain degree of cultural homogeneity is essential if people are to communicate with one another freely without being handicapped by unbridgeable differences between them. The plight of some ethnic sub-groups, which are to all intents and purposes cut off from the mainstream society by language and culture, illustrates the effect on practical freedom of the kind of pluralism which effectively isolates people.

Freedom – loved and feared

Berlin and Gellner between them set out a basic paradox of freedom in two different contexts. Some degree of social cohesion, enjoined and supported by law, is necessary if individuals are to be free. And this is not just because we need protection from encroachments on our freedom by the liberties of others, but because we need a particular kind of social context in which our ideals of freedom can find expression. This may mean no more than having a secure identity, reinforced by social convention. Marriages, for instance, are strengthened by the fact that marriage is a recognised status given social approval, and this allows a freedom within marriage which is lacking if the institution is constantly under question. But for some, this same social approval can also become a trap. Social expectations can create an intolerable burden. The very structures which enable freedom can also destroy it. Both authors are implacable enemies of the kind of totalising approach which sees only a single belief-system, or a single political structure or programme, as invariably right. And so am I. 'A free order', says Gellner, 'is based in the end not on true and firm conviction, but on doubt, compromise, double-think.' A free order needs flexible firmness.

Using this as a starting-point, therefore, I want to break down this basic paradox into what I see as some of its components. And I begin with a story.

An elderly patient undergoing psychotherapy was worried about seemingly trivial choices. She recalled that up to her seventh birthday her parents always gave her presents, which filled her with much pleasure. On her seventh birthday she was taken to a toy-shop and asked to choose. She was faced with a sense of confusion, panic and loss. If she chose one toy, she lost the others. She also risked displeasing one parent while pleasing the other. But the strongest feeling was the most disturbing of all – greed. She wanted all the toys in the shop. Faced with a world of choice, our primitive selves want everything. Knowing that we cannot have everything, we are then faced with a sense of loss.

The power of choice, in other words, is ambivalent. It is both desirable and threatening. Everybody wants freedom, yet in practice most people fear it. What is exposed here in a childish example found classic expression in Dostoevsky's parable of the Grand Inquisitor. Christ's refusal of the temptations to compel obedience by miracle and mystery and authority left his followers with an intolerable burden of freedom. But the Church has corrected that, says the Inquisitor. And he sends Christ away.

T. S. Eliot, conscious of the terrible freedom actually offered by God, put it like this:

Forgive us, O Lord, we acknowledge ourselves as type of the
    common man,
Of the men and women who shut the door and sit by the fire;
Who fear the blessing of God, the loneliness of the night of God, the
    surrender required, the deprivation inflicted;
Who fear the injustice of men less than the justice of God;
Who fear the hand at the window, the fire in the thatch, the fist in
    the tavern, the push into the canal,
Less than we fear the love of God.[3]

In a culture felt to be disintegrating, the fear of freedom can paralyse people. Yet unheroic times can also lead to the opposite reaction. A sense of beleaguerment by pettiness can impel a search for excitement and novelty. There is a strong element of masochism in many of today's recreations – risky forms of exercise from mountain climbing to bungee jumping, gambling, drug abuse, and so on. Young smokers seem to indulge their habit, not despite the risk, but because of it. There are plenty of people in the media and the arts who are willing to satisfy the longing for excitement by pushing out the boundaries of acceptability. The freedom of the artist is to shock. Freedom in a competitive society is freedom to succeed and to exceed. When war is no longer acceptable, and there is little left to conquer, what are the less adventurous people to do in their craving for novelty, except go shopping?

Nietzsche had other ideas: 'The man who has become free – and how much more the *mind* that has become free – spurns the contemptible sort of well-being dreamed of by shopkeepers, Christians, cows, women, Englishmen and other democrats. The free man is a *warrior*.'[4] Freedom, according to Nietzsche, is a continual surmounting of oneself. Interestingly he linked this with polytheism which allowed a multiplicity of norms. It was through inventing multiple fictitious gods, he claimed, that individualism was first honoured. By contrast monotheism, which Nietzsche, like Berlin, mistakenly saw as prescribing a single norm, he described as 'perhaps the greatest danger facing mankind'. The free man creates himself in unpredictable ways through his will to power.

There are echoes of this in post-modernism, though without Nietzsche's seriousness and passion. Freedom, we are told, lies in multiplicity, transience, happenings, play rather than purpose. Freedom, for the true post-modernist, is not to be feared, because nothing ultimately matters, and there is no enduring self to be created. I have recently opened myself to criticism by describing the Internet as post-modernism expressed through technology. The Web is a completely decentred world, a world with almost infinite freedom to communicate and to fantasise, a world which seems impossible to control and which fiercely resists the very idea of control. But how, in such a world, does one distinguish truth from falsehood, or reality from fantasy? Or do such distinctions no longer apply? And if no such distinctions can be drawn, what is the value of the freedom to explore, other than as a kind of game?

This, then, is my first paradox. What we most desire can also be our greatest threat. Freedom is both loved and feared. And though the ones who love it are not necessarily identical to the ones who fear it, the love and the fear are in the end, I believe, inseparable. My second paradox follows from this: more tends to mean less.

Freedom – more is less

Think, for example, of foreign travel. The fact that vast numbers of people now have the freedom to travel has brought huge benefits. But it has resulted in more and more places looking the same. Every airport is like every other airport. So is every branch of McDonalds, and every tower-block hotel. One of the paradoxical consequences of greater freedom is that differentiation is undermined. We are witnessing the homogenisation of culture. World-wide radio, which has been a harbinger of freedom for millions, has also taught everyone the same pop music.

More freedom means less variety. Superficially this is not so. Go into a supermarket and you are overwhelmed by the variety of things on offer – a variety which was inconceivable when some of us were young. It is local differences that are increasingly being lost. One supermarket is very like another, and most of them depend for their supplies on a small number of conglomerates. The specialist supplier is increasingly hard to find. Even those who travel to exotic places and bring back souvenirs frequently have to face the chagrin of finding identical items on sale in the local Oxfam shop.

At a more abstract level, the paradox could be expressed like this: absolute freedom entails the loss of identity. Things are what they are by virtue of the constraints within which they exist. Things which are similar to one another express their different identities by using their constraints in different ways.

This principle can be seen at work in present concerns about ethnic identity. An ethnic group, or maybe a nation, forms its identity within the constraints set by geography, history, culture, language, inheritance and, frequently, shared suffering. Sometimes it is imperative to remove, or at least diminish, some of these constraints in the interests of peace, or development, or survival, or justice. But to remove them without putting any alternative constraints in their place, in the light of some ideal of absolute freedom, is a recipe for disaster. Liberalising legislation, which sweeps away all differences, leaves people bewildered and vulnerable to domination by powerful elites. This was the story of the French Revolution. It was the story of Communism. And it could be the story of our own day, when the elites are those who control the media and the market, and who in the name of choice are in practice leading us more and more in the direction of a mass-market mediocrity.

Freedom – uniformity and diversity

There is a further paradox here because, as I said earlier when referring to Gellner, a certain homogeneity of culture is essential if we are to communicate with one another, and build a free society on the basis of this mutual exchange. But if homogeneity degenerates into the kind of uniformity which undermines the sense of individual identity, the result is likely to be a strong and destructive counter-reaction. The nub of the problem is to find meaningful forms of differentiation between people, groups, places, cultures, and sexes too, which do not simply lock people into stereotypes from the past. Freedom has to be set within a context of meaningful goals, which are not all identical, but which give it content and provide an inspiration for creativity. This is Berlin's positive freedom – but it does not have to be based on the false premise that there is only one rational goal. The lesson of pluralism is that it is precisely through a diversity of goals, and in a diversity of contexts, that identity has to be shaped and affirmed.

Absolute freedom without constraints or goals is self-defeating. More tends to mean less. Feel free to break promises, and you exclude yourself from the benefits of a society based on trust. Refuse to accept that some choices are binding, and you lose any sense of personal destiny. Sit lightly to marriage, and you never discover the freedom enjoyed by those who live in a secure relationship, nor can you free yourself from the burden of constantly having to be perfect. And the converse is also true. Less absolute freedom can pave the way for more freedom with significant content. It is a familiar point made repeatedly by those who stress the need to sacrifice freedom in the acquisition of skills. Enjoying the freedom to compose or play one's own music entails hours of subjection to the disciplines of learning and practising. The same is true in the moral sphere: abiding by sensible social conventions can enhance our freedom to relate to one another. Thus the much-maligned virtue of modesty can provide a context for nuanced behaviour in which deep encounters do not have to become drearily and predictably sexual.

Freedom and theology

These are familiar moral and theological themes, but they do not depend solely on theology. They are inherent in the nature of freedom, and they take us back to what I was saying earlier about the discovery of one's true self. To hold an ideal for oneself – and that, in the end, is what personal morality is about – is to be searching for some kind of inner integrity and consistency. It is this which makes positive and enduring relationships with other people possible, and thus opens up new realms of freedom. But integrity and consistency can only be won at the cost of restraining some freedoms in the name of greater ones.

For Christians, repentance is one of the necessary roads to such an ideal. Unfortunately it is nowadays widely misunderstood. The essence of repentance is not to grovel, nor is it to work up feelings of guilt. It is to accept responsibility for what we are, and to seek empowerment for change. It is an exercise in freedom, just as the discipline of prayer is an exercise in freedom, because both are means of opening ourselves to transcendent possibilities. To repent is to acknowledge that I am what I am, but that I do not have to be locked into what dismays or disgusts or demeans me, because I am loved by one who knows where my true good lies. To know that we are loved for what we truly are, despite what we feel ourselves to be, is liberation. It conveys the energy needed to live a new life.

Berlin, as I have indicated, was suspicious of this kind of thinking. He correctly saw that it can go horribly wrong, in that it can become an excuse for imposing an ideology. The dangers inherent in religion are that it can enlist people's deepest feelings and strongest commitments in causes which, while claiming to be driven by transcendent love, trap them in bigotry, prejudice and oppression. We don't have to look far to find examples. And if we ask why this happens with such depressing regularity, I think the answer frequently lies in an inadequate concept of God.

Berlin saw that if there is only one rational answer to questions about the nature of the true self, or the good life, or whatever, then the temptation to impose it on other people is irresistible. Monotheism, with its tremendous emphasis on the unity of God, and the consequences which may seem to flow from this about a divine plan for humanity, can encourage this tendency towards unitary solutions.

Politicians and clergy in Northern Ireland or the Middle East have no inhibitions about telling us exactly what God wants. Nor do some nearer home.

A Trinitarian faith ought to be more subtle. It contains within it principles of diversification which ought to safeguard it against such dangers. Those who believe that the fullest revelation of God's nature has been in a particular life, lived in a particular historical setting, have a strong motive for taking other particularities seriously. If Christianity were simply an idea, then it might be possible to express it once for all in a single formula. Because it is centred on a series of historical events, these can be interpreted and reinterpreted in countless different contexts. A Trinitarian faith also points to the God-givenness of inspiration, and this too opens it up to a huge diversity of manifestations. The Spirit blows where it will. The unity at the heart of all things, which faith perceives, cannot be grasped as such, but only glimpsed through this diversity. And that puts an onus on believers to respect, and listen to, and question, those who differ from them – in the belief that it is by opening ourselves to diversity, without ceasing to believe in an ultimate unity, that we are led in the end to a fuller apprehension of truth.

I shall return to one of the practical implications of this later. Meanwhile the point of my rapid theological excursion was simply to illustrate how a freedom disciplined by religion does not have to fall into the kind of monolithic oppressiveness which Berlin perceived. When it is true to itself, Christian faith is capable of providing the kind of balance between universality and diversity, discipline and openness, on which the mature exercise of freedom depends.

But how does this balance – between constraint in the interests of a necessary unity; and openness to actual diversity – actually work? Iris Murdoch identified freedom with the capacity to attend, to fix our minds on some perceived reality and allow it to address us. Teaching children to attend ought to be one of the primary aims of education. Attention is the basis of creativity. It is a major component of prayer.

[It] is not an inconsequential chucking of one's weight about, it is the disciplined overcoming of self. [It] is not strictly the exercise of the will, but rather the experience of accurate vision which, when this becomes appropriate, occasions action. Attention [imperceptibly] builds up structures of value round about us, [so that] at crucial moments of choice most of the business of choosing is already over.

This is in contrast, she adds, to the kind of freedom which involves 'conceptualizing as many different possibilities of action as possible: having as many goods as possible in the shop'.[5] Freedom, as it were, focuses on necessity. It is about being real. Thus far Iris Murdoch. She is expressing in secular, aesthetic terms what Christians have always understood by the phrase, 'whose service is perfect freedom'.

Mary Midgley, in her book *The Ethical Primate*, gives an interesting evolutionary slant to this idea of directed attention as the basis of choice.[6] Choice is both possible and necessary, she says, because our evolutionary history has given us a plurality of aims. This is not an accident, but is inherent in the way evolution works. Machines are built with a single, fixed purpose. Organisms can evolve because they have built-in flexibility, none more so than human beings. We also have the capacity to reflect on the conflicting desires which this flexibility generates – and to project our thinking into the past as remorse and thanksgiving, and into the future as hope and fear. On top of all this, we have somehow to harmonise these different aims and insights in ways which do not undermine our integrity as human beings and our relationships with others.

This is a picture of what we are, in the first instance spelt out by Darwin. It is miles from the Nietzschean vision of the sovereign, independent individual exercising his 'will to power'. We are free – but our freedom is in the end freedom to attend to the complex realities which make us what we are, both internally and externally. That includes shaping an environment – physical, mental, and social – which does not merely protect us from doing harm to each other, but which actually helps to build harmony out of conflict. I am repeating what I said earlier about freedom being set within the context of meaningful goals. This is true of us as individuals. But how far must these goals also be social ones?

It seems to me to follow from the nature of the complex balance between unity and diversity, freedom and constraint, that individual freedom must depend at least in part on our relatedness to others. The pursuit of freedom is not a zero-sum game, in which one person's loss equals another's gain. We increase freedom by sharing it. I am merely restating the familiar insight that freedom is indivisible. So if it is true that the more we give, the more we have, then what must be done to ensure that this mutuality of freedom actually occurs? This is a very large subject for the tail-end of a chapter, but I want briefly to indicate a way of approaching it in terms of the distinction between procedures and principles.

Procedures and principles

It seems to me characteristic of our times that, in tackling complex issues, we have come to rely more on procedures than on principles. It is immensely hard, for instance, to decide on the basis of principle what a just solution to some conflict might look like. Everybody involved is likely to have their own ideas. But it is not so hard to agree on fair procedures through which to work towards a solution.

In medical ethics, for example, today's watchword is consent. This has become a procedural concept which is increasingly used to by-pass intractable questions about right and wrong. Nobody states explicitly that it can completely replace moral considerations, but in the case of abortion, say, it looks very much as if this is what is happening.

Democracy is another particularly interesting example, because there has been a strong tendency to commend it, and even to define it, primarily in terms of procedures – and young democracies frequently fail for precisely that reason. In fact, democracy is not just about voting, or majority rule, or representation – though desirably it includes all these. Unless it is also rooted in an attitude of mind which acknowledges the possibility of being wrong, of not getting one's own way, and includes a willingness to relinquish power, the procedures cannot save it from being manipulated by those who believe that they cannot afford to be seen to be wrong or to suffer rejection.

Attitudes and principles are in the end more fundamental than procedures. That is why ultimately any arrangements for enhancing each other's freedom require more than minimal government willing to guarantee only freedom from interference. In a democracy there has to be public debate about the common good. It is always a fallible, shifting debate which allows room for differences – and it is a long way from the dictatorial kind of social order so abhorred by Isaiah Berlin. But the debate cannot take place at all if the society is morally rootless, because corporate freedom, no less than individual freedom, depends on the beliefs and constraints which give it significant content. The only alternative to internal restraint is external force.

The spiritual challenge to modern conceptions of freedom lies here. There is no future, I believe, in Churches trying to reimpose their own norms and assumptions on a now diversified culture. But they can and should inject into public debate a strong moral critique of the principles undergirding public life, and of the ways in which power is exercised. They should hold up a complex vision of our essential unity as human beings, and of our God-given diversity. They should not succumb to the modern fashion for avoiding discussion of the good, on the grounds that people are likely to disagree about it. Instead they should defend the view that the true dignity and freedom of human beings includes our ability to agree on worthwhile aims. And they should expose, by every means possible, the illusion that there can be freedom without some constraining vision of what that freedom is for. In addition, those who have a secure spiritual basis ought to be able to face the prospect of being wrong, without lapsing into the cynicism or despair which can so easily become the secular substitutes for repentance and humility. Michael Polanyi, who was much exercised by questions about freedom, set out the purpose of his great book *Personal Knowledge* in these words: 'The principal purpose of this book is to achieve a frame of mind in which I may hold firmly to what I believe to be true, even though I know that it might conceivably be false'.[7]

That is the statement of a man secure enough in his own belief not to fear freedom, constrained enough by his belief to give his freedom real content, and open enough in his belief to welcome the freedom of others. It is a reminder that true freedom has spiritual foundations.

13

Religion and the national Church

It was about 35 years ago that the then Dean of King's College, Alec Vidler, invited a group of Cambridge theologians to meet informally, read papers to one another, and to think critically about the state of religion in England. We were conscious of an element of complacency in the churches at that time – an unwillingness to face some of the intellectual and moral challenges which were becoming increasingly evident. So in 1962 we published a modest volume of essays called *Soundings*, just before the beginning of the torrent of change which hit us during the 1960s and early 1970s. Alec Vidler's own essay, which concluded the book, was called 'Religion and the national Church', and it is from this that I have taken my theme.

Vidler was suspicious of religion. He reflected on one of his heroes, the nineteenth-century theologian F. D. Maurice, who was deeply critical of religious systems and schemes and parties, and the sort of niggling in which religious people love to indulge, to the neglect of the centrality of God. 'Religions separate people from one another and tempt them to boast of what they possess and others do not; the gospel is the proclamation that they already belong together as children of one God and Father of all'.[1]

Vidler also reflected on Dietrich Bonhoeffer's enigmatic remarks from prison about 'religionless Christianity' and 'holy worldliness'. After the excitement aroused by their publication in 1953, the ideas were beginning to be pushed to one side. Vidler asked how it was possible for faith in God to be at the centre of secular life, rather than as a marginal activity, concerned with snuffling around people's sins, like today's tabloids. He asked too how the Church, as an embodiment of Christian community, could be kept free from the domination of organisers and legalisers.

All this turned his mind towards the merits of a national Church with indeterminate membership, a Church marked by intellectual integrity, candour and honesty, a Church solidly rooted in the gospel, but not so cleaned up and tidy that everybody could tell just what it stood for. He quoted with approval a saying that the distinctive role of the Church of England is the 'apostolate of the indevout'.

Perhaps it is not so difficult to write these things as Dean of King's College, for King's – certainly in those days, and I suspect also today – is in many respects an embodiment of them. There is the creative interplay between a lively, critical, enquiring, largely indevout community, and a glorious tradition of worship; a secular society of scholars which is yet dominated by, and known all the world over, for its chapel. The idea that it is possible somehow to recognise the centrality of God in a world preoccupied with its own business, does not seem so absurd when one sits in these stalls, or when one just walks across the bridge, looking and meditating on what this place actually means.

But it is not a vision with much popular appeal among Christians today. The pressures are all in the opposite direction, towards greater distinctiveness and definition. The religious success-stories are found in those churches which demand a high level of commitment. The idea of an apostolate of the indevout would be regarded in many quarters with derision – a betrayal of the essential challenge of the gospel. The Church of England is frequently criticised for making things too easy for its members, inoculating them against Christianity, as some put it, by giving half-believers the comfortable illusion that they are all right. Even the aesthetic glories of worship in King's can be grounds for suspicion to those whose spirituality demands something more intimate and personal.

In such an atmosphere the idea of a national Church seems more and more anachronistic – and it is no secret that there are pressures on the Church of England progressively to loosen its ties with the state. I believe that they should be resisted, and for reasons very like those put forward by Vidler in 1962. Much has changed since then. Of course churches have to be more active and outward-looking, more concerned to win members and deepen their commitment. But this must not be done at the cost of withdrawal into some kind of religious ghetto. Our concern is with God – the God who is to be found in the mainstream of life, the God who is less concerned with scales of devoutness than are those of us who like to measure religious performance, whether in ourselves or others. A national Church needs members with a deep commitment to maintain its life, and, thank God, there are those ready to make that commitment. But it also needs openness, liberality, a willingness to accept that the vast majority of people have never been very devout, and are never likely to be – yet that they need somebody to hold in trust for them those rituals, those beliefs, that awareness of the transcendent, without which life contracts in on itself and can become small and mean.

Politicians frequently tell Church leaders these days to get on with the business of religion and to leave the politics to them. One sees their point, and I concede that there are times when Church leaders show political naïveté. But this division between political and religious, public and private, actually conceals a disastrous misunderstanding of what it is that enables civilised societies to exist. There is no going back to the kind of society in which a single set of beliefs and values prescribes what should be done. A national Church in today's world must not imagine that it can lay down criteria to which everyone must conform. Beliefs and values have to be argued, not simply imposed. I am attracted by a thought expressed by a Canadian writer: 'Civilisation is formed of men and women locked together in argument'.[2]

But being a pluralist society does not absolve us from having some kind of basis on which that argument can take place. And a minimum basis, surely, has to be that we argue within an inherited tradition of argument which is always open to new levels of insight and meaning, because somewhere within it there is an awareness of the transcendent. Who is going to keep that door to the transcendent open, unless within the heart of a society there are those with precisely that task?

Let me put the point concretely. To go into King's College chapel is to be cut down to size – by the building itself, by what goes on it, by the story of which it speaks. To glimpse the transcendent there is to find our own concerns relativised, put in perspective. That is important because it can help to rescue us from the idolatry of our own ideas, prejudices and self-concern. But merely to do that, without offering us the hope of some greater truth to which we can reach out, could be destructive. The alternative to idolatry is nihilism, the abyss of relativism in which all meaning and truth is lost.

To keep open the door of the transcendent means treading the narrow path between hope and despair, between searching and belonging, between knowing and confessing our ignorance. That is one of the things liturgy can help us to do. And perhaps also it is why we need an apostolate of the committed *and* of the indevout. Maybe the anomalies of being a national Church in an increasingly pluralist society look less strange in the light of this particular task. To keep open the door to the transcendent, to stand for the centrality of God in a world which largely ignores him, does not actually *require* there to be a national Church. But it is a task which a national Church can and should perform, and it would in my view be foolish to throw away the opportunity to do so. The very idea of a national Church entails holding the door of the transcendent open – for everybody.

Our Ascension Day liturgy is a reminder of this. The ascension is about the movement from the particular to the universal. This Jesus, who was known to a handful of disciples at a particular time and in a particular place, is raised in glory to become Lord of all. His manhood, which was once the manhood of a single person, is taken up into the godhead, that all humanity may be exalted. Christian witness in the self-confident world of higher learning may seem small and weak, yet it holds a truth which is true for everyone. We cannot be fully human unless we look beyond our humanity to that which transcends it. Nor can we reach out effectively towards the transcendent without the grace of God, who first reached out to us.

14

William Temple

It is one of my lifelong regrets that I never saw or heard William Temple. But it is to him that I owe my serious introduction to theology. I can still vividly recall going into a bookshop one day in 1949, seeing there a big volume entitled *Nature, Man and God*, deciding that I was interested in nature and man and God, and going home to devour all 520 pages. Thus William Temple introduced me not only to theology, but also to philosophy, ethics, art, politics, poetry, and much else besides.

Today he looks down from his portrait in Bishopthorpe Palace – serene, benign, alert, powerful, a giant among men. Serene, I think, is the key word; not complacent. He was certainly not complacent about the state of the world or the state of the Church. He felt deeply about the tragedies and injustices, the pain and ugliness, he saw around him. But his faith was serene, and his thinking had a serenity about it which shines through all his voluminous writings. He knew what he believed; he knew how things fitted together; he knew how faith and life and social concern and politics should be related to one another. And because he knew, he could express his thoughts with matchless clarity and precision. He could weave together the thoughts of others into a coherent whole. One can see, too, how he managed the extraordinary feats ascribed to him in being able to speak spontaneously and at length on complex issues, and make sense of them. The underlying pattern was there in his mind already.

Yet, though Olympian, he also deliberately exposed himself to the raw sides of life. I have no doubt that Manchester taught him much; and the Workers' Educational Association; and the General Strike. Perhaps the General Synod might have taught him something too. But I was delighted recently to come across an account, written in the last year of his life, of his involvement as an undergraduate in the Oxford

Medical Mission in Bermondsey. He described how the boys in the club where he worked had to take prayers each evening on a set text. One of the boys, aged about 17, was terrified at the prospect but was eventually persuaded to do it by Temple. Temple wrote, 'Trembling all over he read the story of Daniel in the lions' den. At the end of it he shut the Book and said: "There's lots of lions in these 'ere Bermondsey streets; well, the Lord can deliver you. Let us pray." ' Temple went on; 'Yes; I think however long I live, that will be the best sermon I shall ever hear'.

Olympian – yet rooted firmly enough in the real world to know that a gospel which cannot speak directly to young people in Bermondsey, or Moss Side, or Bury, is no gospel at all. As we think of what has happened to young people in our own society, we can see that Temple's deep concern about them – his worry about the consequences of youth unemployment, and his understanding of how the Fascists had exploited this for their own purposes – still has something to teach us.

But 50 years on, the coherent system, the confident intellectual claims, the assumptions about how a society works and about the power of reasoned argument to change it, look very different. Not that it has all gone. The welfare state is at least in part one of Temple's legacies. His insistence that the Churches have a role and a duty in trying to articulate Christian principles for the guidance of political action has stood the test of time. His stress on community as the linchpin of social theology is needed today even more than it was then. What has changed is that we can no longer rely on the shared aims and understandings which undergirded his thought.

Looking again recently at *Nature, Man and God*, I found it almost unreadable. The world Temple knew has been through a process of disintegration – intellectual, social and global. One symptom of the change is that some politicians now speak with approval about the gross and growing differentials in pay between the highest paid and the lowest paid. It is claimed that political attempts to narrow this gap would damage performance and create more unemployment. When views to the contrary are expressed – views which would certainly have been shared by Temple – we have become accustomed to their being dismissed as 'the politics of envy'.

One of the more disturbing features of all this is the apparent absence of any concern about what such great disparities in income and wealth do to the sense of community. The way people feel about each other *does* matter. But there are even deeper causes of unease than this. One of the consequences of a huge increase in freedom of choice is lack of commitment and steady loyalty. If people can simply walk away from what they do not like, such communities as exist become purely self-chosen. The kind of community in which people are going to learn from others who are different from themselves is fatally weakened.

Work itself is in process of fragmenting into more and more individualistic efforts, symbolised by the growing number of small businesses, and the lone worker with the home computer. No doubt there is much that is good in this – just as there is much that is good in the pluralism of society, in our greater freedoms to be different, in the greater possibilities for personal enterprise, in the breakdown of national economic barriers, in the ideal of less political interference. It is a mark of our times that the prestigious and enormously valuable Templeton Prize for religion should have been awarded to a major apologist for democratic capitalism, Michael Novak. Equality as an ideal, perhaps an unrealistic ideal, has given place to enterprise: without enterprise, we are told, without the struggle to keep up in an increasingly competitive world, there will be nothing to share except equal poverty. It is a hard message to resist – but can it be allowed to dominate the whole social and political agenda?

I believe that Temple would have recognised that the world in which he lived had to change. Part of our problem now, in a world which distrusts powerful leaders and immediately cuts them down to size, is our need for those with the stature and vision to draw together our present fragmented experience, and illuminate it with the gospel. We need those with prophetic insight who can identify the real roots of injustice. We need prophetic voices which can be heard above the din of contemporary chit-chat. And we need that mature rootedness in Christ which can save us from grabbing nervously at the latest fashionable formula, whether theological or political. But we also need to stand fast to Temple's conviction that the theological and the political must overlap. Politics without moral vision degenerates into cynical expediency. A theology which has no implications for the way in which a society should order its life cannot claim to be faithful to Scripture.

But how? How, 50 years after Temple, can we begin to bring the broken fragments together again?

One way *not* to do it is for the Churches themselves so to absorb the spirit of the age that 'success' becomes the only criterion. It is a temptation forced on us by financial stringency and by the attractions of hard-line Christianity as an answer to bewilderment. We need to be very cautious, I believe, about a kind of church commitment modelled on successful business enterprise, which is content to leave behind those who struggle in matters of faith, or finance, or misfortune.

But neither must we sanctify failure or condone indifference. We witness to a crucified and risen Lord who is present with us in the world's pain and brokenness, and who by being present is a constant source of hope and renewal. Our main task as Churches, I believe, is to hold in trust for our world a faithful awareness of Christ's presence, as the one in whom all things find their true meaning and salvation. And it is our major public responsibility to make that presence known and accessible. A Church which does not somehow speak of the presence of Christ in the midst of everyday experience has nothing worth saying.

The actual discovery of what this means, however, usually has to happen in quite particular circumstances – in the transformation of this person's life, in the building of that community, in the removal of some piece of injustice, in the stilling of some fear or the healing of some hurt. Christ has always been known in the particular. So in a world of bewildering diversity and complexity, in which individuals can feel powerless and insignificant, a reminder of Christ's presence in the small things of life, where each of us can actually make a difference, may be a good starting-point.

The vision has to expand. The Christ who is known where two or three are gathered together in his name, is also Lord of all. The gospel is universal. I am not advocating a recipe for narrowness. But even William Temple began his world outreach in Bermondsey. And he knew the lions in the streets. And he knew that the Lord can deliver us.

15

The Anglican Church and the unification of Europe

Britain is no longer an island. The fact that it is now possible to travel to Brussels by train symbolises a profound change which, over the years, will gradually affect our island psychology as well as our modes of travel. Britain's ambivalence towards the mainland of Europe has a long history, and the agonised debates which seem to dominate our politics are not just political manoeuvres. They spring from deep questions about identity – an identity formed by the many centuries through which our boundaries have been clearly defined and inviolate. Insularity has for us meant stability, security and ultimate sovereignty.

But this is by no means the whole story. If the sea was a barrier round Britain, it was also a means of transport. It was trade, and especially sea-trade, which gave us our empire – in the case of many parts of it, almost by accident – and which created the English-speaking world. And the effect of this was the very opposite of insularity – a consciousness of links, allegiances and responsibilities on a global scale.

I have begun with this broad and familiar picture because I do not think Britain's attitude towards European unification can be understood without it. Nor is it possible to assess what the Anglican Church might have to offer without seeing it against this background of both distinct identity and global outreach. In European terms the Anglican Church does not fit any of the more familiar European models, in that it claims to be both Catholic and Protestant. In global terms the Anglican Communion is a remarkable example of growth happening almost by accident, and in some instances against the wishes of the mother church in England. The refusal of the English bishops to allow the early American colonists to consecrate their own bishops, for example, is a classic instance of failure to acknowledge the degree of independence which was essential if a world-wide community was to be maintained.

Partnership in Church and Commonwealth

In 1991 our Church's General Synod published a report on the Anglican Communion and the Commonwealth, comparing them as types of association which, despite their almost accidental origins, might have something to teach the world about how to live together peacefully and co-operatively. The report is entitled, significantly, *From Power to Partnership*, and it spells out how a form of association can change, and a new pattern in human society can evolve, as people adapt to new circumstances without losing their sense of sharing a common history. I intend to dwell on it a little, as I believe it may have some lessons for us in Europe.

The Commonwealth is, in many respects, a very loosely defined organisation. It is hugely diverse. It includes people of many different faiths, ethnic backgrounds and political allegiances. It has virtually no power, except the power to persuade, and ultimately to expel. Yet it is an association valued by its members, perhaps precisely because it bridges so many of the deep divisions in today's world. Why else would South Africa give high priority to returning to it, after her long expulsion, as soon as her own elections were complete? In his sermon in Westminster Abbey to celebrate South Africa's readmission, the then Archbishop Desmond Tutu spoke about 'the return of the prodigal son'.

The report is realistic about the Commonwealth's weakness and relative ineffectiveness. Yet it sees this transition – from an empire based on power, to a partnership based on mutual respect and the bonds of history, as a sign of hope, a gift from God. 'We might see it as a *gift* to the world of international affairs standing for the possibility of quality relationships which as a benefit – not a *raison d'être* – serve the interests of its partners.'[1]

The Anglican Communion is likewise a loose confederation of churches, covering much of the world and not confined to the Commonwealth, but having this same character of sharing a common history, a common ethos, and held together by mutual respect, by a very slender central organisation, and by bonds of affection. The parallel is not exact because Churches are also held together by specifically theological factors, such as a shared faith and common ministry. But Anglicanism has never been confessional in the sense of having a specific statement of doctrine which, as it were, defines the Church and distinguishes it from others. Nor can it nowadays share a completely common ministry, in that some members do, and some do not, accept the ministry of women priests and bishops. As in the Commonwealth there is no central power which can dictate what Anglicanism is. The ten-yearly meeting of all Anglican bishops, the Lambeth Conference, offers guidance and makes recommendations, but it cannot dictate to separate national Churches. These are recognised as having their own autonomy within a family of Churches related to one another, sharing a common symbol of unity in the Archbishop of Canterbury, and pledged to work together. The relevant word, as in the Commonwealth, is partnership – a commitment to be together in our allegiance to Christ, in our rootedness in a common history and in our mission to the world. But this vocation has to be worked out in very different cultural contexts, through what the report calls 'earthed exploration of what Christ and culture mean for each other, [and] how a human church bears God to people'. This attention to different cultural contexts lies at the basis of the policy of provincial autonomy.

Here, then, on one level is the form in which Anglicanism has developed a world-embracing sense of unity. But there are also other characteristics which make up part of the Anglican ethos – though they are perhaps most clearly seen in the Church of England. These provide one possible model for unity in diversity. A perceptive Scottish theologian, writing about our agonised debates on the ordination of women to the priesthood, coined the phrase 'communities of disagreement'. She describes this particular disagreement about women as a gift,

> . . . not just because it opens up deep and wide theological questions, but because it touches the levels of pain and passion which test what it means that we love our enemies. The world is used to unity of all sorts . . . unity in resistance, communities of party, creed, interest. But it is *not* used to such possibilities as this: that, for example, those who find the exclusion of women from the priest-

hood an intolerable apartheid and those who find their inclusion a violation of God's will, should enter into one another's suffering. Somewhere in there authority lies.[2]

The disagreements remain. There has been suffering. But there has also been a readiness to stay together, to work at the issues, to pray for further guidance, and to accept the essential provisionality of our institutions and of our judgements. Part of this ability to live together comes from a sense of history which teaches the lesson that one or other side in such a deep disagreement is never wholly right or wholly wrong. Part of it comes from having what we call 'a dispersed authority' – a structure full of checks and balances which never allows one point of view wholly to dominate another. Part of it is rooted in a sense of the worth of individuals which encourages tolerance. Part of it is summed up in a favourite Anglican word, 'comprehensiveness'. This is how the report describes it:

It is an attitude of mind which Anglicans learn from the thought-provoking controversies of their history. It demands agreement on fundamentals while tolerating disagreement on matters in which Christians may differ without feeling the necessity of breaking communion. It is not compromise, nor a sophisticated word for syncretism. Rather it implies that the apprehension of truth is a growing thing . . . and there must be a continuing search for the whole truth in which the Protestant and Catholic elements will find complete reconciliation.

There is a price to be paid for this kind of openness to differing viewpoints, this understanding of faith as a journey in mixed company rather than as a possession to be received once for all. Some people find themselves bewildered by what they perceive as Anglican indefiniteness. Others find in it space to grow. Some people wonder if a body so diverse can actually achieve anything. Others find the respect for human freedom exhilarating, and a spur to creativeness. It is also important to note that there is a price to be paid for unity without diversity, the end-product of which is usually tyranny or sterile conformism.

Translating this typically Anglican sense of how to live together back into Commonwealth terms, one might speak of a dialogue of cultures. The fact that the Commonwealth contains large Muslim populations offers a particular challenge to demonstrate the possibility of effective dialogue between Christian and Islamic cultures, even in times of growing mistrust between them. As many are beginning to realise, this is an important area of dialogue within Europe itself, where history has in some ways been more painful, and may therefore benefit from being set in a larger world context.

The dialogue of cultures which takes place within the Commonwealth is capable of extension. Major issues like peace-keeping, racism and human rights could be tackled more adventurously, encouraged by the example of South Africa. But even in matters like sport, the Commonwealth ethos may have something to offer. The Commonwealth Games are often referred to as 'the friendly games' – they are characterised by a competitiveness which does not degenerate into hostility or into a determination to win at all costs. They are more a celebration of unity than a substitute for warfare – whereas I am afraid one has to wonder sometimes whether in the European Games the reverse may be true. The dialogue of cultures is, of course, made easier by sharing a common language and a common heritage – but it still manages to survive strong assertions of ethnic and linguistic identity.

The co-operation of ecumenism

I have concentrated so far on this analogy between the ethos of Anglicanism and the ethos of the Commonwealth because it sharply poses a question: What kind of unity are we seeking when we speak of European unification? Is it something more close-knit than this, and if so how are we to cater for an acceptable degree of diversity? It might be said that the unity expressed in the Council of Europe is not unlike what I have been describing. There is a definite membership, and there are definite standards of membership in terms of democratic government, respect for human rights and the rule of law. But there is also a breadth of membership which is attractive to Christians, who have consistently warned against the dangers of exclusivism in the European Community. There are also possibilities of mutual help, within its very limited budget. But the constant complaint is that the Council has no teeth, except through the Court of Human Rights. My impression is that politicians do not take much account of it, because it is more about partnership than about power.

Must we look, therefore, towards the kind of unity which involves a real degree of power-sharing? I turn to a different model, the model of unity *between* Churches as it has developed in Britain during the past 15 years or so. This model began to take shape around 1985, after some 40 years of seeking unity through a Council of Churches. Councils of Churches, when they were created in the period around the second world war, were intended to be the voice of the Churches speaking together. It was assumed that the Churches would gradually allow the councils to take responsibility for corporate policy-making – and they have indeed implemented valuable programmes, notably in the relief of refugees and in the fight against racism. Both are areas in which it has been obvious that the amalgamation of resources was the most effective way of getting the work done. Councils of Churches represent a great vision – but what in practice has tended to happen is that they have become repositories for ecumenical enthusiasm which has then become more and more detached from the day-to-day life of the Churches themselves. There are times when councils no longer speak *for* the Churches, but speak *to* them, properly urging the Churches to be more ecumenical, while themselves being increasingly unrepresentative of what the Churches actually are. This criticism can be levelled against the World Council of Churches, and I have myself spoken out publicly about the narrowing of its ideological perspective, and the danger that its policies will be dictated by a small body of bureaucrats with a particular theological commitment.

One can see something broadly similar happening within the European Community. The Community ought to be 'us' in our role of working together with our European partners. In Britain, I am sorry to say, the Community is predominantly thought of as 'them'. And this seems even more true of the European Commission. Brussels is made to appear, however illogically, as some sort of foreign agent. A distrust of instruments of unity inevitably follows when the instruments become too far removed from the bodies they are trying to unite – and this can happen no matter how compelling the ultimate vision of unity and the good which is expected to flow from it.

The new method of ecumenical working in Britain deliberately stays much closer to the actual life of the Churches themselves. The new Council of Churches for Britain and Ireland, and its national counterparts, are co-ordinating and facilitating bodies, exploring areas of co-operation, seeking commitment by the Churches to common policies, enabling the Churches to act sometimes with each other, sometimes on behalf of each other, but always keeping the final powers of decision within the Churches themselves. It includes many more denominations than the old British Council of Churches – indeed it covers virtually all the Churches in Britain – and is the co-ordinating agent for a large series of local and regional ecumenical bodies.

Even with this method of working it has proved convenient to delegate some forms of action to separate ecumenical commissions which do specialist work in the name of all the Churches. As in the old British Council of Churches, racial justice and inter-faith relations are the two most prominent areas in which this kind of approach works best. In most other areas the Churches are learning to co-operate through very light central structures, and so this wide range of Churches, from Roman Catholics and Orthodox at one end to independent Black Pentecostal Churches at the other, have found the method acceptable. It is slow. It entails a mind-shift in those normally responsible for making decisions. The amount of consultation required can become tedious. There have to be constant reminders of the purpose of it all, and there are still awkward problems which have not been solved in trying to operate the system in the four nations, as well as in the British Isles as a whole. Nevertheless the mind-shift is gradually beginning to happen. It is becoming more and more difficult to think in purely denominational terms. Furthermore, the fact that the process is rooted in local co-operation gives substance to the belief in subsidiarity. Over the years Churches in Britain have learnt by bitter experience that unity from the top down tends to create further divisions.

This, then, is another model of unity which the Churches are beginning to experience, and which might have lessons for our secular European experience. It is a question of what kind of powers are held by the instrument of unity. Is its role eventually to take over functions from the separate entities, whether Churches or states, and to make decisions for them? Or is it primarily a co-ordinating and facilitating agency through which separate states can reach agreements while retaining their own powers of decision-making? A growth in the number and permanence of effective agreements will, in the long run, constitute a kind of union, and at that point the two approaches may merge. But if the experience of the Churches is anything to go by, the two approaches feel very different in action. One way of describing it is as the difference between federalism and confederalism. Federalism envisages a central authority which allows a certain degree of decentralisation and delegation of powers. Confederalism is about the coming together of separate authorities for certain specific purposes. In a confederation, power is delegated *to* the centre, not *from* it. My impression is that much discussion of European union, certainly in my own country, is confused by the failure to distinguish between these two.

Interpenetration in the Diocese in Europe

So far I have used the model of the Anglican Communion and the model of ecumenism as ways in which the Churches, and particularly the Anglican Church, can help to set some goals for the unification of Europe. I turn now to a third model, that represented by the Anglican Diocese of Gibraltar in Europe. Those who know the diocese will need no reminder that it is a curious, scattered, somewhat anomalous body, which began as a series of chaplaincies for expatriates, and is now the forty-fourth diocese in the Church of England. As the European Community has developed, the diocese has become increasingly important, not only for Anglicans working on the Continent, but also as a Church which has put down deep roots and is beginning to become indigenous. This is evidenced by the fact that it is no longer exclusively English-speaking. And it looks as though it may develop a distinctive ecumenical role. Just as the Church of England has been learning from Lutheranism that the differences between Christian traditions are not necessarily identical with the form they have taken in England, so on the Continent there is value in the witness of a tradition which does not fit easily into the usual polarisation between Catholics and Protestants. The Anglican Diocese in Europe is very small by continental standards, but it may have a significance beyond its size precisely because it is so different.

Alongside and within that diocese there are numerous other Christian links between the Church of England and other Churches in Europe. I mention only the newly developed links between the Church of England and the EKD (German Evangelical Church) through the Meissen Agreement, and the hopes of much closer unity with the Nordic and Baltic Lutheran Churches through the Porvoo

Declaration. These are fundamentally theological and practical agreements about the healing of ancient divisions between Churches, and the opening up of new channels for exchange and information. In their beginnings they only involve quite small numbers of people. But they are a sign of the breaking down of barriers, and in the long run they will generate many new links between people, parishes and countries, through their creation of new opportunities for working together and learning to understand one another.

This model of unity through the presence of a diocese, through agreements, and through exchanges, I am going to call 'interpenetration'. Interpenetration is the mixing up of things which have formerly been separate; it is the provision of opportunities to meet people, to encounter new traditions and to form new links, and so to create the vital substructure of unity. This process is going on all the time in secular contexts as well as in religious ones. But perhaps the religious networks have an advantage, in that they are likely to be more consciously aware of what they are doing, and why they are doing it. They are motivated to see these small links and exchanges as part of a larger design. Unity for Christians is not an option. It is part of the necessity laid upon us by the gospel of reconciliation, and the promise that in the end all things will be gathered up into the unity of God himself.

Unity through interpenetration, through becoming familiar with one another, through innumerable small commitments and contacts, is much stronger and more resilient than unity engineered from the top down by negotiators. But it takes time to develop, and Churches which are used to thinking in terms of centuries, rather than years or weeks, can find it hard to sympathise with politicians who set themselves deadlines for success determined by the date of the next election. Perhaps, therefore, one lesson to be learnt from all our Churches about the unification of Europe is that, if it takes so long to grow towards Christian unity, we should not be surprised when political union runs into difficulties. Nations, like religions, are the carriers of cultural, corporate and personal identities, and there are no short cuts to political union, apart from conquest. But the message is not simply a negative one. In the last few decades most Churches have shown an astonishing capacity to change. When I started my ministry 40 years ago it was not possible to say the Lord's Prayer with a Roman Catholic. Nowadays the commitment of the Roman Catholic Church in Britain to close co-operation with other Churches is clear, firm and extensive. As an Anglican, 40 years ago I had virtually no contact with members of other Churches in Britain, still less with the Lutheran and Reformed traditions on the Continent. Today most Anglicans accept that ecumenical relationships are entirely natural – indeed, so natural as to be slightly boring. There are some 600 united local churches in England where denominational barriers have almost completely disappeared.

Unity is possible, therefore – but it has to grow through developing an openness towards one another and a tolerance which encourages trust. It needs an institutional expression which facilitates co-operation rather than forcing it, and which keeps in close touch with its constituencies. And it involves a kind of interpenetration, a mixing-up made possible by our presence in each other's communities. I strongly suspect that the political unification of Europe will have to follow the same pattern if it is not to provoke counter-reactions by threatening the identity of its constituent entities.

Interpenetration already takes place: we are irrevocably involved with one another through trade, through our linked economies, and through our shared interests. Much of the discussion about sovereignty in my own country ignores the extent to which, in today's world, many major decisions can no longer be taken by individual governments acting on their own. It seems obvious that sovereignty is no longer indivisible and absolute, but a matter of degree. But there are still proper questions to ask about diversity and distinctiveness, and about the powers of central institutions, and about working in partnership rather than the creation of some new European superstate.

My concern, though, is not with the politics of European unification, but with trying to see what lessons, if any, the Churches may share with those who long for a more united Europe, and what practical help they might give. I have pointed to three models of unity through partnership, through centrally facilitated co-operation leading to confederation, and through interpenetration. They are not mutually exclusive, neither are they exhaustive. But they have in common the sensitivity to proper diversity, and they all need time to grow.

Aims for increasing unity

I turn finally to practical steps the Churches might be taking to promote greater political unity – and here I draw on a recent debate in the Church of England's General Synod, when we tried to set ourselves some European aims for the immediate future. We identified four such aims.

1 Greater unity among the Churches themselves. It would be unreal for the Churches to advocate political union if we cannot unite among ourselves. But it could also be dangerous to move into closer political union for reasons of pure expediency, and without any agreement about its moral and spiritual significance. From the start, the European vision may have had economics as its driving force, but it has always had some greater concept of human flourishing as its goal. And that is why it so important that we search together for some expression of 'the soul of Europe' – a search requiring the involvement of all the Churches. I vividly remember attending my first Brussels meeting of Church leaders, looking round the table, and asking, 'Where are the Roman Catholics and the Orthodox?' The Churches will not be able to contribute to the process of unification, unless we can articulate a vision which is not falsified by our own disunity.

2 This aim of unity leads to the second aim, which is 'to work with other Churches in seeking to ensure the most effective presentation of the Christian gospel in contemporary Europe'. Western Europe is probably the most secular society in the world. I will not attempt to go into the reasons for this – but among them must surely be the miserable record of religion as a divisive force, a cause of bitter and brutal wars, a means of oppression and supposed justification for some of Europe's atrocities. Against this background it is difficult for many people to hear the claims of traditional religion, and we have to show ourselves worthy to be heard by our penitence for the past, by our spirit of reconciliation in the present, and by our determination to fight the social evils of our day in the name of justice, peace and integrity. The preaching of the gospel, therefore, is inseparably bound up with the kind of reconciling work which needs to be done in Europe as a whole. If a 'soul of Europe' is to be discovered, it is more

likely to be discovered in this process of active reconciliation than by simply dwelling on our common Christian heritage.

3 The third aim set by our Synod is to support the development of our Anglican Diocese in Europe, not by turning it into a proselytising body, but by encouraging partnership with other Churches; by making it a welcoming home for Anglicans from all over the world who are working in mainland Europe; and by providing opportunities to discover how our particular pattern of unity in diversity actually works. As European Churches we share many common problems, and I was greatly impressed on a recent visit to the EKD in Berlin by the amount of mutual learning which was possible in a few brief days together. I learnt some lessons, which I shall not forget, about forgiveness in a formerly East German congregation, 60 of whose members had been giving information about their fellow Christians to the secret police. There is so much rich, and often painful, experience to share, that retreat into isolation would be an impoverishment for all our Churches. So our commitment as Anglicans to mainland Europe is real, and is increasing.

4 All this provides the context for a fourth aim in which co-operation between Churches is essential – namely, the attempt to articulate a Christian voice in the shaping of the new Europe. There are many aspects of this – spiritual, ethical, social, political, technical – but let me give just one example. Biotechnology, and in particular the issues raised by rapid advances in genetics, have implications for all these aspects of our life together. A special feature of genetic developments is that they frequently cannot be confined to a limited group of organisms, or to a clearly defined place, or even to an individual country. Once started, genetic development is hard to control. This is why it is so important to be alert to the wider consequences of work done in this field, and why it is a prime subject for international supervision. But if we find it hard to agree on such matters in Europe, what hope is there for doing so globally? And this is only one example among many of a new range of problems which, however much we value diversity and freedom of choice, have to be regarded as inherently international. The environment belongs to us all.

For the Churches to have a perceived role in helping to shape European thinking on such matters, as on many others, and for us to discover a greater unity among ourselves in the process, would, I believe, be a modest but useful contribution to a safer, more just and more united world. And that surely must be the ultimate aim underlying our more immediate concern for European unification.

III
THE MEDIA

16

Gerald Priestland

My most vivid memory of Gerald Priestland is of an evening we spent together in a revolving restaurant at the top of a skyscraper in Cambridge, Massachusetts. We were both attending the same conference – a gathering of several thousand scientists and theologians convened by the World Council of Churches. He poured out to me his frustrations about the conference – its overloaded agenda, the chaotic nature of its proceedings, and the half-baked claptrap in which some participants seemed to specialise. As I was feeling much the same, we commiserated over an unfamiliar alcoholic concoction, the kind with paper umbrellas stuck in it. It was a gloomy evening.

But when later he broadcast his report on the conference, he was mostly positive. He saw clearly how important it was to understand what science and technology were doing, not only to Western society but to the world, and to set it in a moral context. He recognised that the World Council of Churches was up to its neck in politics, not because it wanted to be politicised, but because its members were exasperated by politics and were trying to put some Christian ethics into it. And he acknowledged that only the Churches could have brought together that kind of gathering for that degree of serious and open discussion of deeply moral issues.

That was in 1979. I recall the occasion because it seems to me characteristic of the man. He had a temperament which often made it hard for him to enjoy what was actually going on, yet a determination not to put people down or make them look foolish. He wanted to understand them, to learn from them, and to tell the truth as he saw it. He always denied any suggestion of being a theologian – indeed, he constantly described himself as a very tentative believer, a searcher, one whose job it was to engage in a well-disposed exploration of religion. And it was perhaps this sympathetic openness which brought him such a huge following. I remember him talking on a later occasion about his embarrassment at being regarded as a kind of religious guru, and his alarm at the overwhelming response to *Priestland's Progress* – his series of quite heavily theological Radio 4 programmes in which he described his religious search. What disturbed him most was that people were turning to him rather than to the Churches. He coined the phrase 'the Church of the unchurched' to describe people outside the Churches, engaged in a religious search like his own. And he challenged the Churches to tackle what was clearly an enormous unmet need.

It is a challenge that the Churches have not hitherto had much success in meeting. Straightforward evangelism has only limited appeal, because the unchurched to whom Gerald Priestland spoke so effectively are precisely those who are unwilling, or unable, to hear what the Churches are saying, if it comes to them in the form of direct assertion or covert persuasion. In speaking to them as an independently-minded searcher, he had a priceless advantage: he could circumvent hang-ups about authority and suspicions about bias.

In the years since his death, the hang-ups and the suspicions have grown worse. What was already by then an inhibiting distrust of authorities, authority figures and established institutions, is fast developing into a climate of outright mockery and contempt.

A few years ago I used on television the phrase 'culture of contempt', which I had borrowed from a perceptive columnist in a religious journal. I still get letters about it because it obviously struck a chord. Gerald Priestland never, so far as I know, expressed contempt for what he was reporting. He would have been profoundly uneasy about the contemptuous tone of much of today's comment, not only on the Churches, but on other basic institutions in our society – the monarchy, parliament, even the judiciary. Contempt hijacks understanding; it stops communication; it is less concerned with truth than with demonstrating the author's cleverness. The kind of perceptiveness which commentators of Gerald Priestland's generation were able to bring to deeply serious issues is progressively being replaced by the snap comment, the debunking aside, the flip dismissal.

You will say that I am exaggerating, and in a sense I am. I am describing a tendency, not a fully established state of affairs. There is still good reporting and perceptive comment, even about religion. But there have been disturbing changes in the way in which the major institutions in our society are perceived and described, and the media must share part of the blame.

People talk about a crisis of authority. What we are witnessing is more than a justifiable reaction against the abuses of authority, but is rather a reaction against the concept of authority itself. It therefore cuts at the root of beliefs, attitudes and institutions which have traditionally held societies together. It discounts the accumulated wisdom of past generations. It sees history as no more than a record of human folly and corruption. Cynical contempt is one of the extreme forms of this rejection.

When the media indulge in this cynical contempt, they usually defend themselves by saying that their aim is to reflect the nature of society, not to change it, and they would claim that they are merely expressing the anti-authoritarian flavour of modern liberal culture. The truth, I suspect, is more complex. There seems to be a kind of vicious circle whereby the media feed back into a culture certain tendencies, which may indeed have had their origin elsewhere, but which are magnified by constant public reiteration, and which thus provide the apparent basis for more and more extreme versions of themselves. The culture of contempt, in other words, feeds on itself. And the appetite for it grows, especially among those who work in the kind of corporate culture where direct criticism of authority is dangerous, where debate is stifled, and where disillusionment with those in control is allowed to fester.

But where are the origins of this growing reaction against the whole concept of authority, this unwillingness to recognise that there are traditions and institutions which are the carriers of tried and tested values of continuing importance, validity, and relevance to humanity? It is not enough, in my view, simply to point to the general spirit of criticism which has permeated and shaped Western culture from its beginnings. The kind of questioning found in the Hebrew prophets and the Greek philosophers, the challenging of assumptions by which science advances, the rejection of dogmatic authority since the Enlightenment – all these may at times have been uncomfortable, but their effect on the whole has been good and positive. What they all had in common, though, was the belief that such questioning would lead to a more profound apprehension of truth. The modern crisis of authority lies in the weakening, or even loss, of this shared assumption. There is an awful suspicion in some quarters that there are no universal and objective truths to be found: there is only my truth or your truth; my morality or your morality; our culture as only one among many, no better and no worse than any other. The present crisis of authority is that authority is perceived to have no basis; in the end, everything boils down to a matter of individual opinion and personal choice.

Again I am exaggerating to make the point. But I believe that there is a real and devastating shift, from the exercise of a critical spirit in the search for truth, towards a kind of criticism which does not believe in truth but merely wishes to deflate all claims to it.

How has it come about? It is obviously not unconnected with the spirit of criticism which, in the past, has been so fruitful in helping to shape our culture by exposing abuse and falsehood. Siren voices tell us that what we are witnessing now is simply an extension of that process, and that there is nothing to worry about. Human beings will find ways of living with the new freedom to think what they like and do what they like, basing their lives on the belief that there is no ultimate source of truth or goodness to which they can appeal. Humanity has survived massive cultural changes in the past, and will survive in the future – so they say.

That sounds fine and noble for those who already know where they stand and who are used to sophisticated mental gymnastics. But would any of us actually want everybody – and I mean everybody – to pursue the policy that there is no truth or morality beyond what individuals believe? And what are we to make of the counter-reaction, the insistent demands for strong leadership and clear values, and the growing attractiveness of highly authoritarian forms of religion? We have to reckon with the fact that there are powerful forces pushing many people in both these directions.

In public discussion of the Internet, I have drawn attention to the possible long-term impact of the information revolution in reinforcing a self-regarding individualism, and further eroding the sense of community. It is here, perhaps, that we can identify another of the fundamental causes of the present crisis of authority.

The enormous quantity of available information, quite apart from the way it is presented, can have a disorientating effect. I remember as a young research student going into the University Library in Cambridge, and each time feeling overwhelmed by the sheer vastness of knowledge. It seemed foolish to imagine that as an individual, paddling as it were in the shallows, I could ever make any contribution to it. What value could my own thoughts possibly have in the context of all that accumulated learning? There is indeed a proper place for humility – an acknowledgement that each of us only scratches the surface. But the recognition that, for every assertion, there is some-where a counter-assertion, does more than induce humility. It actively undermines what we think we know by putting our puny under-standing in such a vast context that we despair of finding solid foundations. To be overloaded with information reinforces the sense that knowledge is just an endless succession of human opinions, and that there are no abiding truths and principles by which human beings ought to live.

In their own way the media contribute to the disorientation I have been describing, simply by virtue of the flood of images and ideas which can wash over those exposed to them. To go straight from Bosnia to *One Foot in the Grave*, to be treated as having a two-minute attention span, to be assumed to need more and more stimulation by increasingly startling presentations, to be bombarded by a succession of instantaneous experiences, to be endlessly diverted, to have no time to pause and reflect – all this is to have everything reduced to the same level of significance – or insignificance.

Let me stress that I am talking about misuse, about possible ways in which things which may be good in themselves can subtly change our perceptions. It is the same point I was making earlier about the Internet. To have almost limitless power to call up any image, to convey and receive information without any restraints, to create, as it were, one's own world, could reinforce the dangerous perception that life has no purpose beyond individual self-gratification.

There is much which could be said positively about the information revolution. Knowledge on the whole is to be desired. The heart of my worry about what is happening in today's revolution is that it fits all too neatly with other tendencies in our society – the supermarket mentality, the unbridled assertions of rights and freedoms without their corresponding responsibilities, the worship of the great god *choice*. We seem to be losing sight of the more ancient wisdom that it is precisely the existence of constraints which brings out the best in human beings, and that the antidote to superficiality is a firm sense of the boundaries within which life must be lived.

To give an immediate personal example: in preparing this lecture I was very conscious of boundaries – boundaries of time and subject-matter, and the boundaries set by radio as a medium. Without them I would not have had to think so hard about what I wanted to say, and how to say it. Any serious purpose, in fact, needs constraints to give it focus and direction, and to concentrate energy. This is equally true of the most serious purpose we can undertake – the attempt to make sense of our lives.

But how can this be done in a culture which seems to be losing its awareness that there are truths, values and responsibilities which transcend our individual opinions, our selfish desires, and the mad scramble for personal fulfilment? How can we escape from the ultimate incoherence of unbridled relativism and subjectivism, as they progressively saw off the branches on which they are sitting? How can we identify once again some of the constraints and boundaries which have been thrown away with such abandon? How, in a word, can our culture recover an awareness of the reality and significance of God? In the end it is the weakening of this awareness which lies at the heart of our problems. God used to be perceived as the guarantor of truth. This is not to claim that human beings can ever finally grasp the truth, or that we can ever wholly free ourselves from bias and misunderstanding. But to believe in God is to believe that there is truth to be known – truth which is not simply of our own making. It is to believe that there are constraints on the way human beings should live – constraints which are not merely matters of cultural conditioning. It is to believe that there is dignity and purpose in human life which goes beyond individual self-fulfilment, which roots us in a meaningful universe, and which holds out for us a larger hope.

It may seem like an easy clerical platitude to assert that much of what is wrong with our contemporary culture is that it has no place for God. The days when God was the dominant feature of everyone's landscape were not noticeably happier or more peaceful than our own. Indeed, the kind of God many people seem to have believed in has been at least as much a source of division as an upholder of the value and the connectedness of things. But when we look deeper, and spell out the extent to which some awareness of God, whether conscious or not, has undergirded beliefs about truth, goodness and human destiny, the picture begins to look different. On this level it is neither slick nor platitudinous to claim that the most urgent need in our modern Western culture is to recover that sense of a stable, meaningful and demanding ultimate reality.

But how can this be done in the face of what I have been describing – and in particular after an information explosion which appears to discredit all claims to absoluteness?

It seems to me that one of the great strengths of Christian belief about God is that it is rooted in history. God is not a philosophical idea but a presence manifesting himself in countless historical circumstances. There should therefore be no difficulty in acccepting that our knowledge of him is always historically conditioned, always dependent on particular times, places and circumstances, and is thus gloriously rich and diverse. The variety of different Christian beliefs and practices ought not to cause surprise, still less embarrassment.

An older generation of atheists used to try to confound Christians by pointing out contradictions in the Bible. But contradictions, or at least deep differences of perception, are what one would expect if faith is essentially about discerning and responding to the presence of God within a chaotic jumble of events. Nevertheless it is a sign of the reality of what believers are responding to that, within all this diversity, there remain strong family resemblances, a strong sense of shared experience, a strong awareness of the same gracious and loving holiness at the heart of things.

This is not enough as a Christian answer to the information explosion, but at least it is a reminder that belief in God is not about adopting and clinging to some narrow, restricted and historically circumscribed set of ideas. It is about seeking and encountering a reality which lies beyond the conditioning, and which meets us in the varied circumstances of our own lives.

Probing further, one becomes aware of a deeper form of diversity. A mature religion always includes an element of paradox. The reality being expressed is greater than can be contained in a single set of concepts. There is the paradox, for instance, of freedom and grace. Christians claim both that God has made us free and responsible for our own actions, and also that our lives are surrounded and supported by his gracious love, without which we can do nothing. This may seem like a contradiction – but in fact anybody who has been loved knows the truth of it in experience. We are never more free than when we are totally bound to another. It is a truth which can only be expressed paradoxically.

To take another example: God we are told is 'wholly other' than his creation; he totally transcends it; he is the reality that lies behind and beyond all things. Yet it is also a characteristic part of religious experience that God is known in and through creation, and in the depths of human life. It is a paradox carried to its extreme in the Christian belief that this transcendent God revealed himself in the human life of Jesus.

I stress this element of paradox in belief in God, because it is important to us also as human beings in enabling us to come to terms with the tensions and contradictions in our own lives. Belief in God, in other words, is a richly complex process. It is the exploration of a tradition which encompasses and illuminates the whole of human life. It can only be threatened by a sense of the limitlessness of knowledge if this rich complexity is lost, if it is narrowed down to a single set of ideas, or one-sided interpretations, or simplistic answers.

But unfortunately what dominates all too much of the present religious scene is just that kind of lust for simplicity and certainty which is the denial of paradox and of the need to live with paradox. Is God male or female? we might be asked – answer yes or no. Does God approve of homosexuals? – in a single sentence please. I am reminded of the classic request sent by a student to a Christian enquiry agency: 'We are doing God this term; please send me full details and pamphlets'.

In an age of soundbites, the cards are stacked against presentations of faith which actually try to tackle fundamental issues of the kind I have tried to highlight. I wonder how Gerald Priestland would have coped in today's climate of opinion. At least he recognised clearly the intractable dilemma which haunts the religious reporter. He once described it in these memorable and wise words: 'All journalists', he said, 'me included, over-simplify. It is our greatest art – our greatest crime.'

17

Preachers from outer space

The Church of England tends to have a bad press. This can be disheartening for ordinary church members, because nobody likes to belong to an organisation which is always being criticised, even if they are aware that much of the criticism is misplaced. Often there is genuine bewilderment about things which are supposed to have been said or done, and my own postbag is frequently inundated with letters from puzzled or angry people. It is difficult to respond to these feelings without being accused of knocking the media or appearing over-defensive, but it may be useful to look briefly at how and why such false impressions can be generated. I leave on one side the possibility that, in some instances, there may be genuine malice, a desire to do the Church of England down: I am not in a position to fathom other people's motives.

My first major encounter with the Press happened nearly 40 years ago when I was interviewed for a tabloid about the theological implications of life on other planets. I made the fairly obvious point that the incarnation in Jesus of the second person of the Trinity was significant for human beings on earth, but that if there were creatures in outer space, then presumably God had made himself known to them in ways appropriate to their form of life. The newspaper reported this under the banner-headline, 'Preachers from outer space', and the article which followed was wholly given up, as far as I recall, to describing the imaginary characteristics of Martian clergy.

On the face of it this was a simple instance of mishearing. But it also revealed a set of assumptions about the sort of things clergy are expected to say. There is in fact a special tone of voice in which newspapers tend to report Church affairs. Differences of opinion are invariably 'unholy rows' which quickly 'plunge the Church into turmoil'. Clergy are usually depicted as making pronouncements (mostly denunciations) 'from their pulpits'. Headings to articles are apt to appear in Gothic script. Journalists suddenly break into phrases like, 'Yea, verily' – apparently oblivious of the fact that this owes more to Frankie Howerd than to the Authorised Version. Nuanced statements are first over-simplified, then fed to a known critic for comment, who promptly describes them as 'hypocritical'.

All this nonsense reflects a general incomprehension among many journalists of what the Churches are about, and a mild desire to ridicule an institution which supposedly makes great claims for itself. For some of it we have only ourselves to blame. If journalists are not provided with good human stories, they will fasten on trivialities for their entertainment-value. And never forget that entertainment is now the primary purpose of very large sections of the mass media.

But there are other forces at work as well. In a fiercely competitive industry there are strong temptations to concentrate on whatever is sensational, divisive or bizarre. The public image of most of our institutions, therefore, frequently bears little relation to what actually goes on in them, and the constant harping on scandals contributes to the undermining of their authority. The Church is no exception. Even so, the newsworthiness of misbehaviour among church people still derives, thankfully, from its being so rare.

One can sympathise with reporters who have been told to get a story at all costs. One senses the desperate hunt for a soundbite or for some startling disclosure and, when found, the 'good quote' displaces all the careful explanation, however much it misrepresents the main thrust of what has been said. I am not denying that there is also much excellent reporting. But an awareness of the pressures which tend to give a slant to news means learning to treat much of it with more than a pinch of salt.

There is another factor which makes life difficult for those aiming at simplicity in reporting on religious matters. Religious language is not entirely straightforward. It depends on symbolism, paradox, and words and images whose meaning has been stretched to carry an additional significance. Words like love, sin, holiness, communion, look decep- tively easy, but frequently mislead. The paradox of a Church claiming to be the Body of Christ, yet often behaving like a very imperfect human institution, can all too easily be portrayed as hypocrisy. The claim that Christians are sinners like everyone else, yet conscious of being justified by God's grace, cuts no ice with headline writers.

It is healthy to have these paradoxes challenged from time to time. But those who challenge them often fail to see that it is precisely in these tensions, and in attempts to use words in more than their ordinary meanings, that the human spirit reaches out to God. People who, in their own technical sphere, regularly handle complex ideas and processes, often have absurd expectations about the simplicity and straightforwardness of religious insights. Much easier to concentrate on squabbling clergy – which then becomes, for the most part, what the public expects and understands.

Thus if those who long to convey something more feel at times like preachers from outer space, the reasons are not hard to discern. But this is no excuse either for complacency or for depression. In the end, the gospel is conveyed more effectively by what we are and what we do, than by what we say or what is said about us.

18

Riding the storm

This beginning of his signs did Jesus in Cana of Galilee, and manifested his glory; and his disciples believed on him.
(John 2:11)

It might seem a bit odd for Jesus to begin manifesting his glory by
creating some 600–700 litres of wine at the tail-end of a party. No
wonder preachers find this a somewhat difficult story. It is made more
difficult by the fact that, unlike other stories in St John's Gospel, it is
not followed by a theological explanation.

St John's Gospel is constructed round seven great miracles, or signs
– miracles of healing, of giving bread to the hungry, of raising the
dead. Each is followed by a longish discourse which draws out
the meaning; each except this one. This story ends, 'and his disciples
believed on him'. We are left to wonder why, and what it means.

Clearly it is not just a story about Jesus rescuing his friends from a
social disaster. A dozen bottles would probably have seen to that, not
600 of them. The general thrust of the story in the context of the
Gospel as a whole is not hard to discern. It is a story about new life –
lots of it. Here, at the very beginning, St John tells us about a whole
new world-order. If mere water can become wine, then a new order
has indeed begun in Jesus. 'And his disciples believed on him.'

But we can go further. The water-pots were there, we are told,
'after the Jews' manner of purifying'. In other words, the water represented the old law, concerned as it was with ritual cleanliness, with the
old way of doing things. The wine represents the new way, now being
experienced by the Church for which St John was writing – the way
of resurrection life, the banquet of wine promised in the Kingdom of
heaven. This is probably why St John tells us that the marriage took

place 'on the third day' – a phrase which had only one meaning for Christians, the day of resurrection.

But why so much wine? Because the resources of God are without limit. We can compare it with the huge quantities of bread in the feeding of the 5,000. And there are also echoes of the very last words of the Gospel where St John writes: 'There are also many other things which Jesus did, the which if they should be written every one I suppose that even the world itself could not contain the books that should be written'. In other words, what we are being shown here in a small slice of time is something which spills over into an endless future. The litres of wine, the mountains of bread, the books without number, are all images of something too big to handle.

But we can go further. Bread and wine immediately remind us of the Eucharist. John, alone among the evangelists, does not mention the Last Supper. There has been much speculation about why not. One possible answer is that he does it here. In telling his story of Jesus to well-established churches, he had no need to remind them of the origins of the Eucharist. But he reads it back, as it were, into the life and ministry of Jesus, into the blessing and distribution of endless quantities of bread and wine. The Eucharist, in other words, is not just focused on the death of Jesus, but on the constantly renewed gift of resurrection life.

But we can go further. St John loves multiple meanings. The stories he tells are packed with symbolism and subtle allusions. And there is one allusion his Greek readers would almost certainly have picked up, even though it may seem strange to us. The idea of turning water into wine was already familiar in Greek mythology. It was symbolised in the rituals of the cult of Dionysus, the god of wine – Bacchus, as he was called by the Romans. And it is a curious coincidence that when, very early in the life of the Church, Epiphany began to be celebrated as the feast of the manifestation of God's glory in Christ, a feast centred on this story of turning water into wine, the date chosen was 6 January, the feast-day of Dionysus.

It is important not to read too much into a coincidence. But what St John may have been hinting at, and what the early Church may have picked up, is the good news that one greater than Dionysus is here. Jesus, in this first sign, fulfils all that was hoped for in a pagan cult which seemed to promise life but in fact only symbolised chaos and lawlessness.

In pagan mythology Dionysus was the god of animal energies, of drunkenness, revelries and orgies, the god of excess, the god who also represented the destructive side of human nature, the dark, dangerous, mocking forces which lie only just beneath the surface of civilised life. It is perhaps significant that, in more recent times, some of the thinkers and critics who have wanted to escape from what they have described as the baleful, restrictive aspects of Christianity have used Dionysus as a symbol – Nietzsche being the prime example.

And we can see Dionysian characteristics in our own society and sometimes in our own selves – in the breakdown of authority, the delight in mockery, the growth of irrationality, the over-indulgent displays of emotion, the tapping of the unconscious, the breakdown of order and the kaleidoscopic existence into which so many people are forced.

Television has been described as Dionysian – and it has been contrasted with radio, which is much better at conveying ideas, and which thrives on conversation, rationality and order. Chaotic images don't come across well on radio – but the constant shifting of attention, the images of violence, the stunning of the mind, are meat and drink to television.

What Dionysus stood for is still highly relevant at the end of the twentieth century. All these newly released energies may seem to promise a new, more vigorous kind of life. But St John is telling us that what Dionysus stood for has been taken up in, and transformed in, Christ.

Yes, water can be turned into wine, as Dionysus promised – but not in the chaos of unbridled self-indulgence; rather as part of an ordinary human celebration where Jesus is present.

Yes, there are huge resources of untapped energy in human life which can easily become destructive; but they are as nothing compared with the energies which flow from God; and perhaps our salvation lies in learning how to discern within them the hidden face of Christ.

Yes, there are threats of chaos and dissolution; yes, many of us are conscious of travelling in unknown territory where the landmarks are fast disappearing; but in the midst of us there is still a calm and powerful presence, not perhaps answering our immediate anxieties but waiting for the right moment – 'Mine hour has not yet come'.

This was the first of the signs in which Jesus manifested his glory.

180

And if there are, as I have suggested, hints of a more turbulent background against which the sign is to be understood, then it is perhaps especially a sign for our day. Christ is *in* the turbulence. And all we need is the faith to walk with him, through the eye of the storm.

IV

EDUCATION

19

Maps and dreams

I take my chapter title from a book by a Cambridge anthropologist, which may at first sight seem a long way from the theme of continuing adult education. It is an account of a year spent studying a tribe of hunter-gatherers, known as Beaver Indians, in a remote part of north-west Canada.[1] Their territory was about to be crossed by the projected Alaska natural gas pipeline, hence the idea was to map their movements, and so to plan as to minimise the impact of the pipeline on their way of life.

In the event Hugh Brody, the anthropologist, did much more than this. He lived as a member of the tribe, and journeyed with them as a friend. In his book the even-numbered chapters describe his scientific studies of their way of life, the maps he drew of their hunting patterns, and the social and political pressures on them from the encroachment of the so-called civilised world, including indiscriminate white hunters. The odd-numbered chapters describe what it is like to be a Beaver Indian from within. They have maps too – dream maps; an inner sense of place and its possibilities. Choices about hunting grounds are not made rationally or systematically, but arise spontaneously out of apparently chaotic conversation. Plans are not agreed first and then implemented, but are made in the process of being implemented. These were people with a high degree of skill, which was almost wholly inarticulate. For guidance they looked back to the stories of the elders who had first hunted their quarries in dreams, and then relived the dreams in actuality. In their limited world it was an extraordinarily effective way of behaving. The standard Western image of the American Indian as a drunken layabout proved to be wholly false when they were operating in their own environment.

Maps and dreams – two different ways of learning, knowing and behaving. For Brody, in his attempts to guide the pipeline planners, they were complementary – and both were necessary if wise and sensitive decisions were to be made. I hope that the parallels with present educational concerns may be instructive.

The educational world in recent years has been through an intense period of map-making. Plans, directives, numerical assessments, statistics, exhortations, threats and guidance have flowed in all directions in ever-increasing abundance. It is a frightening thought that, if this is what education is about, then in a culture of perpetual learning the map-making will never cease. It might seem as if there will be no time or inclination to dream. But we know this is not true – or ought not to be true. Planners have a job to do, but the most important aspects of learning are not found in plans at all.

The inspiration of 'dreams'

When I look back to my own school-days, I can see that what gave me a love of books, and to that extent set the future course of my life, was the experience of being read to. I do not just mean the kind of reading done to infants, but serious reading to a group of 14 or 15 year-olds by someone who knew how to read well. I can still mentally enjoy those sessions, and I can still vividly remember what was read, and the tone of voice in which it was read. As soon as I left school, I searched second-hand bookshops until I found a copy of one of the books which had particularly impressed me. It was called *Letters from a Self-made Merchant to his Son,* and was subtitled, 'Being the letters written by John Graham, head of the house of Graham & Company, pork-packers in Chicago, familiarly known on 'change as "Old Gorgon Graham" to his son, Pierrepont, facetiously known to his intimates as "Piggy" '. My copy is dated 1903.

It is not a famous book – in fact I would be surprised if many people had even heard of it. It is full of homely wisdom and improbable anecdotes. Since it begins when Pierrepont has just joined the freshman's class at university, the first theme, naturally enough, is education.

I didn't have your advantages when I was a boy, and you can't have mine. Some men learn the value of money by not having any and starting out to pry a few dollars loose from the odd millions that are lying around; and some learn it by having fifty thousand or so left them and starting out to spend it as if it were fifty thousand a year. Some men learn the value of truth by having to do business with liars; and some by going to Sunday School. Some men learn the cussedness of whiskey by having a drunken father; and some by having a good mother. Some men get an education from other men and newspapers and public libraries; and some get it from professors and parchments – it doesn't make any special difference how you get a half-nelson on the right thing, just so you get it and freeze on to it. The package doesn't count after the eye's been attracted by it, and in the end it finds its way to the ash-heap. It's the quality of the goods inside which tells, when they once get into the kitchen and up to the cook.

And so on, until you know a great deal about what makes a self-made merchant tick, and quite a lot too about curing and packing pork. A little later, the strains of education are beginning to tell, and Mr Graham Senior writes: 'When I told you that I wished you to get a liberal education, I didn't mean that I wanted to buy Cambridge. Of course the bills won't break me, but they will break you unless you are very, very careful.'[2]

I wanted to give you a flavour of the book, because I would like you to imagine it being read to 14 year-olds today. I believe that the sessions were memorable because the man reading them actually lived the part, and Graham & Company's pork-packing house in Chicago became part of my dreams.

I recall a similar experience which sparked off a lifelong love of poetry. It occurred the first time I watched Laurence Olivier's film of *Henry V.* Its immediate effect was to send me to my father's copy of Shakespeare, from which I read most of the plays over a period of a few weeks. Olivier's version is now derided by superior people as war-time jingoism, but what it did for me was to reveal the sheer power of words.

You must forgive me for these personal reminiscences. My point is simply that education happens and continues in ways which cannot easily be planned, but which depend heavily on the impact of personalities. Not exclusively, of course. Old Gorgon Graham made the point that there were many ways of getting a grip on it. But the encounter with another mind, another imagination, can be, at least in my own experience, uniquely enriching.

This is one reason why I am suspicious of too much reliance on computer-learning. It is a wonderful way of gaining information; it is very cost-effective; it can be enthralling, even mesmerising, to a far greater degree than much face-to-face teaching. But although it allows a high degree of personal interaction, what the student is in the end interacting with is not a person, but a database. I speak here in some ignorance of the actualities of learning in this way, because I have never done it. So I would want to ask, does one encounter another mind in computer-learning – and if not, what is being lost educationally? In many years of adult teaching in theology, there usually came a point when I could say to students, 'You now have a broad, general grasp of the subject. In this next stage, concentrate on getting to know one writer more thoroughly. Try to get into his mind.'

Allan Bloom's book, *The Closing of the American Mind*, seems to me to be making a similar point.[3] His thesis was that students no longer read great books. If all is relative, if comparisons and judgements are merely a matter of taste (as current intellectual fashion would have us believe), then the idea that there are great minds worth encountering, and great books worth reading, falls to the ground. The story of Bloom's own book almost proves his point. For a period of two or three years, everybody was reading him. He was the flavour of the month. Then tastes and fashions changed. He was deemed politically incorrect, because greatness offends against the principle of equality. And who is to say what is great anyway? By 1993 he was dismissed contemptuously, in an article in the *Journal of the Higher Education Foundation*, as an example of 'the Canute-like reflex-anti-post-modernism of the "right" '. I like that quotation. Every word of it is loaded, and the reliance on invective seems to me a perfect illustration of what happens when the idea of intrinsic greatness can no longer be entertained.

If Bloom was, after all, saying something important, and if education is indeed about the encounter with other minds, preferably great ones, then it is useful, I believe, to distinguish between what triggers off the desire for education and what satisfies it. In my own case the trigger experiences, though important to me, might have had little impact on somebody else. The post-modernists are surely right to stress the relativity of the things which fire our imaginations, and in that sense there is an infinite number of ways into the learning frame of mind, which accepts education as a lifelong endeavour. But I am not at all sure that the same relativity applies to the actual content of education. It may not be possible to draw up a list of great books which must be read, great ideas which must be tackled, and great minds which must be encountered. There are nevertheless some things which an educated person ought to know. The scientist in me is still sufficiently strong to believe that the scientific description of the universe which has emerged over the last three centuries, while always corrigible, is yet sufficiently true to be an essential part of any educated mind. And the theologian in me would say the same about St Paul's exhortation, 'Whatsoever things are true, whatsoever things are honourable, whatsoever things are just, whatsoever things are pure, whatsoever things are lovely, whatsoever things are of good report, if there be any virtue and if there be any praise, think on these things' (Philippians 4:8). Goodness, beauty and truth are not simply in the eye of the beholder. Despite all the arguments about relativism, somehow in our encounter with these qualities we are conscious of touching reality.

Education is important, in other words, because there are things worth knowing, and doing, and being. But when the desire has been triggered, what actually carries it forward, and motivates it?

At the stage in my life when I was considering whether I ought to continue as a scientist or seek ordination, I used to have tea regularly in our laboratory common room with a group of highly distinguished scientists. On one occasion I was impertinent enough to ask them what drove them to do their research. The question went round the table, and there were unconvincing murmurs about building foundations for better medicine, doing good in the world, and so on. But the predominant answer, and in the end I suspect the only fully honest one, was curiosity.

Curiosity, and the need to break out

In such company, one advantage of curiosity as an explanation is that it has good scientific credentials. Scientists know what curiosity is, and can understand its survival value. Most animals have exploratory instincts, and in the most successful there is an appropriate balance between curiosity and fear. Curiosity unrestrained by fear could be suicidal; fear unredeemed by curiosity is a recipe for stagnation. So in the animal world there is also that mixture of exploration and cautiousness which scientists can recognise in themselves.

Another way of describing it might be to talk about the need, both in animals and in humans, to build mental models of our environment. Our minds instinctively focus on things that are strange, but not too strange. A child in a car, for instance, will notice oddities in the car itself, but is unlikely to be concerned with the passing scenery, which is too far outside its normal experience. When the very strange intrudes itself, then the likely response is fear.

All this has obvious educational implications. The driving force in education is the same as the driving force in research, and at every level one can observe educators trying to harness curiosity. The whole demeanour of a good teacher in a primary school is calculated to excite curiosity. And at the other end of the scale – when, say, television is trying to operate in its educational mode – curiosity is a large part of the bait. I think of a programme like *How do they do that?*, which begins with the familiar but puzzling. We are all presumed to have seen what 'they' (whoever they are) do to amaze us. And curiosity compels us to watch.

A learning society, therefore, must certainly discover how better to harness curiosity. But if I am right in focusing on what cannot be planned – the inner life, the dreams of those being educated – there must be more to it than that.

Take the case of Alan Bennett's parents. Judging by the popularity of his most recent book, *Writing Home*, almost everyone must know about Alan Bennett's parents by now. He draws a very touching picture of the limited world in which they lived. It is not that they were unintelligent or afraid to explore. His father was always pursuing new enthusiasms, and there is a hilarious description of travelling on a Leeds tram during his father's double-bass playing phase. Nor were they incurious. In fact they liked nothing better than to watch other people and to speculate about them. As they saw it, the root of their problem lay in the lack of a proper education. Alan Bennett writes:

My parents always felt that if they had been educated their lives and indeed their characters would have been different. They imagined books would make them less shy and (always an ambition) able to 'mix'. Quiet and never particularly gregarious, they cherished a lifelong longing to 'branch out', with books somehow the key to it. This unsatisfied dream they have bequeathed to me.

He writes elsewhere: 'It was class and temperament, not want of education, that held their tongues; "stopping on at school" might have loosened them a little but it never entirely loosened mine, and I stopped on at school one way or another until I was twenty-eight'.[4]

'Class and temperament' – is he just identifying the sources of fear and inhibition which, in their case, held curiosity and adventurousness in check? Or was their problem of a different order? They cherished a 'lifelong longing to "branch out" ', as he puts it. To my mind that concept of branching out provides the key which can take us beyond curiosity towards something altogether more profound.

Branching out was for Bennett's parents a typically meek description of what others have described in more radical terms – breaking out, escaping, transcending. It is what adolescents have to do. But it does not stop with adolescence. The desire to break out is at the root of our human restlessness, our sense of unfulfilment, our awareness of possibilities unrealised, of more to come. This is not just unsatisfied curiosity. It is the fruit of an unsatisfied spirit.

Pascal put it like this:

The greatness of man is so evident that it is even proved by his wretchedness. For what in animals is nature we call in man wretchedness; by which we recognise that, his nature being now like that of animals, he has fallen from a better nature which once was his. For who is unhappy at not being a king, except a deposed king?[5]

Pascal locates our difference from animals precisely in this sense of restlessness and dissatisfaction. We may not want to use the language of the Christian doctrine of the Fall, but it points to something real in human experience. There is an open-endedness about human nature which drives us in ways which are sometimes destructive and sometimes marvellously creative. It is not just a question of animal instincts gone wrong, curiosity run riot – but it is the capacity for self-transcendence, a capacity which opens up a whole new world. In Pascal's case, it was a world he felt he had lost. In the case of Alan Bennett's parents, it was a world they were too inhibited to enter. For us, with our concern for education, the capacity for self-transcendence must surely be seen as the main motive power waiting to be harnessed.

Let me give some examples. Michael Polanyi – to my mind one of the most interesting of the philosophers of science – uses the notion of 'breaking out' to describe what happens in the process of scientific discovery. For most of the time, our minds dwell in and delight in a framework of thought which enables us to handle our experience and gain some control over ourselves. But there come times when the framework has to be demolished, when we let ourselves enter a realm where everything is uncertain, when experience is more like the dream-world of the Beaver Indians than the map-making of the anthropologist, when contemplation is more real than analysis, before a new framework emerges.

Polanyi then interestingly compares this with the experience of Christian worship. He describes the tension between guilt and sur-render, the alternation between prayer for grace and the joyfulness of praise. The Christian worshipper, by working within these tensions, is continually attempting to break out, to cast off the human condition, even while humbly acknowledging its inescapability. He goes on:

> Christian worship sustains, as it were, an eternal, never-to-be-con-summated hunch: a heuristic vision which is accepted for the sake of its unresolvable tension. It is like an obsession with a problem known to be insoluble, which yet follows, against reason, unswerv-ingly, the heuristic command: 'Look to the unknown!'. Christianity sedulously fosters, and in a sense permanently satisfies, man's craving for mental dissatisfaction by offering him the comfort of a crucified God.[6]

When I was teaching theological students in Birmingham in the 1960s, I used that last sentence as a text for a whole course of lectures on prayer.

Polanyi described one form of breaking out, given shape and energy in a religious tradition which, at its best, has been one of the pioneers of education. We can see what happens when it is *not* given shape by looking at some of the studies of religious experience under-taken by the Alistair Hardy Research Centre. One such study set out to discover how many people had experienced something which could be broadly classified as a kind of inner breaking out of the shell of ordinariness, an experience of transcendence, of unexpected meaning – and what they had done about it. The answer was that about two-thirds of the people interviewed had had such experiences, and most had done nothing about them, because they had no language in which to express what had happened, or no expectation that other people would understand, or no belief that such experiences could be significant.[7]

Interpreting such evidence in terms of the thesis of this chapter, I would say that the motive power to self-transcendence was there but the means of harnessing it was not. Maps are needed – maps from which we shall eventually break out – to give shape to our dreams.

I have spoken in religious terms – but in fact neither the power nor the means of breaking out need necessarily be religious. The worlds of art, music and literature are constantly trying to break out of the frameworks which once sustained them but now restrict them. There is an interesting case-study in the person of the post-war French philosopher, Michel Foucault, whose whole life was directed to this pursuit of transcendence, to the creation of an authentic self in ways which were the very opposite of religious. His means of breaking barriers was by transgression, by deliberately flouting social and moral norms, even the norms of reason. Nor did he despise dreams. He saw the dream as 'a privileged domain for thinking through the unthought – a shadowy clearing where, in a moment of vision, a human being can, as it were, recognise itself and grasp its fate'.[8]

I do not quote Foucault in order to commend him, but simply to illustrate the range of thinkers who have tried to give shape, by various means, to this aspect of our human experience. I think we can also see in this larger-than-life character an articulation of the impulses which drive many young people into criminal adventures. It is the tragedy of those who can only *be* something in ways which are shocking.

There are huge reservoirs of feeling, dissatisfaction, longing and hoping, waiting to be tapped – and it seems to me that the first task of a learning society is to recognise that they are there. From my Christian perspective, I have a means of interpreting them; and I believe that the simplest and most fruitful way of coming to terms with our immense human possibilities is to see them as the reflection in each of us of our creation in the image of God. This is the ultimate ground for believing in the open-endedness of human personality. But I also acknowledge that the Christian faith has sometimes worked against this open-endedness, and has trapped people rather than liberated them. I find it particularly distressing when Christian minds appear to be closed to anything but a very limited version of faith. This is a cast of mind in which maps leave no room for dreams.

So I return to the Beaver Indians. Maps were needed for them if they were to survive in a world in which it was no longer possible for them to continue simply as they were. Planned, lifelong education is a necessity for us if we are to survive in our world – a world in which new skills and insights are needed in every generation. But there must also be scope to tap down into the deep and permanent roots of our humanity, the ultimate source of our motivation. The Indians, cut off from these roots, forced into a way of life which was alien to them and in which they were de-skilled, became layabouts. Their dreams became alcoholic stupors. The picture is not totally unfamiliar, even in Britain. I hope, therefore, that those who look to the educational future of this country will give due place to those aspects of it which cannot and should not be mapped, which touch and motivate people in the deepest recesses of their lives, and which give substance to their dreams.

20

The case for a national RE syllabus

In this chapter I reproduce verbatim a keynote speech made at a conference of educationalists on the subject of religious education (RE). It was the second in a series intended to raise the profile of the subject, which at the time was suffering through not being included in the National Curriculum. RE syllabuses in schools are determined locally, after consultation with committees known as SACREs, which are representative of local religious bodies. My impression is that, since the conference (which took place in March 1995), the National Model Syllabus has gained ground, though it remains voluntary.

Nearly three years ago, here in this very room, I made a plea that RE should become part of the National Curriculum. I tried to rebut the argument that multi-culturalism necessitates local control through SACREs. I claimed that RE is a serious academic subject which needs good professional resources, and that it was unlikely to attract these so long as it was relegated to a marginal position, both nationally and at the level of planning school timetables. And I described the vicious circle in which the subject might continue to be caught if its low status in schools further depressed teacher-recruitment, further lowered the standard of teaching, and thus led inevitably to further relegation. I urged those with a concern for RE to work together to demonstrate that agreement on a national RE curriculum was possible. And so it is with immense pleasure that I acknowledge the work which has been done in preparing model syllabuses through co-operation between different faith-communities. I am quite incompetent to judge a syllabus, but to my unpractised eye they look good, and it is encouraging to learn that they are already having their effect on local Agreed Syllabuses. I warmly congratulate all those involved.

Today we question whether this national collaboration can be taken further, not for the sake of administrative tidiness, but always with the aim of improving the teaching of the subject, and improving its status within the educational world.

Last month I spent a morning in a junior school in East Berlin. It was during the half-term holiday, but even so there were children and teachers in the school continuing over the holiday for the sake of children whose parents were at work. I was particularly struck by one young RE teacher who had a degree in theology. RE throughout Germany is confessional, and those of different faiths and traditions have a right to be taught by someone who professes that faith. This has disadvantages, as we know, for the cohesion of society, and the principle of religious division is deeply rooted in German history. But what I found most impressive was the seriousness with which the subject was treated, and the amount of professional resources allocated to it. This particular young teacher also took voluntary classes in RE for the children of church members after school hours, and all this was but a preparation for confirmation classes which lasted for three years.

You may ask, are the German people notably more religious as a result of such huge effort? The answer, I suspect, is no more clear than it is here. But at least there is not the dreadful ignorance about the content of religious faith that one so frequently finds in this country. And there was a strong sense that adults owed it to their children to give them a solid grounding in religious teaching. Maybe it is easier to feel strongly about such matters if you have lived for 45 years in the German Democratic Republic, and your school has had to be carved out of a half-derelict building still pitted with shrapnel scars, and without maintenance or repairs since 1939.

Are we serious about RE? There is still plenty to be worried about, despite John Gay's exhortation not to be glum. This audience will, I am sure, need no reminders of the somewhat negative conclusions of the OFSTED report, particularly in relation to secondary schools. I quote from the summary: 'the vast majority of secondary schools did not provide enough time to teach the agreed syllabus in Key Stage 4 and few provided a basic RE course for post-16 students'. Even at primary level OFSTED found that 20 per cent of the schools did not teach RE, and that in 50 per cent of the schools the RE syllabus was inadequate.

This was before the new model syllabuses – but those syllabuses are not going to change the endemic problems of there not being enough specialist staff, not enough time for teaching, and not enough resources to teach with. Nor, unless something drastic happens, is OFSTED's overall verdict likely to be reversed: 'Much RE teaching is confined to a rather dull exposition of basic Christian beliefs, with little attempt to examine Christianity as a major world faith or as a belief system affecting people's daily lives'.

Furthermore, things are likely to get worse if LEAs can no longer afford RE advisers or the provision of resource centres, if the contribution of colleges to teacher training is diminished, and if schools find themselves more and more subject to the pressures of the market. If the downward trend is to be reversed, those concerned about RE are going to have to build on the degree of collaboration already achieved, and to press the case for the subject as a central and essential part of education. This has to be done without falling into the opposite error of attempting to define too precisely what needs to be taught. It has always been a temptation within Christianity to define what cannot in the end be completely formulated, and to regulate what must in the last resort depend on individual response. Indeed, one can go further and say that there is a necessary element of open-endedness in any living faith if it is to be a genuine exploration of the boundaries of experience. But that is to anticipate. My immediate purpose is to stress that more collaboration at the centre must not result in more rigidity, but must be directed towards better quality, and better interaction with the whole educational process.

If a national syllabus were to achieve general acceptance, that would not make SACREs redundant. There is always going to have to be sensitive adaptation to local circumstances, and that will require the well-balanced local knowledge which SACREs ought to possess. Effective RE must entail some practical co-operation with local faith-communities, and that too could be provided and monitored by SACREs. The principle of local interest in RE is much too strong and valuable to abandon – but a subject which is seen as merely local can easily become idiosyncratic, or unduly influenced by powerful individuals, or relegated to a place of secondary importance. By contrast, a generally accepted national syllabus could attract the best writers, publishers and resource providers, and should enormously assist in the process of training RE teachers.

But, apart from the need to climb out of a vicious circle of decline, how would one justify greater emphasis on RE, in a context where all subject-areas are struggling for time and resources, and where RE still bears the stigma of supposedly not being a proper academic subject? How do we answer the charge that, in a modern society, schools should not be expected to give major attention to subjects which belong more properly to the faith-communities themselves, especially when overt religious practice involves such a small percentage of the population?

Let me start with some pragmatic arguments, the first of which I do not particularly like, but which I believe needs to be stated. It is the 'learning about right and wrong' argument, and it has been given a new twist by a recent European study of the inverse relationship between religious adherence and crime. In very broad terms, the rise and fall of Protestant church-adherence in Britain over the last 150 years closely parallels the fall and rise in the number of indictable crimes. There are numerous objections one can raise to that sort of correlation, not least the objection frequently voiced by Simon Jenkins of *The Times* that it is only the fear of crime which has risen, not crime itself. But could anybody write today what Geoffrey Gorer wrote in 1955?

> In public life today the English are certainly among the most peaceful, gentle, courteous and orderly populations that the civilised world has ever seen . . . The control of aggression has gone to such remarkable lengths that you hardly ever see a fight in a bar, when football crowds are as orderly as church meetings . . . the orderliness and gentleness, this absence of overt aggression calls for an explanation.

The explanation given was that this social orderliness corresponded with a high degree of internal and external social restraint through Protestant morality. It had its down-side, and it would be foolish to wish it back without radical transformation. Stated crudely, the idea that firm and widely disseminated moral teaching, rooted in a religious and conformist culture, cuts crime is not an attractive reason for raising the status of RE. But those who press this argument in more subtle ways have some evidence on their side. We are in danger of producing a morally bewildered generation, and while there is no educationally valid way back to a heavy-handed moralism, there is a responsibility on the educational world to help in building some moral foundations. In doing this RE is only one resource among many. By far the most important factor is usually the general ethos of the school and the quality of relationships. But where RE is taken seriously it can act as a focus for interpreting and criticising that ethos as part of the ordinary educational process.

A second pragmatic reason for justifying a major role for RE lies in the growth of irrationalism. It may be true that only a small proportion of British people are active adherents of some religious body. But a remarkably high proportion profess some religious principles and some residual belief. And especially among the young there are increasingly weird and wonderful religious ideas. Religious impulses do not disappear when a particular culture finds it hard to handle them. They reappear in other guises, usually ones which have very slender connections with reality as ordinarily perceived. It would be foolish to over-emphasise the importance of New Age religion, but the fact that most major bookshops carry shelves of books on astrology and the occult, and various kinds of healing, and keys to self-knowledge, offset by a small row of presentation Bibles and white-bound Books of Common Prayer in a dingy corner, is surely a straw in the wind. I say this not out of religious envy, but in some alarm at where these new preoccupations may be taking us.

One of the strengths of the main-line religious traditions is that they have for centuries wrestled with great human problems, related in subtle and profound ways to the world around them, and have tried to produce coherent responses to the questions asked of them. They have, in a word, striven to be rational, and they have tried to bring strong and sometimes dangerous religious impulses within a framework which can contain them and channel them wisely. It does not always work, as we see to our cost in many parts of the world today. But religious movements which actually undermine rationality seem to me to be doubly dangerous. We need to be alert educationally to their implications for knowledge as a whole. We have to take seriously the fact that there is a lot of religion around in today's world, and that the antidote to irrationalism is not irreligion but rational religion.

This leads me to a third pragmatic reason for stressing the educational importance of RE. It is that, in the last 20 years or so, religion has become one of the main forces in international politics. Look at almost any part of the world where there is serious trouble, and the chances are that the root-problems will either be religious or will involve quasi-religious issues of ethnic or national identity. One of the failures on the political level during this period has been the slowness to come to terms with the power and influence of religious feeling.

I am not suggesting that primary school children need to do RE in order to understand international politics. What I am saying, though, is that to be religiously literate is nowadays an essential part of growing up to be a responsible, informed citizen. Religion is not an adjunct of the heritage industry. It is a living force in the world, and a primary motivation for a large part of the world's population. To be ignorant about it is to be just as disabled as to be ignorant of science or mathematics.

Other pragmatic reasons for giving RE a proper share of the school timetable are frequently cited. Though I would not give it the central place that some people do, the cultural heritage argument remains a strong one. So does the argument that some basic religious knowledge is needed to illuminate other subject-areas like English and History.

But I turn now to the claim that religion is intrinsically important in education, and that RE therefore needs to be studied, and properly resourced, for its own sake. The claim is that religion is an essential part of knowledge and of human experience, and that it is uniquely capable of relating all other subjects to some vision of the whole, and drawing out their practical implications for human life and community.

This is not a fashionable point of view, and it seems immediately to be thrown in question by the sheer difficulty of defining the subject, agreeing its content, justifying its claims, and accounting for religious diversity. I want to finish, therefore, by indicating very briefly how such objections might be countered, and to do so in a way which I hope is educationally helpful.

Broadly speaking, there are three ways in which the charges against the intrinsic value of RE might be met.

1   Confessionalism

I referred earlier to the very comprehensive teaching programme I encountered in Berlin. This is possible because it is confessional: it is grounded in a particular confession of faith. Teachers have no problems about expounding a religious tradition to those who already belong to that tradition. Confessional teaching is, or should be, possible in our own church schools. This need not imply narrowness, or lack of intellectual integrity, or failure to give due weight to other religious traditions. To teach from a point of view, and to combine this with critical insight, is no less legitimate in RE than in English or History or in any other subject, where to aim at complete, objective detachment falsifies the nature of the subject itself.

As we all know, there are strong pressures from outside the educational world to push RE in a more confessional direction. These have very understandably created alarm, both in different faith-communities and among teachers themselves, and I am glad to say that the Church of England, through its official bodies, has on the whole sympathised with this alarm. I do not myself think that in our present cultural diversity, confessional teaching in schools is possible or desirable, outside the rather special circumstances of independent or aided schools, and even there it needs to be handled with care. There is a proper fear of over-zealous dogmatism.

2   Essentialism

By essentialism, I mean searching for common elements in different religious traditions in such a way as to mitigate their distinctiveness. It is the exact opposite of confessionalism, and it tackles the problems of definition and diversity by concentrating on some generalised 'essence' of religion. All faiths and none can be studied side by side, because there are phenomena in human experience to which they all in their different ways relate.

This approach acquired a bad reputation as a result of the 1944 Education Act. Essentialism can result in a bland mixture of nothing-in-particular. But there are intellectually respectable ways in which an essentialist approach to religion can be explored, and these are not to be regarded as any less worthwhile because of the danger of being confused with the very widespread, if un-thought-out belief, that all religions are essentially going the same way.

The study of spirituality, as an alternative to religion, assumes an essentialist approach. It has the advantage of directing attention towards actual feelings and experiences, and the means by which these are developed and explored, rather than towards divisive doctrines and traditions. Prayer and mysticism employ much the same techniques around the religious world. And there are theologies, too, framed in such broad terms that they can speak to religious phenomena in general.

When I first began to teach in the 1950s, the theology of Paul Tillich was in the ascendant. He had a convenient definition of theology as being about that which concerns us ultimately. It was in many ways a helpful and suggestive insight. It took theology out of the realm of complex metaphysical claims and counter-claims, and located it in what was seen to be central to, and constitutive of, human experience. To be religious is to be aware of an ultimate concern – and by that definition, religion is hard to escape.

Like most essentialist definitions of religion, the formula was too all-embracing. Anything and everything can become an object of ultimate concern, just as almost anything can be included under the heading of spirituality. Whereas it is precisely the particularity of religious claims which gives them their power, and we falsify them if we try to homogenise them.

Furthermore, it is not possible to understand the religious struggles of our day unless this high degree of specificity is appreciated. People do not die for religion in general, but for a concrete faith. Nor do people live in the light of some generalised ultimate concern, but usually in the light of a faith in which some quite distinct symbols, stories and rules of thumb have for them become centrally important. People may come to recognise broadly similar hopes, feelings and assurances in each other's experience, and may also be able to identify broadly similar life-questions. All the major religions have something to say about the meaning and purpose of human life, human identity (both personal and social), human destiny, our human restlessness and our capacity for self-transcendence, and our ways of coping with failure. In making the point that these are common religious themes, generalised descriptions of religion can be helpful. But a religious education which justified itself by sticking to such generalities would, in my view, have failed in its task. I believe that there is a tougher task to be done, a more educationally demanding one, and one which more clearly justifies RE's place at the centre of the curriculum.

3 Critical solidarity

I want to turn on its head one of the most common objections to RE. Theology, we are told, is not a proper academic subject because it is based on faith, or – worse still – on mere opinion. This is indeed true of many of the ways in which religion is taught. What this understanding of religion ignores, though, is that one of its primary tasks has been to witness to the essential mystery of the heart of things, and from this perspective to ask critical questions about everything else. Are there limits to what scientists may do in the pursuit of knowledge, for instance? By what criteria do we decide that some new insight is progressive? How far is it possible to 'explain' human actions? By holding open a door to that which surpasses knowledge, critical religion has the effect of relativising all claims to absolute certainty.

Confessionalism, as I have tried to indicate, has great strengths, but it can also become narrow and exclusive, and it is by definition dependent in the last resort on a particular commitment. Essentialism solves the problem of diversity, but in doing so assumes likenesses which may in fact be misleading; it reduces the sharpness of religious insight by removing its distinctiveness. What I have called 'critical solidarity' does justice to the distinctiveness of faith, while at the same time encouraging the search for religious reality in terms of questions rather than answers. It seems to me to be peculiarly well-suited to an age which is suspicious of answers and which is over-crowded with contradictory and evanescent ideas.

The classic form of critical religion is the *via negativa*, the description of God in terms of what he is not. One of the most attractive features of Eastern Orthodoxy for many of our contemporaries is the doctrine of divine darkness, the absolute unknowability of God, with whom nevertheless it is possible to find union. A more modern and Western way of putting it might be to say that it is precisely in the knowledge that there are questions about God, and in the wrestling with those questions, that God is to be found, loved and obeyed.

Of course, we need the language of faith, and stories and symbols, through which to do this. These embody our distinctiveness. But the most profound of these are not clear and simple, with meanings which lie on the surface, even though it is true that a child can use them. It is worth noting that in Christianity even credal statements have a strong negative implication. The famous definitions concerning the person of Christ are in no sense explanations. Rather, they set limits beyond which attempts at explanation should not trespass, if they are to do justice to the essential mystery which the words are there to safeguard.

Critical solidarity, of the kind I am attempting very briefly and inadequately to describe, asks questions not only about religious knowledge, but about all knowledge. It is the enemy of self-sufficiency and dogmatism, of those who are not willing to ask fundamental questions about their discipline, their values, their identity, their aims, and their purpose in teaching. It is in this sense that I would claim a central place for it in education, not because it can aspire to knowledge which other disciplines do not possess, but because it is concerned about the nature of the ultimately real, and knows that this is a problem which will not go away.

The self-searching which this requires entails an openness to dialogue. Civilisation, said somebody, is based on conversation. In entering into conversation we express a degree of solidarity, of identification with each other's common concerns. But conversation also explores differences. And conversation against a background of openness to the transcendent allows those differences to illuminate deeper levels of our own faith.

I have sketched an approach to religious understanding and dialogue which may seem a long way from anything which might be written into a syllabus. My purpose is simply to stress that there is available here a tough-minded approach to religion which can not only secure it a proper academic status, but which also has something important to offer the remainder of the curriculum. I hope the work being done by the church colleges on their *Engaging the Curriculum* project will encourage thinking along these lines. It is going to take a massive effort to translate insights into the nature of the theological process into usable teaching material. That is why we need to pool our resources, and do it together.

V

MORALITY

21

Veritatis Splendor: a response

The interest aroused by the papal encyclical *Veritatis Splendor* (*The Splendour of Truth*) at the time of its publication in 1993 was remarkable. Admittedly media speculation about controversial amendments, and the anticipation of further ructions on the subject of contraception, played their part in this. In the event, however, these issues were deftly side-tracked, and the predominant reaction was one of gratitude to a Church leader able to speak with such firmness in a time of moral drift. Pope John Paul II has made a contribution to moral thinking which cannot be ignored by those outside his own communion.

First, though, it is important to realise that, despite the claims of *Veritatis Splendor* to be expressing a universal truth, it is addressed primarily to the theological teachers of the pope's own Church, much of it written in coded language and with criticisms of practices which outsiders may find hard to identify and evaluate. It is clearly stated to be a disciplinary document, intended to put certain moral theologians in their place – and as such it should be interpreted as part of the continuing tension between the Roman Catholic Church's scholars and its magisterium. These are topics on which outsiders would be unwise to say too much. The important question is whether, against such a background, a universal message is possible, and whether it is one which other Christians and the wider public can actually receive.

The insistence that it is possible to discern moral truth, and that the key to such discernment is Christ, must surely be the right starting-point for any Christian leader. A purely relative morality is no morality at all. The essence of moral experience lies in meeting that which is sheerly obligatory, and which is seen to have universal reference. Kant taught us this 200 years ago. And these two qualities of givenness and universality go a long way towards substantiating the claim to truth. Furthermore, for Christians the location of what it is to be truly human in the person of Christ is not, or ought not to be, a matter of dispute.

For non-Christians the identification of Christ as God's truth is obviously highly problematic, but there may nevertheless be a way for them to appropriate some of what the encyclical is saying in a less starkly Christocentric form. The pope hints at this in the first words of the encyclical, 'The splendour of truth shines forth in all the works of the Creator and, in a special way, in man, created in the image and likeness of God', referring to humanity's role in creation as the foundation of all that follows. Moreover, the growing sense of the failure of secular systems of morality is at least opening the way for many people to think that morals need some transcendent basis. There is a possibility, therefore, that a universal message may still be perceived in the encyclical, despite its limited ecclesiastical provenance. That, at any rate, is what seems to have happened in the welcome given to it by secular commentators who have rejoiced in the fact that at last somebody knows what he stands for. Moral firmness is what the world needs, so it would seem, even if the basis of that firmness is not shared.

But if the idea of moral truth is natural to Christians and attractive even to some who do not share Christian beliefs, can it actually be vindicated in the way in which the pope sets out to do so? And does it lead to the conclusions about intrinsically evil actions, which have proved to be the most controversial part of what he has written? Other commentators have given their own answers to these questions. Here I can do no more than indicate some worries of my own, writing from a traditional Anglican perspective.

It hardly needs stressing that, in philosophical terms, the notion of truth is enormously difficult, and that outside a religious context the notion of absolute truth is frequently dismissed as absurd. Relativism tending towards nihilism has gained its hold on post-Enlightenment thinking, as belief in a transcendent reality has waned. This certainly ought not to deter theologians from making high claims about truth, but it does impose on us an obligation to face some of the problems, and at least to be clear about how the word 'truth' is being used.

A comparison with scientific truth may be useful. Most scientists believe, explicitly or implicitly, that they are steadily approximating towards truths which in some sense exist independently of those who are studying them. But few would claim that the process is ever likely to be completed, or that anyone can tell what absolute truth might look like, or what meaning might be given to the concept. Scientific truth, in other words, is to be approached rather than finally attained – but this does not mean that there are no reliable staging-posts for understanding along the way. It is the absoluteness of truth which will always remain elusive.

Can theologians validly claim any more than this? Does revelation overcome the human limitations inherent in any purely secular discipline? Not, surely, if we take seriously the insight that revelation has to be received by fallible human beings; nor the belief that revelation is as inexhaustible as the study of the natural world. To claim that Christ *is* the truth is not the same as claiming that this truth is known in its fullness, or can ever be. This much is obvious, even on the level of New Testament scholarship – and is still more so in the richness of response which has in practice been evoked by the person of Christ.

In the encyclical we are told that truth is discerned through the developing tradition of the Church, and by appeal to its teaching authority. Para. 27 states:

> Within Tradition *the authentic interpretation* of the Lord's law develops with the help of the Holy Spirit. The same Spirit who is at the origin of the Revelation of Jesus' commandments and teachings guarantees that they will be reverently preserved, faithfully expounded and correctly applied in different times and places.

The key words are 'authentic', 'guarantees' and 'correctly', and in the next paragraph the reference to the Church's magisterium completes the picture. If this is a claim about progressive approximation to absolute truth, then it can probably be sustained, with the proviso that it must allow for the possibility of criticism and revision. But if it is beyond criticism, such a claim to absoluteness could only be made on the basis of a claim to infallibility. The usual reply to such a charge is that such teaching is authoritative rather than infallible. Indeed, infallibility is defined in such restrictive terms that absolute claims can only be made explicitly on very rare occasions. The existence of the possibility of infallibility, however, can shed an aura of uncompromising authoritativeness over the teaching of the magisterium, which gives plausibility to claims like those made in Para. 27 without actually asserting infallibility as such. Authoritative statements deemed not to be open to criticism nevertheless draw on the concept of infallibility.

The difficulty here for Anglicans like myself is fundamental. It is not just about the plausibility or otherwise of those few doctrines actually defined as infallible, but about the notion of truth implied in the very idea of infallibility. Statements of truth which seem, as it were, to have 'arrived' in some final form can have the paradoxical effect of diminishing the very truth they seek to express. They not only leap over all the difficulties inherent in the notion of absolute truth itself, but they can close off that sense of the infinite mysteriousness of reality which lies at the heart of faith.

In much the same way the idea of an infallible moral truth seems to subtract the haunting sense of unfulfilment from morality – the continuing awareness of further undisclosed obligations, which makes saints particularly aware of their own sinfulness. In fact, a morality composed of such truths would be reduced to the single virtue of obedience. I gladly acknowledge that this is not what the pope is actually saying, and that the notion of absolute moral truths is used to set firm moral limits rather than to prescribe the whole content of morality. But I cannot help noticing the danger-signs.

There is an instructive parallel with transubstantiation. When it is believed literally, transubstantiation destroys symbolism. If the reality signified is identical with the signifier, there can in some respects be an actual reduction in meaning through forfeiting the possibility of symbolic overtones. It is more difficult, for instance, to identify the Body of Christ as received in the Eucharist with the mystery of ourselves within his Body the Church, if the primary emphasis is on his actual flesh and blood. Over-literal truth-claims, in other words, tend to exclude other creative possibilities. I am reminded of how, in the very different context of a Communist society, I was struck by the repeated use of the adjective 'correct', and by the drastic narrowing of spirit which this represented.

All this is not to say that belief in moral truths, and continual striving towards them, are necessarily subject to the dangers which I have been trying to describe. On the contrary: they are the conditions for moral growth. It is the supposition that it is possible to arrive which needs to be questioned.

When translated into the notion of intrinsically evil acts, the problematic character of absolute moral truths becomes even more apparent. This feature of the encyclical has already been much criticised on a variety of grounds. Is it possible, for instance, to isolate

individual acts from their intentions, contexts and potential consequences? May not supposedly good actions, which pay no heed to
consequences, be as evil in their own way as carefully calculated
actions which pay no heed to principles? What should be done when
all possible courses of action are, in different ways, classified as intrinsically evil?

This last question receives a partial answer in the final moving
section of the encyclical on martyrdom. But even this does not get to
the heart of the issues raised by moral conflict. It is not too difficult
to draw up a list of intrinsically evil actions by sticking to extreme
forms of behaviour viewed in isolation. The drawing of lines which
must not be crossed is the rudimentary groundwork of morality. But
the real work of moral wrestling only begins when principles are in
conflict, when the lines drawn do not fit actual circumstances, when
more than individual integrity is at stake. And it is when this kind of
moral wrestling begins that, the longer the list of intrinsically evil
actions, the more intractable the problems become. The encyclical
unfortunately does not make it clear precisely what counts as intrinsically evil, and what does not. The argument is constructed on the
basis of unquestionably heinous crimes like genocide – but seems to
hint at much more. Does it, or does it not, for instance, extend to such
matters as artificial contraception, which perhaps only a proportion of
Roman Catholics would regard as sinful? And if it does, is not this an
example of the aura of infallibility seeking to extend itself into realms
where that kind of certainty cannot be had?

The pope has made a powerful and challenging contribution to
moral theology for which all who care about such matters must be
grateful. In indicating where I part company from it, I want also to
reaffirm its importance. I hope it will be regarded as setting an agenda
for discussion, and that reactions to it, albeit critical ones, will be
accepted as a necessary part of a continuing ecumenical dialogue.
Moral teaching which claims universality must in the end seek universal reception, no matter how august its source. And that means that
encyclicals should be corrigible, after publication as well as before it.

22

Evangelium Vitae

One of the tasks of moral leadership is to draw lines which should not be crossed. Another is to distinguish between things which are different. In his encyclical, *Evangelium Vitae* (*The Gospel of Life*, 1995), the pope shows himself better at the first than at the second.

As an eloquent defence of the gospel of life against what he calls 'the culture of death', the encyclical fulfils a noble purpose. It is impossible to doubt the pope's sincerity, or the urgency of the task he has set himself in combating by all possible means the threats posed in today's world to the sanctity of life. He must surely be right in his repeated assertion that the protection of human life, and especially life in its weakest forms, is not only a Christian imperative, but also the essential moral foundation for any truly human society.

But it is the details which give cause for concern. Are there really no moral differences between contraception, embryo research, abortion, capital punishment and euthanasia, that they should be lumped together within a single 'culture of death'? Biologically speaking there are very different issues at stake, so the first task of criticism must be to ask how seriously the pope takes biology.

It clearly counts for something. In fact, the need for people 'to respect the biological laws inscribed in their person' forms part of his justification for preferring so-called natural methods of contraception.

But if moral theology is thus to take account of biology, then it must surely pay some attention to one of the most fundamental biological principles, the principle of gradualism. In the biological world there are few sharp dividing lines. One thing develops or merges into another. Even life itself is hard to define, and the precise location of the transition-point from non-living material to living organism is to some extent arbitrary. The same is even more true of the transition from pre-human to human life in the story of evolution.

By relying exclusively on biblical material for his description of human life, the pope faithfully echoes traditional Christian teaching:

The life which God gives man is quite different from the life of all other living creatures, inasmuch as man, although formed from the dust of the earth, is a manifestation of God in the world, a sign of His presence, a trace of His glory.

As a statement about the present role which human beings now occupy, the theological claim is compatible with a biological understanding of human origins. But we need to know whether the biological understanding is, for the pope, also part of the total picture. Was there, for instance, some moment in prehistory when human life attained its unique value and significance? Or can we think in terms of a gradual growth of distinctive humanness, allied perhaps with the gradual growth of the brain and of human language?

The difference is not merely theoretical, because gradualism in evolution is complemented by gradualism in embryology. The absolutist argument against abortion and embryo research depends on the assumption that human life, in some reasonably full sense, begins at the moment of conception. The pope admits an element of doubt in this assumption, but counters it with the statement that 'the mere probability that a human person is involved would suffice to justify an absolutely clear prohibition of any intervention aimed at killing a human being'.

But suppose that there is not even a 'mere probability', in that the claim simply cannot be squared with what is now known about the early stages of embryological development. The argument by which the claim is defended rests on an ambiguous use of the word 'human'. The pope makes the point that something new begins at the moment of conception, and adds 'It would never be made human if it were not human already'. Many things are human: our genetic structure is human; every cell in our body is human. But what is at issue is the existence of 'a new human being' – and that, at the very minimum, requires some identifiable cells which are going to distinguish that human being from all the other products of conception.

Biological gradualism blurs the sharp lines which the encyclical tries to draw – and while it is possible fully to sympathise with the pope's overwhelming desire to protect life, it is also important to see that this cannot be done by ignoring what is known about the nature of life. The lengths to which the pope is prepared to go are shown by his failure to acknowledge any circumstances in which abortion might be permissible, not even to save the life of the mother. The idea that there might sometimes have to be a choice between evils disappears in face of the blunt assertion, 'No circumstance, no purpose, no law whatsoever can ever make licit an act which is intrinsically illicit'. This takes us a long way from acting on the basis of 'mere probability'.

In its treatment of euthanasia the encyclical is on much firmer ground. The presumption underlying this debate – that postnatal human life must not be deliberately destroyed – may in some cases pose awkward problems of definition, but the principle is rightly seen as the foundation of law and morality. The pope's stand against the excessive claims of personal autonomy, the belief that human beings can do what they will with their own bodies, rests on his earlier analysis of freedom in *Veritatis Splendor*, and is in my view profoundly important. But even here there are some difficult issues which are not faced.

Just as life is not easy to define, so death now has fuzzy edges. The fuzziest appear in the persistent vegetative state (PVS), about which the encyclical says nothing. Yet there is a deeply serious question posed by PVS. How much of a human body needs to be dead before it can be said that the human being is dead? Transplant surgery, again not mentioned in the encyclical, assumes that only the brain-stem needs to be dead. It would be interesting to know how the pope relates this conclusion, and all that follows from it in modern medicine, to what is implied in the encyclical about, say, the abortion of anencephalic infants.

Criticism of this kind should not be seen as detracting from the general thrust of *Evangelium Vitae*. In a world intent on manipulating life to suit its own purposes, these things need to be said. But to be heard they need also to be based on sounder biological insight.

23

Learning about right and wrong

The papers they had finished lay
In piles of blue and white,
They answered everything they could,
And wrote with all their might,
But though they wrote it all by rote,
They did not write it right.
(A. C. Hilton after Lewis Carroll,
from *The Vulture and the Husbandman*)

I have tried to imagine some of the components of a test for 14 year-olds on right and wrong. Why is it right to keep promises? Does this apply to politicians? Which is worse – to steal £50 from a handbag or to lose £50 millions by faulty accounting? On what basis do some people decide that the commandments about theft, murder, and family life are more important than those about adultery, envy, and sabbath observance? These would be some of the easier questions – but even with them, it is not absolutely clear how one would write them right.

Learning about right and wrong, in fact, is not about learning by rote lists of right and wrong things to do. It is about becoming a morally responsible person; and this happens in a multitude of different ways. What is experienced or observed in the playground is as important, perhaps more important, than what is said in the classroom. A school where bullies rule and where discipline is slack teaches lessons about unfairness, and may store up hidden anger, which erupts in later life as contempt for social order. Similar conclusions can be drawn in a home where the parents are unpredictable, and where there is no obvious relationship between punishment and wrongdoing.

215

They can be drawn too in a society where effort seems to go unrewarded, and where success too often seems to belong to the ruthless or the morally dubious.

The point is an obvious one. Personality is formed and morality is learnt, for the most part, by unconscious absorption of values and attitudes from our surroundings. There is a place for rules, of course, and for explicit teaching about them. Rules of thumb – the acceptance for example that stealing is wrong – can provide a moral base-line against which those who are effectively fiddling the books can be challenged to examine what they are doing. Stories too can act as reference points, but for most people nowadays the Good Samaritan has, sadly, given place to *Neighbours*. The soaps are our modern parables, hyped-up versions of morality tales subtly conveying their own standards.

Many people respond to moral dilemmas by appealing to a kind of proverbial wisdom which, because the sayings usually contradict each other, can easily be adapted for any occasion. 'Honesty is the best policy', and 'Look after Number one', can between them be used to justify almost any action. People also acquire a degree of moral insight through their own experiences, especially through painful ones, and also through the experience of friends. We also tend to absorb the moral values implicit in our favourite newspaper.

Learning about right and wrong, in other words, is a complex and lifelong operation. If it is to have any coherence, the mass of experiences, impressions, and influences need somehow to be welded together. This is why thinking about morality – by trying to analyse how we are behaving, and why, and whether our values and motives are the ones we really want – is an essential element in moral growth.

At the deepest level of all lies belief. When a crowd of thugs beats up an old man in the street, it is because they have ceased to see him as a human being with feelings like themselves. At the other extreme, when a mother dashes into a burning house to save her baby, she doesn't do it because anybody has taught her to do so. For her, that little bundle of life is the most precious thing on earth. When people behave generously towards one another it is because they see other people as part of the same human family, linked to one another and dependent on one another. It is the way we see the world which shapes our behaviour.

This is why morality has usually been linked with religion. It is common to see the link in terms of commands issued by divine authority, and this is where most believers begin. To refrain from adultery because God says it is wrong is a good way to start thinking about moral obligations. The belief that God has forbidden something can set up inner defences, and help to nurture strength of character. Defences built *because* of fear of divine retribution, however, while solving some behavioural problems, may do so at the cost of stirring up inner resentment or by feeding subservience. Jesus went deeper by pointing out that the wish to commit adultery may be no less destructive than the act itself.

The truest motive for refraining from adultery is that, by undermining fidelity and trust, it destroys a precious human quality. In Christian thought, one of the key characteristics of God is summed up in a word variously translated as steadfastness, faithfulness, or mercy. Here is the rock on which the life of faith is built – and it is against the background of this belief that the possibilities of reflecting such steadfastness in our relationship with another human being are to be grasped.

This is one example among thousands of how a morality rooted in belief actually works. In a pluralist society we must expect different beliefs and different nuances in morality. But there are limits. We rightly draw the line at beliefs which devalue other human beings, which inculcate violence, or which promote bigoted intolerance. But these, unfortunately, are the attitudes which may well be unconsciously imbibed, unless the public life of our society is strong and generous enough to show a different face.

24

Moral confusion

I was talking some months ago with a government minister about the problems of teenage pregnancy. One of the prime objectives of his department was to reduce it by all means possible, including the provision of contraceptives to those under the age of consent. I asked him how he squared this with the law of the land, and what he saw as the educational implications of a policy which explicitly assumed sexual relations between quite young children. His answer carried the clear implication that there was virtually no contact between different government departments on such matters, and that each pursued its own policies regardless of how these might affect the others.

This impression of a high degree of dislocation at the centre of our system of government is reinforced by those who have analysed the relative inability of the Cabinet to influence detailed departmental decisions. The result, in terms of teenage sex, is a highly confused set of messages, which I suspect simply reflect the confusions of our society. Pamphlets extolling the wonders of non-penetrative sex, homosexual or heterosexual, may be fine in terms of AIDS prevention, but can also be highly inflammatory for those with an experimental turn of mind. Sex education, which plays down mummies and daddies, and describes oral sex for the benefit of 12 year-olds, may help a handful of children to interpret their experience, but what is it doing to the remainder? Contraceptive slot-machines in school lavatories give the message that casual sex is to be expected.

Of course, there are arguments on the other side. The relaxation of sexual inhibitions has gone too far to be reversed, so we have to learn to live with its consequences and take what precautions we can. Moralising about sex, we are told, is likely to be counterproductive. Good advice will not be heard unless it starts from the premise that young people, and even children, are going to be sexually active.

And yet, I wonder. There are already some small signs of a backlash against this permissiveness. There are young people grateful for the moral support given to them by those willing to stand against the prevailing assumptions. The changes in homosexual lifestyles resulting from AIDS may have been driven by fear, but they demonstrate that patterns of sexual behaviour are not fixed and that, given a sufficient motive, they can respond rapidly to new knowledge. The message is clearly not getting through nearly so quickly to heterosexuals, and a cynic might say that there will have to be many more deaths before it does. Perhaps more should be said about the frightful statistics from Uganda, Tanzania or Zaire.

One of my daughters recently worked in a rural African culture where the HIV infection-rate was doubling every year. In that kind of culture it was actually possible to co-ordinate the efforts of the various public bodies, health, education, social services – even the witch doctors – to produce a coherent, integrated policy, focusing on education and primary care, and not afraid to identify the root-problem of promiscuity.

Why are our much more elaborate and professional services in this country apparently so reluctant to do the same? I have criticised the confused messages from government – but the same confusion can reign at the point of delivery, where a reluctance to raise basic moral issues with individuals can effectively legitimise self-destructive behaviour. There are, of course, real problems about tackling such moral issues in a society which likes to think of itself as pluralist. But this is not an excuse for failing to talk about them, whether at the level of government policy-making or at the level of personal consultation. Talking need not entail agreeing, nor even trying to persuade. Unless we talk about serious moral matters, however, they will simply go by default. And there will be no central core of understanding and commitment around which some greater coherence in policy-making might eventually be formed.

25

A nasty murder

She put her hand to the nail, and her right hand to the workman's hammer. And with the hammer she smote Sisera, she smote off his head, when she had pierced and stricken through his temples. At her feet he bowed, he fell, he lay down: at her feet he bowed, he fell; where he bowed, there he fell down dead.
(Judges 5:26)

It is a wonderful piece of poetry. But adhering to the lectionary, as I usually try to do when preaching, has its hazards. There is a certain irony, on this of all occasions, in celebrating a particularly vicious murder. And not just murder – treachery too, an appalling abuse of hospitality against someone who was not at that time counted as the enemy. Worse still, in the eyes of the Old Testament, this defeated soldier suffered a violent death at the hands of a woman. Jael, the wife of Heber the Kenite, is extolled as a heroine. And the verdict on her unspeakable act is unequivocal: 'So let all thine enemies perish, O Lord'.

F. D. Maurice preached on this text at Lincoln's Inn in June 1851, and found himself in some difficulty in trying to explain it while remaining loyal to a high view of biblical inspiration. His sermon twists and turns, making much play of the natural human qualities of Jael, and emphasising the understandable exultation of Deborah, the prophetess who sang the song. Maurice flirts with the idea of progressive revelation: perhaps God was not showing his whole mind to a primitive people who, in that chaotic and barbaric age, were not capable of receiving it. But in the end he plumps, rather unconvincingly, for the idea that God can teach us through the mistakes and wickedness of others.

Had he known it, ideas were even then developing which would have spared him some embarrassment. Within a decade or so, Darwinian beliefs about evolution were beginning to transform even the reading of Scripture. In fact, one of the great gifts Darwinism brought to religion was the insight that religion itself might have evolved. It might therefore be possible to identify crude and superseded religious beliefs and practices, which had played their part in the development of the higher religions, but which could now be discarded. Deborah and Jael, according to this scenario, were to be seen as part of the story of the growth of national identity and religious loyalty – but are in no way examples of how we ought to behave now. Science thus came to the rescue of religion, and religion was tempted to take on science's own cult of progressiveness. Science is always pushing out the bounds of understanding, and it is characteristic of it that its latest insight is usually the best. Old religion, on this interpretation, likewise gives way to the new.

But evolutionary interpretations of religious knowledge have not worn well. Is it always true that newest is best? I suspect not in Gray's Inn. How are we to decide what is higher in religion and what is lower? Can we simply assume that we are standing at the peak of religious development? And if we are, how then do we explain the actual mess we have made of our world? The idea of inevitable human progress has for many years seemed like a rather sick joke. The giants of religion seem to belong more to the past than to the present.

So the history of biblical interpretation moves on, and we look to a different idea – the embeddedness of religious faith in a series of different cultures. Religious beliefs and practices differ because they belong in different contexts. Some cultures are welcoming to religious faith, and some are hostile. Ours nowadays is mostly hostile. Deborah, with her bloodthirsty song, belonged to a culture in which assumptions about right and wrong were very different from those in our day. One subtle difference is that the concept of righteousness, at least in early Hebrew culture, was rooted not so much in laws about such things as murder (although there were such laws), nor in fixed ethical norms, but in relationships. To be righteous was to measure up to the claims which a particular relationship made upon you. And that meant, above everything else, loyalty: ruthless loyalty if need be. In the culture of the Book of Judges the relationship was fiercely tribal. What mattered was victory – victory by almost any means. As F. D. Maurice rightly said, Deborah was not a teacher of ethics.

But an awareness of cultural differences, like a theory of religious progress, can go too far. We worry less than F. D. Maurice did about whether a biblical song condones murder, because we relegate it to its place and time, which is not our place and time. We relativise it – and in so doing, we open the way to relativising everything else. Far from believing nowadays in moral absolutes – given once for all in the past – or in moral progress – with our own most advanced insights in the forefront – many nowadays are deeply conscious of the relativity of moral insights and, in consequence, are in great moral confusion. If cultural conditioning sets the terms of our morality, then the moral challenge to what we are, and to the kind of world we create for ourselves, is blunted and destroyed. In much popular understanding, morality is in the end self-chosen. 'It's my life. I do what I want.' The only widely recognised constraint is, 'Do no harm'.

I wonder, though, whether today's moral confusions need be seen in quite such desperate terms. The Song of Deborah is not just an old, outdated song. It is part of a continuous tradition of faith as recorded in Scripture. And what makes that tradition special is the sense that it is more than a merely human story. Human life is shown to us in its openness to another reality – in its responsiveness, or lack of response, to God.

I spoke earlier of the Old Testament assumption that righteousness is about measuring up to the claims which a particular relationship makes upon us. Throughout the Bible, that fundamental relationship is seen as being with God. True, it is a concept which feels strange to many people today. But if we can see it as the underlying assumption even in a brutal story of tribal vengeance, then perhaps we can use it as a golden thread to trace some moral continuity with all that has grown out of this tradition of faith. Cultures, circumstances and particular moral perceptions may change – but if, in the end, what morality is about is the claim made upon us by the relationships in which we stand, then we have a base-line. Morality is precisely not about doing what I want, but about responsiveness; above all, responsiveness to that overarching relationship in which all others are included – our relationship with God.

There is often annoyance when Christians claim (as we frequently do) that in the end there is no true morality without God. On one level, of course, the claim is untrue: there are many fine, non-religious people who prove that it is untrue by the quality of their lives, and who often put Christians to shame. But if the golden thread of biblical tradition is at least right in this respect – that morality has to do with the claims made upon us by the relationships in which we stand – then the question of who has claims upon us is paramount. It is the same question that was asked of Jesus – Who is my neighbour? And his answer set no limits.

What we find in the history of moral development is that the claims consistently widen. Tribal loyalties give place to national loyalties, which give place to all-embracing human loyalties. Our present proper concern with suffering in remote parts of the world witnesses to what has happened to our moral sense. So one of the keystones of morality becomes its capacity to be universal. And when that happens, before we know what we are doing, we are using again the language of religion. The identification of an overarching, all-encompassing relationship with God both expresses, and gives point to, the universal character of all those other relationships which lay claim upon us. To see *that* is one way in which belief in God becomes grounded in our moral perceptions.

This may seem a rather abstract way of spelling out the religious basis of morality; so let me end by trying to put it more simply. Christian morality is not primarily about obeying a set of rules given us by God. If it were, then people could (as many of them do) accept the rules and leave out God. Of course rules are important. We need them for day-to-day living. But they are not primary. The first and most basic demand made by Jesus was, 'Follow me'. The heart of Christian morality is to know God and be known by him, and so to see all other relationships in that light. To leave out God is to leave out what matters most.

The moral distance between Jael, the wife of Heber the Kenite, and Jesus of Nazareth, may seem almost infinite. But there is a thread which joins them. The bloodthirsty poem which celebrates the murder ends with words about God which span the ages: 'Let them that love him be as the sun when he goeth forth in his might'. Love of God formed the climax of hope and aspiration, even in that chaotic age. Love of God is the theme which binds the Scriptures together. Love of God shines in the face of Jesus. To love God and serve him is the invitation held out to all humanity.

26

Age of consent

The demand for equality in the age of consent rests on the false assumption that homosexuality and heterosexuality are simply two sides of the same coin. This is not to say that homosexuals are any less valuable as people, or significant in their relationships, or morally responsible, than heterosexuals. Nor does it entail that they should be forbidden to express their sexuality in appropriate ways. Nor is it an invitation to moral denigration of the kind all too often indulged in by those to whom the very idea of homosexuality is abhorrent. To say that two ways of life are not equivalent is not to condemn one of them out of hand. But it is to put a question-mark against policies which presuppose that there is no essential difference between them.

The educational world has provided fertile ground for those who, in their anxiety not to disconcert potential homosexuals, lean over backwards in proclaiming that all sexual orientations are equal. The recent episode of the children banned from *Romeo and Juliet* because it was exclusively heterosexual illustrates the absurd lengths to which such ideas can be taken. Successful lobbying and strong media influences have given homosexuals a much higher profile than their numbers actually warrant, with the result that claims to equal attention are no longer felt to be preposterous. In a mature society, people should be sensitive towards, and accepting of, those who differ from themselves. It does not follow from this, however, that there are no distinctions to be drawn, or that a society should not be able to safeguard certain principles in appropriate laws.

The point at issue is the one which bedevils all modern societies which are moving in a pluralist and multicultural direction. I say 'moving', because it is not true that Britain is already pluralist, nor necessarily desirable that it should be. Indeed, it is by no means certain that a fully pluralist society could survive. The questions are always:

What norms do we need? Are the core values of society strong enough to permit a variety of recognised departures from those norms? When are laws needed to express and to buttress the norms themselves?

The current general debate about moral values is a symptom of anxiety that perhaps the norms have been eroded too far. An indication of this may be the recent concentration on the indiscretions of public figures, given that the norms are frequently expressed in the lives of symbolic individuals rather than in laws. When a few years ago the bishops of the Church of England published their study document on sexuality, the distinction they drew, between what might be permitted among the laity and what was required of clergy, was widely criticised as discriminatory. The reason for it, however, was precisely this perception of the symbolic and public character of the clergy's role.

In society at large, role-models are weak, and are weakened even more by our present 'culture of contempt'. It is all the more important, therefore, to ask searching questions about the possible effects of relaxing the law. The law may not be very effective in dissuading individuals from doing what they want to do, but it defines a public standard of behaviour. If sensibly administered, it can be educative and persuasive without being oppressive. But, equally, to abolish laws, or to change them drastically, can be educative in ways which are not always anticipated by those who seek to do so. What might seem to be an education in justice can easily be read as an invitation to experiment; and, as always tends to happen, the experiments soon begin to reach down well below the newly permitted lower limit.

Even more significantly, though, a change in the law also conveys the message that distinctions which might have been enshrined in the old law are no longer significant. It is not sufficient to counter this by saying that the law should not have been interfering in people's private lives anyway. Sexual behaviour in every culture is set within a context of law and custom, because the freedom of people to associate with one another depends on knowing where the boundaries lie.

For young people, the absence of clear boundaries can be particularly damaging – and one of the interesting results from the recent Wellcome survey of sexual attitudes was the number who felt that they had had sexual experience too young. There are also significant differences between the sexes. It looks as though the unrestrained and promiscuous character of many young male homosexual adventures is related to the fact that women are more likely to channel sexuality into commitment, and that without their presence therefore, this restraining influence is no longer felt. It is widely observed that girls usually mature emotionally a year or two before boys. In other words, there may be a biological rationale for an age discrimination between men and women, and the present distinction between male homosexuals and lesbians may not be as indefensible as is often claimed.

Those who are persuaded that there are no distinctions at all to be drawn between homosexuality and heterosexuality will find no difficulty in reducing the age of consent to 16. As one who holds that there is a distinction, rooted not only in these biological differences but in the belief that there are proper and improper uses for the human body, I would not want a signal to be sent to young people that sexual choices are of no concern to anybody but themselves. Nor do I want to maintain unreasonable laws which are largely ignored, and which sometimes in the hands of the vindictive or the unscrupulous lead to tragic convictions. I believe it was right to reduce the age of consent from 21 to 18, thus signalling that homosexuality in young men is neither to be treated as uncontroversial nor to be penalised beyond the age of maturity. A reduction of three years provides an opportunity to assess the social consequences. A reduction of five years would have assumed more knowledge about how or why people become homosexuals than we presently possess. And it would have removed a distinction which remains real, no matter how vociferous the protests against it.

27

Abortion

Some recent well-publicised cases have rightly aroused public concern about the way in which the 1967 Abortion Act is being implemented. It seems that in some, perhaps many, places there is now effectively abortion on demand, and there are strong arguments for a formal review. Everything possible should be done to prevent public opinion polarising into the confrontation between pro-life and pro-choice, which has had such dire consequences in the USA.

Neither extreme is convincing. The pro-life position blurs the important biological and moral distinctions between different stages of antenatal life. Whatever people's theoretical beliefs about the status of the embryo, most would agree that an early miscarriage is not as tragic as the birth of a still-born baby. This is not just because of the greater hopes invested in the latter. An embryo is morally significant, and should be cherished on the grounds that it is capable of developing into a person – but it is not yet a person in any full sense of the word. Personhood is gradually acquired during the process of gestation, which is why a late abortion raises bigger moral questions than an early one.

The pro-choice position, in reacting against pro-life absolutism, seems to deny any moral value at all to the growing embryo. But 'a woman's right to choose' cannot be the sole criterion when there is another life at stake. There is no right to do away with a life when it is inconvenient, even when it does not have fully developed person-hood. This is not to say that a woman's desires and interests should be ignored: the whole point of the Abortion Act was that her needs should be weighed against the interests of the life in her womb, with the implication that the duty to protect the foetus becomes more compelling the more advanced the pregnancy. There is also a difference in moral weight between medical and social reasons for abortion, and the ever-present danger that the latter may be trivialised.

The careful balance intended by the Act has been upset by an interpretation whereby allowing any pregnancy to go to full term is deemed to constitute a greater risk to the mother than terminating it. Hence abortion on demand. Behind this moral abdication on the part of many doctors lies a growing reluctance among professional people to give moral advice to, or to take moral responsibility for, anybody else. The modern emphasis on patient autonomy, which has rightly redressed the balance against medical paternalism, can be taken to the point at which the interests of all others involved are ignored. There are enormous social pressures in the direction of individual self-fulfilment. But the fact is that nobody is wholly autonomous; everybody's life affects other people – and that includes those on the way to becoming people. Hitherto it has been assumed that the necessity for two doctors to agree is a sufficient safeguard against abuse, but there is growing evidence that this need be no more than a formality. It is time to think again.

The notorious case of the octuplets raises different issues. The fact that the mother was given fertility treatment without her partner's knowledge and after already having had several children, suggests a degree of medical compliance with the patient's wishes bordering on irresponsibility. It has been claimed that she was intending to use her pregnancy to trap her male partner into transferring his attention from her rival. Whether or not this is true, the possibility that it might be true – if not in her case then in others – makes it clear that the present procedures are open to abuse.

Fertility treatment must necessarily involve two people. It makes no sense to increase a woman's fertility *in vacuo*, without a potential partner in view. It seems entirely reasonable to insist therefore, that both should be consulted about the treatment, and both should agree to it, and accept the responsibilities it entails.

The larger question – of whether prolonged and costly fertility treatment should be freely available to all – goes to the heart of current dilemmas over NHS funding, and for the time being is likely to prove insoluble. The progress of medical research ensures that the range of treatment-options is always going to outstrip the resources to pay for them, while at the same time it feeds public expectations. In the long run, most treatments become standardised, less expensive and hence more available to most of those who need them. But in the short and medium term, there are bound to be inequities as some people benefit from treatments denied to others. A frank recognition that this is so, coupled with some self-denial about rushing to claim 'rights', would help in what are bound to be difficult and disappointing decisions. Politicians can assist by not trying to make political capital out of alleged injustices, and by not arousing unreasonable expectations. The choices are hard enough already.

28

Loving God

Hear O Israel: the Lord your God is the only Lord; love the Lord your God with all your heart, with all your soul, with all your mind, and with all your strength.

(DEUTERONOMY 6:4)

The words are so familiar and so fundamental that it is easy to assume that we know what they mean. What sort of picture comes into mind as we hear them? What does it actually mean to love *God*? Contained within the text are many layers of meaning, and all I can do is to try to unwrap a few of them.

We begin with the outer covering, 'Hear O Israel: the Lord your God is the only Lord'. It is a statement about God, and it is an appeal to the people of God for loyalty. There is only one God. God has ceased to be the name of a class of objects – gods – the gods of Egypt, of Babylonia, or wherever. God is the name of the only divine reality, and to suppose that there could be other divine realities is to empty the word of meaning.

To say this is not to pre-empt all our inter-faith discussions, or to make a take-over bid for all other religions. It is to define what, when we speak out of our Jewish-Christian traditions, the word 'God' means. There is and can be only one Lord – the focus of meaning and ground of unity for all that is.

But what do we love when we love him? Jewish tradition would answer, 'We love his law'. Later in Deuteronomy we read, 'You shall love the Lord your God and keep for all time the charge he laid upon you, the statutes, the laws and the commandments'.[1] Loyalty, in other words, issues in obedience. But it is important to see that this is not grudging obedience, it is not an irksome load which somehow has to

230

be carried. Running all the way through the Old Testament, and particularly through the Psalms, is a deep sense of delight in the law as that which reveals the mind of God. Psalm 119 is a huge acrostic of 176 verses, each of which expresses in a different way the psalmist's joy at knowing the commandments of God.

Christians too can express this same sense of delight in the word of God, in the revelation of God in Scripture, in the comfort and guidance which the Scriptures convey. This, then, is a second layer of meaning in our text. We love God in his word.

But to love God and to love the Bible are not quite the same thing. And it can be disastrous to confuse them, thus putting the Bible beyond criticism. The Bible may give us our access to God – but it is God we must love.

So we move to a third level of meaning – one which takes us beyond the original Old Testament significance of our text, into the heart of the Christian mystery. We love God in the word made flesh. Sometimes this is interpreted in very personal terms, as a simple love of Jesus. There are many today, as there were in the Middle Ages, for whom intimate companionship with Jesus is central to their spiritual lives. Deep attention is paid to what Jesus might have said or done, or might be saying now in face of our contemporary problems. I must confess a certain alarm when this is taken too literally. When pious people ask such questions as, 'What would Jesus have done about the privatisation of British Rail?' I am strongly tempted to answer, 'He would have walked'. There are limits to what can be said about his character and qualities as described in the New Testament, and it is not hard to slip over into fantasy.

For others, the central mystery of the word made flesh is expressed in more theological terms. The significance lies not so much in reconstructions of the character of Jesus as in who he was, and what he did. Our love for God is a response to the love of God who pours himself out in a human life and a human death, the God who comes to us in sacrificial love. It is by being loved that we are enabled to love: 'We love him because he first loved us'.[2] And so the command to love becomes a human possibility through the action of God which enables its fulfilment.

This level of meaning in our text takes us, as I have said, near the heart of it. But there is still another question: What more are we doing when we love God than being loyal to him, and loving his word, and his actions, and his goodness as we see it in the face of Jesus? What about loving him in his world, in all that is good and beautiful and true? What about loving him in music and art and the wonders of nature? Loving him in the happy faces of children, and the tragic eyes of those who suffer? Loving him in all our fellow human beings, so that love of our neighbour becomes part of our love of God? And that includes loving him in ourselves, in those God-inspired feelings which draw us to the source of life. The Spirit has no name, because the Spirit is us – God in us, enlivening us, directing us, opening our eyes to God's reality. He takes our name to make it part of his, in building up the Body of Christ.

Theologically alert readers will have noticed that I have been describing the Trinity: God as the source of all, God who reveals himself, and God who inspires us to respond to his love from the depths of our own being, 'with all our heart, with all our soul, with all our mind, and with all our strength'.

It is no coincidence that, when St Augustine set out to write about the love of God, what he actually wrote was his great treatise on the Trinity. That is perhaps one reason why an exposition of what it means to love God can seem surprisingly difficult. But focusing on the Trinity may remind us of a truth which could otherwise be pushed into the background.

Loving God is not just about loving him in his revelation of himself through his word and his works; this is revelation through the Son. Nor is it just about delighting in his presence and his power, and receiving his love poured into our hearts; this is the experience of the Spirit. It is also about loving God in his transcendent mystery, as Father, and source, and ground, of all. And it is precisely because God, in the ultimate mystery of his being, surpasses all our knowledge of him that it is safe to worship him with all our heart and soul and mind and strength. To give utter devotion to what our own minds are able to grasp is to fall into idolatry.

It is easy to love an idea of God, or a picture of Jesus, or an expression of faith, or an experience of happiness. It is easy to close our minds to what is strange or threatening, or not immediately comprehensible or lovable. It is easy to retreat into facile certainties in the mistaken belief that love requires them. St Augustine agonised over the question, 'How can we love what we do not know?' He was answered 1,000 years later by an unknown English mystic who asked, 'How can we know what we do not love?'[3]

Love comes first – the love which is willing to know and not to know. The love which is delight, desire and devotion.[4] Delight, because by God's grace we know something of his loveliness – yet we do not know enough to justify our denying the delight that others have in him, maybe in different ways which we find hard to recognise; desire, because knowing and not knowing is a constant stimulus to exploration, and leads us to the great ocean of God's truth where all of us are out of our depth; devotion, because only one who infinitely transcends us can receive the totality of love, and return it enriched and enlarged.

This God, both known and unknown, is the only Lord, the source and goal of love. And it is this God, both known and unknown, whom we worship, and should be seeking to hear and to serve and to love. It is this God, only to be known in loving him, who pours his love upon us, eager to receive our response to it, in the offering of heart and soul and mind and strength.

29

Innocence

Have you noticed how the Christmas stories are centred on four journeys? First there is the journey to Bethlehem, back to the place of family origins, back to royal David's city, the place of promise, back to the past. One might almost say, back to basics.

Then there is the journey of the shepherds to see this great thing which had come to pass – a journey made in surprise and hope, and ending in wonderment.

The journey of the Magi is a powerful symbol of the world's search for an answer to its problems. The fact that the tradition alternates between wise men and kings somehow pinpoints the world's dilemma about whether the answers lie in knowledge or in power.

Finally there is the journey into Egypt – the journey of escape, the flight from Herod's murder squads, but a flight which leaves a terrible trail of slaughtered innocents.

For many people today, I suspect, Christmas has this same character of a journey – a journey of the heart: a quest perhaps for some echo from the past, something remembered and partially lost; some hope and wonderment glimpsed; a search for meaning, with a star to guide us. Or is it an escape, a flight from too much harsh reality?

The journey of the heart may take us back to childhood, to Christmas celebrations as they used to be, with their magic still untarnished; times when in imagination it always snowed, and Father Christmas always came, and Uncle George forgot his grumpiness, and the eyes of children were bright with innocent excitement.

Or the journey of the heart may take us forward, beyond the tragedies and sufferings of today's world to a scarcely expressible hope: a world in which neighbours no longer bomb and shoot each other; a world in which people no longer starve and die of neglect, are no longer sucked into the evil machinations of those who want to exploit them; a world in which people no longer hate each other.

Both journeys have their attractions at Christmas time. But whether we look backwards or forwards, there are dangers. Cynics might be right to dismiss the backward look as mere nostalgia – the dreaming-of-a-white-Christmas syndrome. They might be equally quick to label the forward look as mere Utopianism, a baseless optimism. And it's true that Christmas nostalgia soon fades after the second appearance of cold turkey. And Utopianism is shattered by the next news bulletin.

Despite the cynics, though, the search, and the hope, and the journey, are not to be dismissed so easily. They represent a feeling after something real, however elusive, however naïvely expressed – something which must not be abandoned, whatever the sneers, and whatever the disappointments.

I think particularly this Christmas of the search for lost innocence. With our consciousness of a society in deep moral trouble, it is the innocence of Christmas Day which grips the heart: the innocence of Virgin and Child; the innocence of murdered babies, which gives their feast-day its name – Holy Innocents. And it is the shining innocence of Christ himself in the gospel story which both convicts us and uplifts us.

Yet innocence is not a quality by which today's world sets much store. It tends to be equated with ignorance and gullibility. The innocent are pitied and ridiculed for not being streetwise, for their lack of experience, for having lived what are presumed to be sheltered lives. The year 1993 has faced us with gnawing doubts about the innocence of children. We are increasingly conscious of how disastrously young minds can be polluted with images of horror; how quickly they become well-educated in what the poet Traherne called 'the dirty devices of the world'. And even where innocence exists, what can it do in face of the murderous struggles around it? What can the children of Bosnia, or countless other troubled areas of the world, hope for except to grow up quickly, or to escape?

The search for lost innocence can easily begin to seem like a vain or misguided dream. But if innocence enables us to retain the clarity of childlike vision, isn't this what our world needs? 'Back to basics', if it means anything, must surely mean seeing our way through the muck and muddle of today's confused values to a few simple truths about human life – that we are made for God, and made for goodness.

If innocence is about the purity of heart which sees God in everything, then surely this is the vital counterpoise to a world of contrivance, self-interested calculation and studied effect – the self-conscious chic world of those awful weekend colour supplements. If innocence is about seeing the best in people, rather than the worst in them, then surely we need a few innocents among the carping, critical destructiveness of so much of what passes for public life.

Innocence is not about ignorance – though some forms of ignorance may be worth cherishing in a society avid to fill minds with the products of other people's diseased imaginations. If we have that kind of ignorance, we can count ourselves lucky. But true innocence goes beyond this. It is all there in St Paul's classic description of the love which 'thinks no evil; rejoices not in iniquity, but rejoices in the truth; bears all things, believes all things, hopes all things, endures all things'.

Today's message is that such burning and shining innocence is not a dream or a delusion. It has been made actual for us in the life of Jesus. If we set out this Christmas on a journey of the heart to Bethlehem, whether in wonderment like the shepherds, or in puzzlement like the Magi, we too may find its source. And in worship we shall taste its reality. That is the secret of a happy Christmas, a Christmas vision which endures.

VI

ENVOI

30

A farewell sermon

I have searched the Scriptures for guidance on preaching a farewell sermon – and the results are not encouraging. Moses, if we are to take the Book of Deuteronomy at its face value, gave the Israelites 26 chapters of reminiscence, instruction and exhortation, with a special four-chapter supplement on blessings and cursings, topped up with a solo song of no less than 43 verses, and concluding with an individual blessing for each of the tribes. He then prudently disappeared.

St Paul in his famous parting address to the Ephesians made much of how awful things were going to be after he had gone, and concentrated on warning them against his successors. This is the very last thing I would want to do; I go into retirement confident that the future is in good hands.

Our Lord's final discourse to his disciples, as St John presents it to us, comprises three chapters of unparalleled complexity. Though I have spent much of my ministry saying that things are usually more complex than they appear, I do not think that this would be the right note to strike here.

So rather than risk the perils of saying farewell, I go back to the beginning, and I want to share with you three golden texts, one in each of our readings.

The story of our salvation begins with three little words in the Book of Genesis: 'So Abram went'. He went, not knowing where he was going, but because he felt impelled to go. He went at an age, so we are told, when even a patriarch might be considered past it, no less than 75 years old. His call was as simple and as open-ended as the call of Jesus to his first disciples: 'Follow me'. And Abram is called the father of faith because everything in the story of salvation follows from one old man's willingness to respond. As far as I can recall, the words,

'So Abram went', are the first words that I underlined in any theological book.

A second golden text, from Thessalonians: 'Faithful is he that calleth you, who also will do it'. This is the motto of Westcott House, and it was part of the folklore of the place that Bishop Westcott used to say, 'Never forget that καλων [translated "calleth"] is a present participle'. He doesn't just call once for all; he goes on calling. The process of going out into the unknown never ends. There is no finality on this earth in the life of pilgrimage. Our assurance lies not in the fact that we have arrived, in the presumption that we have somehow reached the final definitive version of faith. It lies in the faithfulness of God. In a world where so much is changing, and there is so much to tempt people into bewilderment and fearfulness, our great hope is that at the centre of all things there is a reality which is dependable, joyous and loving. 'Faithful is he that calleth you, who also will do it.'

My third golden text is from St John's Gospel: 'You must be born again'. This at first sight may seem to strike a radically different note. New birth is not the same as continuous pilgrimage. It is about our origins; it is about new life given to us before we have even started out; it is about life lived *from* God as well as *towards* God. We could not seek faith unless God had somehow planted it in us already. We are not called by an unknown God, but by one who is already the innermost reality of our own hearts.

I am in danger of falling into a complex Johannine discourse. But if those who see faith as a going out into the unknown, and those who see faith as simply given in a once-for-all gift, are ever to understand one another, it is essential to get this balance right: life lived from God, and life lived towards God. Thank God for the sheer grace which has brought us to where we are. But we hear daily the call to die and rise with Christ.

It is because there are signs that we are losing this balance that I find myself uneasy with those who state too readily that they are born-again Christians, as if this means that they are a class above the rest of us, that they have somehow 'arrived'. And I am uneasy with those Catholics who seem to think of Catholic faith as some kind of total package, simply handed down from the past. What we have received from the past is, of course, hugely important. But God goes on calling us, and the reality of Catholicism lies in the future, when the broken pieces are gathered together, and Christ is all in all.

I am uneasy too about the kind of liberalism which sits too lightly with what we have received as Christians. To be open to new truth does not entail the wholesale abandonment of old truths. Christian exploration is a constant process of rediscovering familiar landmarks in unlikely places, and finding that Christ is there before us.

It may seem all very complex – but I promised not to say that. I have simply given you my three golden texts because they have been important in my own life. I believe, too, that they can help us keep the close and essential connection between setting out to an unknown destination, and the faithfulness which sustains the journey itself, and the grace of God which originates it and makes it possible.

It is not just a journey of the heart; as if the essence of religion could all be contained within our own inner life. It is a public journey in which we depend on each other – a journey through a public domain which nowadays is all too often hostile, or denigratory, or plain indifferent. It is a struggle sometimes to keep hope alive in a society oppressed by a sense of the absence of God. It is sad, too, to contemplate how much effort in the Church has been wasted, and continues to be wasted, in fruitless controversies between the advocates of personal faith and the advocates of public involvement.

An archbishop is called to do much of his work on this frontier. As part of the public face of the Church, he has unique access to the places where public policy is made. He always has to be conscious of the way in which the character of a society can help to support, or serve to undermine, the faith of its members. As one who holds a universal faith, he constantly has to struggle for its public validation. This is a basic reason why those who are up-front in the Church are always trying to apply our faith to understand, and to criticise, and to interpret, what is going on in the world of affairs.

It can be bruising work. We frequently get it wrong. But we rely more than we can possibly say on the support, prayers and friendship of our brothers and sisters in Christ. And that means all of you.

It has been good to try to serve you during these 12 years. From the fact that my wife and I have decided to stay in North Yorkshire, you can see where our hearts lie. So as I step down from this particularly exposed position, let me just say, thank you. And God bless you.

And what of the future?

Old men ought to be explorers
Here and there does not matter
We must be still and still moving
Into another intensity
For a further union, a deeper communion
Through the dark cold and the empty desolation,
The wave cry, the wind cry, the vast waters
Of the petrel and the porpoise.
In my end is my beginning.[1]

That was T. S. Eliot. And it is perhaps he who best sums up what I have wanted to say:

Not fare well
But fare forward, voyagers.

O Lord Jesus Christ who hast created and redeemed me and brought me to what I now am; thou knowest what thou wouldst do with me; do with me according to thy will: for thy tender mercy's sake.

References

Chapter 1: Learning to like each other

Originally a lecture sponsored by the Templeton Foundation, 1993.

1 John Hedley Brooke, *Science and Religion: Some Historical Perspectives*, Cambridge University Press 1991, pp. 331ff.
2 W. Heisenberg, *Physics and Philosophy*, Allen & Unwin 1959, p. 57.
3 Thomas Mann, *Doctor Faustus*, Penguin 1968, pp. 353ff.
4 Russell Stannard, *Science and the Renewal of Belief*, SCM 1982, p. 161.
5 Adrian Desmond and James Moore, *Darwin*, Michael Joseph 1991.
6 For example, in *The Blind Watchmaker*, Longman 1986.
7 H. E. Hamilton King, *The Disciples*, Kegan Paul 1898, p.111.
8 Council for Science and Society 1989.
9 Quoted in David Harvey, *The Condition of Postmodernity*, Blackwell 1980, p. 9.
10 In Imre Lakatos (ed.), *Criticism and the Growth of Knowledge*, Cambridge University Press 1970, p. 228.

Chapter 2: A vote of thanks to Darwin

Originally an Idreos Lecture on Science and Religion, given at Manchester College, Oxford, 1994.

1 *Westminster Review*, April 1960, p. 556.
2 F. J. A. Hort, *The Way, the Truth and the Life*, Macmillan 1894, pp. 93, 88.
3 Desmond and Moore, *Darwin*, p. 472.
4 Frederick Temple, *The Relations between Religion and Science*, Macmillan 1884, p. 121.
5 ibid., p. 115.
6 ibid., pp. 117–8.

Chapter 3: Evolution and ethics

Originally an Idreos Lecture on Science and Religion, given at Manchester College, Oxford, 1994.

1 See Chapter 25 of this book.

2 Temple, op. cit., pp. 136–7.
3 Temple, op. cit., pp. 140–1.
4 Quoted in Hans Gunter Zmarzlik, *Social Darwinism in Germany*, in G. Altner (ed.), *The Nature of Human Behaviour*, Allen & Unwin, 1976.
5 P. B. Medawar, *The Future of Man*, Methuen 1959, pp. 99–100.
6 T. H. and J. Huxley, *Evolution and Ethics*, Pilot Press 1947, p. 124,
7 J. Huxley, *Evolution in Action*, Chatto & Windus 1953, p. 146.
8 E. O. Wilson, *On Human Nature*, Harvard 1978, Chapter 7.
9 A. N. Whitehead, *Adventures of Ideas*, Pelican edn, 1942, p. 32.

Chapter 4: The sacramentality of the natural world

Originally part of a lecture-series given at Durham University, 1993.

1 Alexander Schmemann, *The World as Sacrament*, DLT 1966, pp. 13–16.
2 Pierre Teilhard de Chardin, *Hymn of the Universe*, Fontana 1970, p. 26.
3 ibid., p. 22.
4 John Habgood, *Religion and Science*, Hodder & Stoughton 1972, p. 150; quoted in John Habgood, *Making Sense*, SPCK 1993, p. 22.
5 Bill McKibben, *The End of Nature*, Viking 1990.
6 Thomas Traherne, *Centuries of Meditation*, I 29.
7 Charles Birch *et al.* (eds), *Liberating Life*, Orbis 1990.
8 Isaiah 45: 22.

Chapter 5: The word made flesh

A Christmas sermon preached in York Minister, 1994.

Chapter 6: Life on Mars?

First published in the *Church of England Newspaper*, 1996.

Chapter 7: Is there reliable knowledge about God?

Originally a Gifford Lecture, 1988.

1 Quoted in Idries Shah, *Darkest England*, Octagon Press 1987, p. 115.
2 This is 'the experiential – expressive model', as described in Lindbeck, *The Nature of Doctrine*, SPCK 1985, pp. 31ff.
3 Quoted in John Bowker, *The Religious Imagination and the Sense of God*, Oxford 1978, p. 1.
4 John Ziman, *Reliable Knowledge: An Exploration of the Grounds for Belief in Science*, Cambridge University Press 1978.
5 'Beginning all over again' in A. R. Vidler (ed.), *Soundings*, Cambridge University Press 1962, p. 19.
6 The key work is H. G. Gadamer's *Truth and Method* (English translation Seabury Press 1975). I have also relied on Georgia Warnke, *Gadamer: Hermeneutics, Tradition and Reason*, Polity 1987; Richard J. Bernstein,

Beyond Objectivism and Relativism, Blackwell 1983; W. Pannenberg, *Theology and the Philosophy of Science*, DLT 1976; David Tracy, *Plurality and Ambiguity: Hermeneutics, Religion, Hope*, SCM 1987.

7 Ziman, *Reliable Knowledge*, p. 28.

8 Alasdair MacIntyre, *Whose Justice? Which Rationality?*, Duckworth 1988.

9 Martin Buber, *The Eclipse of God*, New York 1952, pp. 7–8.

10 *We Believe in God*, Church House Publishing 1987, p. 24.

11 Pannenberg, *Theology and the Philosophy of Science*, p. 314.

12 Kenneth Cracknell, *Towards a New Relationship*, Epworth 1986, spells out helpfully the conditions for successful inter-faith dialogue.

13 Klaus Klostermaier, *Hindu and Christian in Vrindaban*, SCM 1969.

14 I take this illustration from David Hay, *Exploring Inner Space: Scientists and Religious Experience*, Mowbray 1987, pp. 3 ff. The book as a whole marshalls impressive evidence for the universality of religious experience, as investigated by the Alister Hardy Research Centre in Oxford.

Chapter 8: What can Japanese industry teach Britain?

Originally a lecture to the Industry Churches Forum, 1994.

1 Ronald Dore, 'Authority and Benevolence: the Confucian Recipe for Industrial Success' in *Government and Opposition*, Vol. 20, no. 2, 1985.

Chapter 9: The Church in society

Originally an address to the Affirming Catholicism conference, 1995.

1 *The Daily Telegraph*, 14 July 1995.

2 Quoted in Grace Davie, *Religion in Britain since 1945*, Blackwell 1994, pp. 189–90.

3 Charles Davis, *Religion and the Making of Society*, Cambridge University Press 1994, Chapter 3.

Chapter 10: The family and the new social order

Originally an address at the University of Leeds, 1995.

1 Bruno Bettelheim, *The Children of the Dream*, Paladin 1971.

Chapter 11: Religion and democracy

Originally an address to a multi-faith conference on democracy, 1993.

Chapter 12: Paradoxes of freedom

Originally the sixth Tom Olsen Memorial Lecture, given in St Bride's Church, Fleet Street, November 1996.

1 Isaiah Berlin, *Four Essays on Liberty*, OUP 1969.

2 Ernest Gellner, *Conditions of Liberty*, Hamish Hamilton 1994, p. 77.

3 T. S. Eliot, *Murder in the Cathedral*, Faber and Faber, 1935, final chorus.
4 Friedrich Nietzche, *Twilight of the Idols*.
5 Iris Murdoch, *The Sovereignty of Good*, Ark Edn, 1970, pp. 36–7, 40, 95.
6 Mary Midgley, *The Ethical Primate*, Routledge 1994.
7 Michael Polanyi, *Personal Knowledge*, Routledge 1958, p. 214.

Chapter 13: Religion and the national Church

Originally a sermon preached in King's College, Cambridge, May 1994.
1 A. R. Vidler (ed.), *Soundings*, Cambridge University Press 1962, p. 242.
2 Charles Davis, *Religion and the Making of Society*, Cambridge University Press 1994, p. 33.

Chapter 14: William Temple

Originally a sermon preached in Manchester Cathedral, to commemorate the fiftieth anniversary of William Temple's death, May 1994.

Chapter 15: The Anglican Church and the unification of Europe

Originally a lecture given to political and religious leaders at Leuven, Belgium, May 1995.
1 *From Power to Partnership*, Church House Publishing 1991.
2 Elizabeth Templeton, *Report of the Lambeth Conference*, Church House Publishing 1988, p. 292.

Chapter 16: Gerald Priestland

Originally the Gerald Priestland Memorial Lecture, given before an audience in Manchester Town Hall, and broadcast live on Radio 4, October 1995.

Chapter 17: Preachers from outer space

First published in the York Diocesan Newspaper, February 1995.

Chapter 18: Riding the storm

Originally a sermon preached at Sandringham, January 1995.

Chapter 19: Maps and dreams

Originally a lecture on continuing adult education, January 1995.
1 Hugh Brody, *Maps and Dreams*, Pelican 1981.
2 G. H. Lorimer, *Letters from a Self-made Merchant to his Son*, Methuen 1903, pp. 1–2.
3 Allan Bloom, *The Closing of the American Mind*, Penguin 1987.

4 Alan Bennett, *Writing Home*, Faber & Faber 1994, pp. 10, 42.
5 Blaise Pascal, *Pensées*, No. 409.
6 Michael Polanyi, *Personal Knowledge*, Routledge & Kegan Paul 1958, p. 199.
7 David Hay, *Exploring Inner Space*, Mowbray 1987, p. 136.
8 James Miller, *The Passion of Michael Foucault*, Flamingo 1993, p. 77.

Chapter 20: The case for a national RE syllabus

Originally a lecture on the need for national standards in religions education, March 1995.

Chapter 21: *Veritatis Splendor*: a response

First published as a preface to *Veritatis Splendor: a Response*, The Canterbury Press 1994.

Chapter 22: *Evangelium Vitae*

First published in *The Independent*, 1995.

Chapter 23: Learning about right and wrong

First published in *The Evening Standard*, June 1993.

Chapter 24: Moral confusion

First published in the *Faculty of Public Health Medicine News*, Spring 1995.

Chapter 25: A nasty murder

Originally the Mulligan Sermon, preached at Gray's Inn, July 1993.

Chapter 26: Age of consent

First published in *The Independent*, January 1994.

Chapter 27: Abortion

First published in the Party Conference edition of *Parliamentary Review*, September 1996.

Chapter 28: Loving God

Originally a sermon preached in York Minster to the General Synod of the Church of England, July 1994.

1 Deuteronomy 11:1.
2 2 John 4:19.
3 *The Cloud of Unknowing.*
4 John Burnaby in *Amor Dei*, Hodder & Stoughton 1938, p. 311.

Chapter 29: Innocence

Originally a sermon preached in York Minster on Christmas Day 1993, not long after the murder of the toddler James Bulger by two young boys.

Chapter 30: A farewell sermon

Preached in York Minster, June 1995.

1 T. S. Eliot, 'East Coker', *The Four Quartets*, Faber & Faber 1940.